D1492644

LAST VOYAGE

LAST VOYAGE

*An autobiographical account of all
that led up to an illicit voyage
and the outcome thereof*

by

Ann Davison

illustrated by
C. Walter Hodges

**READERS UNION
WILLIAM HEINEMANN**

LONDON 1953

This Readers Union edition was produced in 1953 for sale to its members only. Full particulars of RU may be obtained from Readers Union Ltd, 38 William IV Street, Charing Cross, London WC2 or from Letchworth Garden City, Hertfordshire. The book has been entirely reset in 11pt Fournier type and printed at the Selwood Printing Works, Frome, Somerset, by Butler & Tanner Ltd. The illustrations are by C. Walter Hodges and have been specially drawn for this edition only. The book was first published in this country by Wm. Heinemann Ltd.

DEDICATED
WITH ALL MY LOVE
TO THE MEMORY OF
MY HUSBAND

Foreword

THEY said in a friendly way: 'What are you doing now?' And I, believing it was a weapon in my hand, replied: 'Writing a book about it,' at which they looked quite properly appalled, being nice people, and remarked: 'We see – throwing the baby out of the sleigh.'

At first I was inclined to be affronted by this transposition of my flaming sword: but it does seem to fit the case more exactly, so – here goes the baby. . . .

ANN DAVISON

Cirencester
October 1950

Book I
PREPARATIONS

1

'YOU on the same game?' said the man in the pub. He was tall, thin and bespectacled, looking more like an inspector of something than a would-be purchaser of a yacht. 'Looking for a houseboat?' he went on, nodding in the direction of the window and the dock. 'That's about all she's fit for now. . . . She's had it.' He thrust his hands deep into his trouser pockets with an air of finality; then added, a little regretfully, 'Been a nice job in her time, though.'

My husband looked at him jealously. We *were* on the same game in that we were interested in the same craft, but we were not looking for a houseboat. In fact we were not particularly looking for a boat of any sort, and for my part there was a certain bewilderment at our being there at all.

Frank had come home one day with details of a sixty-foot ketch and said that as it was an executors' sale the vessel was likely to go very cheap.

'But what is that to do with us?' I had asked. 'What could we do with a sixty-foot ketch?' I was uncertain even as to what a ketch might be.

'We could live on it, for one thing,' Frank had replied cheerfully, which seemed nonsense to me.

The yacht was lying at Glasson Dock in North Lancashire. It was during the early part of the war, so obviously she would have to remain where she was: on the other hand we were busy with a gravel quarry in North Wales and a small-holding in Cheshire, and I did not see how we could continue these operations by remote-control from a small ship nearly a hundred miles away.

However, Frank was very keen. 'If she's good enough and cheap enough, she might do as a spec,' he said, and I, never having beheld a large yacht at close quarters before, was curious to see what one looked like. So we took a day off from sand and gravel and tomatoes and turnips and journeyed up to Glasson Dock.

The caretaker of the yacht *Mariana* was away that morning and we awaited his return in the local where we met our competitor. Not that he was really competing, as he was careful to point out. He was a yacht-broker, and times being as they were the market was pretty dead, and the *Mariana* was very old, 1899; by the time the war ended, if it ever did, she would probably be a hulk. If she went *very* cheap (he looked at us speculatively) she might be worth a gamble, otherwise. . . . He shrugged and spread his hands and gazed silently out of the window.

Then he said, still staring out of the window: 'You know, last time I was up here I had the most extraordinary deal. Extraordinary.'

He turned away from the window.

'About six months ago it would be,' he said, 'just at the beginning of the winter. I had arranged to meet a chap here to look at a yacht. And he stood in this room, here, where I am now, and looked out of the window and said, "Which is she?" I pointed her out – you could see her from here – he looked at her quietly, said, "She'll do," took a cheque-book out of his pocket and wrote out the cheque then and there.

'Never went near her, never even moved out of this place except to go home.'

He sounded pained at the recollection. 'Bought her just like that,' he said.

'Maybe he knew her,' Frank said.

The man shook his head. 'No, I don't think so.

'And the story doesn't end there. He had her moved down to the Mersey . . . you could still move private craft then with special permission . . . and laid her up at Birkenhead, employing a man to work on her evenings and weekends.

'Well, one evening this chap goes down to her as usual – and she wasn't there. Gone.

'Gone,' he repeated. 'Not a sign of her. Slipped out on the night tide. Then they started making enquiries – vanishing boats in war-time look mighty suspicious – and it was found the owner had gone missing too and taken a girl with him. School-mistress I think she was – there were just the two of them. What do you make of that?'

'Who-ho!' said Frank with a grin.

'Sounds more like cloak-and-dagger stuff to me,' I said.

'Nothing came out in the spy line that I heard of,' said the man

4

positively. 'Everything seemed to be in order. You know, he had even left a balance at the bank. He left his house, his car, everything – just as though he had gone out for the evening.'

'What about the girl? Did they find out anything about her?'

'No,' he said. 'There's no sense to it as far as I can see. But that chap must have known what he was about, right from the beginning when he stood in here and bought a boat off the peg.'

We were thrilled.

'What happened to them?'

He shrugged. 'Your guess is as good as mine. There was an air search over the Irish Sea, but nothing came of it. Personally I think they bought it.'

'Why?'

'Well, they went out in shocking conditions – do you remember the time of gales and snow last winter?'

We did.

'And there *was* some wreckage picked up later which might have been part of their ship. But it may have been a mistake . . . they might have got away with it. Or they might not. All I do know is that it was the queerest deal I've ever had.'

Well, *well*, we said, of all things! This to be going on on our very doorstep, so to speak, and we knew nothing about it.

(*It never for a moment entered our heads that we might enact a similar story one day.*)

We ravelled and picked at the mystery, until the caretaker returned and we all went to have a look over the *Mariana*.

At that time my experience with ships was limited to Atlantic crossings in 10,000-ton freighters, so I hardly knew what I was looking at when we explored the ketch. All I remember of her was a splendid sweep of deck, and the early-Edwardian magnificence below. Dark red mahogany, and bright red plush. Brass candlesticks on the bulkheads. A flamboyantly ornamental oil lamp suspended from the deckhead of the saloon. A chaste tin bath under the floorboards in the owner's state-room.

There was no engine. But there was a very full and elaborate suit of sails.

Frank was delighted with her. He strode up and down alleyways and companion ladders, dreaming ships out loud. By the time he had worked from the forepeak to the counter he had altered the accommodation to allow for engine installation; with a wave of the hand he had her wired for electricity and positively gushing with running water. . . .

I was somewhat exercised over the fittings. The mahogany was oppressively dark, but too good to be painted. Did one live in the dark or commit sacrilege?

We argued this point all the way back to Cheshire.

But in the end nothing came of it all – then.

It was just a day-dream. A pleasant day out. We had other matters to attend to and settled down again to our problems of quarrying, business, land and livestock, and thought the incident closed.

The *Mariana* haunted our imaginations at times. Every now and again we refitted her and argued over the mahogany fittings and how much space would have to be sacrificed for an engine-room.

For me, knowing no other, she became a sort of standard vessel to which all others were to be compared, bigger, smaller, better or worse. But we did not see the *Mariana* again for years, and then it was only as a cloud of sail on the horizon.

Yet she was to be the most important thing that ever happened to us. . . .

2

UNTIL the *Mariana*, ships had not impinged on our married life. Frank had a love for ships and the sea which I was aware of and accepted, as I accepted his thinness, his yellow hair, his china-blue eyes and quick temper, as part of his make-up. But the ships were also a part of the life he led before we met; that shadowy past existence of one you grow to know well which always remains slightly unreal and out of focus. I accepted this ship passion but at the time hardly understood it; to me, ships were something in which one crossed the sea in order to get to the other side.

He used to tell me of his sailing experiences in the North and Irish Seas, and said that as I was the sort of person who liked riding horses, flying aeroplanes, and driving fast cars, sailing small boats would just come naturally to me. A duck to water and all that.

'It's all a question of hands,' he said airily.

As a matter of fact nothing has ever come naturally to me: any small accomplishments I may have have been wrought out of the solid rock of ignorance by sheer hard work. But shortly before we were married we had a short test of the duck-and-water theory, and as I expected I was no duck. Frank's enthusiasm for small boat sailing struck me as being exaggerated, and that it was not so much a question of 'hands' as a determination to endure exacting privations and intense cold.

The test took place on Lake Windermere in a half-decked cutter one shocking afternoon. It was blowing a half gale and pouring with rain. We took Frank's terrier with us because Frank said he loved sailing.

As we rowed out to the little boat at her moorings Revs cast a quick glance at the future and flung himself into the water. We fished him back into the dinghy, press-ganged him aboard, where he dived under the decking and remained there, a damp, disconsolate, shuddering bundle of fur.

I said I could see he loved sailing; Frank corrosively returned with some remark about reef points, at which I looked about for submerged rocks – wrong again; then he hoisted the sails, shouted 'Take the tiller!' and went for'ard to do what appeared to be limbering-up exercises, but which resulted in the sudden appearance of an anchor, coincident with the sudden departure of the boat towards an impregnable phalanx of other craft at a speed surpassing anything I had ever experienced before.

Frank leapt into the cockpit in time to avert disaster and we tore off down the lake, to meet a classic example of a line squall. A situation he handled superbly and with evident delight; but I had hardly time to take in the niceties of technique, being occupied in measuring the distance between us and the shore, '. . . can swim from here . . . can't swim from here . . .' and peeling off my raincoat preparing for the worst and putting it back on again when it didn't happen. That is when I wasn't dodging all the wild things that snarl up and bang in a sailboat.

The water was icy, and everywhere. It cascaded down my neck and up my sleeves until I was as wet inside my clothes as out – and much colder.

Nothing dramatic happened. We did not capsize. It was simply a wild wet rush of bitter cold from beginning to end. We landed unspeakably moist, walking stiffly on what seemed to be frost-bitten stumps.

Frank, dripping, red-faced and joyous, said, 'That was *fun*!'

As I said before, this little trip took place before we were married. I could see sailing was one of those things I would have to do a bit of humouring about.

'A most interesting experience,' I said, and Frank grinned very widely indeed.

'You'll come to it,' he said. 'Sailing is the best fun in the world.'

But for a very long time ships remained for me something in which one crossed the sea in order to get to the other side.

For various reasons Frank had no further opportunity for sailing for many years, but as a gesture or propitiatory offering to the nautical gods, kept a twelve-foot sailboat which was dragged relentlessly whenever we moved, and at the time of our brief encounter with *Mariana* was lying in the stable-yard of our Cheshire holding.

It was not a dinghy, it was a miniature half-decked yacht, pretty but in a bad way. Nearly every rib was cracked, all her planking

8

ripe, and the stemhead appeared to be held together by paint. But Frank used to look at her fondly and say he would *do* something with her one day, and I thought quietly there was no real reason why he should, for once the war was over we would return to our real job in life, flying, which *was* fun.

(And why we were not doing our real job in life, flying, in war-time, will come later. It was a sore point.)

It was through flying we met.

In 1937 Frank was the owner and manager of an aerodrome, Hooton in Cheshire, the owner of a fleet of aircraft and the director of several aviation companies and incidentally of various non-flying concerns. He operated charter, Army co-operation and aerial photography flights from Hooton. In 1937 the flying activities were extended to a season's joy-riding at Blackpool; and being short of a pilot for one of the machines, he advertised.

In 1937 I was a free-lance commercial pilot based near London making a sketchy living doing charter flights, delivery flights, towing advertising banners – on to anything that presented itself in the flying line. I was, without discrimination, prepared to fly anyone anywhere in anything and did so to the best of my ability.

It was a happy-go-lucky, here-today-gone-tomorrow sort of existence. I loved every moment and wore a lucky scarf to keep the favour of a Fortune that allowed of my being paid for doing what I liked best in all the world. It seemed too good to be true. And in a way it was. Free-lance flying was intermittent. There would be a rush, followed by weeks of inactivity when one's savings dwindled in the hectic competitive search for further flights. And one was up against low types, too, who would fly for nothing. Life was a series of feasts and famines in more ways than one.

Seeing this advertisement for a joy-ride pilot I thought good-oh, just the job, and drove straight up to Hooton to see what could be done about it, mentally well-armed for a fight against the inevitable antagonism towards women pilots.

Frank Davison exhibited none of the patronising, There there little woman this is a man's game run home and cook dinners atti-tude I was prepared for. He sat at the other side of an enormous desk in a little office on the aerodrome and silently weighed me up. He had the most disconcerting, penetrating blue eyes I had ever seen. Not a man, I decided, to put up with any equivocation.

'I want a pilot for a 504,' he said. 'Know anything about them?'

9

'I've flown them on banner work.'

His interest quickened. 'Where?'

'London.'

'I think you'll do,' he said. 'You must meet my wife. She's a pilot.'

I met Joy Davison and I got the job.

From then on the flying was fast and furious. The joy-ride contingent was based at Blackpool at Stanley Park aerodrome. There were three of us: Jo King, who lived in a tent on crayfish and flew an Airspeed (no-speed, God-speed) Ferry; Joy with a Monospar; and myself with at first the Avro 504 – regarded even then as pretty stationary aviation but a machine of undoubted character – and later a three-seater Hermes Avro Cadet.

All day long we flew Lancashire holiday-makers – 'Ee, love, are you safe?' on circuits and bumps. Passengers entirely lost their identity and resolved themselves into so many pounds weight determining the length of take-off run. We flew them in all weathers, rain or shine, clear or nearly QBI, when we'd fly so many minutes out and back on a compass course, with eyes like organ-stops watching for each other, and feeling our way down by guess and by God, wondering what joy the passengers were exacting from it all.

In the evenings, flying over for the day, the pilots and ground staff of our own and rival joy-ride concerns piled into my Ford 8 like an out-back market bus and drove down to the Fun Fair to eat pies and ride the night out on the Giant Racer.

Towards the end of the season there was not enough work to keep three machines going and we returned to Hooton, whence I flew daily to Blackpool with a crew of two, George, assistant g.e., and Jimmy, the red-haired Irish ticket seller. Jimmy could sell glass beads in the Kimberley Mines; he once brought me three trippers in bonnets and elastic-sided boots whose combined ages must have topped 210. His politics were of true Irish complexity and agin the English. He joined the RAF during the war because there was a good fight going and he was not going to miss it. He was shot down over Germany and killed.

Sometimes we were caught out by weather coming back to Hooton in the evening and would find ourselves tearing through the murk up the Mersey with our wheels just off the water, and George chanting 'ceiling zero ceiling zero', leaning out from one side of the front cockpit hanging on to the centre-section struts, and Jimmy out of the other, watching for ships.

When one appeared we rocketed up and over, receiving as we went photographic impressions of the glitter of brass on the bridge.

Apart from Press flights – blood-hunts we used to call them – and photography flights, scratting about over featureless industrial towns like a hen on a midden, trying to pick which unidentifiable factory wanted its picture taken, there were what were known as Army co-operation flights. Dull work flying on a set course up and down between two points at a fixed height for hours whilst the Army practised taking gun sights and so on.

We had one rather stirring experience, shortly after I joined Hooton.

Joy took me as second pilot in the Monospar on a night co-op course over Manchester. Something went adrift with the navigation coming home. We knew the layout so well we didn't bother ourselves, but when Hooton should have turned up by the clock, we found ourselves cruising among a lot of rugged mountain-tops somewhere in Wales. Which was not according to the programme laid down. Keen and extensive research brought no sign of the missing airfield, and by the time petrol was giving out we found ourselves on the outskirts of a town we should have recognised as Chester but didn't, and Joy landed on the remaining pints of petrol over high-tension wires into a pocket-handkerchief field surrounded by gasworks, goods yards and other urban impedimenta. It would have been a good show in daylight; at night it was superb.

Frank picked us up in the car, white as a sheet and unspeakably savage.

It all sounds very casual and hit-and-miss from the cold scientific heights of today. It was the tail-end of the pioneering stick-and-string aviation when people were still making the headlines for flying the Atlantic, but as a matter of fact we took our flying very seriously. We had unbounded faith in the Future of Aviation, but we worked hard and played hard without any of this earnest holier-than-thou attitude which seems to put such a blight on the modern outlook.

Frank did none of the operational flying himself, being unable to hold a B licence because of defective sight in one eye. This did not prevent him from having an A or private pilot's licence and he had flown on and off for nearly twenty years. In any case the administration side kept him more than fully occupied. He was forever pressing on, expanding the business so that we were getting more and more flying; at the beck and call of the Press; loaded up with Army co-op, aerial photography, charter – joy-riding from the sands at Morecambe Bay, from Manchester aerodromes, from air displays at RAF stations and in Ireland. More machines were added to the fleet and more pilots joined the staff.

But that was to come.

The first winter I was at Hooton the machines were laid up for annual C. of A. and things were pretty slack. Joy retired to write a book, and Frank and I got talking. We were indefatigable talkers.

It was amusing to find we shared an ancestral background, both our parents coming from the same district on the North-East Coast. It was amusing to find we had both played on the sands at Seaton Carew as children and only missed meeting each other there by thirteen years – the difference in our ages. . . .

It was amusing to find we had both been on the prairie in our early twenties, Frank in Canada and I in the Argentine. Frank had made more of his prairie experiences, having gone there to seek his fortune. He did not make a fortune, but besides being a cowboy with a horse called Hector he did all manner of things.

He swung an axe in a lumber camp; panned gold – and had three little nuggets to show for it; gambled on the grain market and lost the profits in an oil company. He raced automobiles and was nearly killed when his car turned end-over-end three times on the track, blew up and burnt out. He paddled a canoe through lonely unexplored regions of the Peace River country, and drove huskies across the winter snows. He met Dr Grenfell at a lecture and went with him into Labrador to fix an X-ray apparatus and so learnt something about fixing X-ray apparatus. . . .

He brought a cutter back from Labrador single-handed just before freeze-up and sailed her up the St Lawrence.

I could not compete with this – my prairie story was simple though it had a far-reaching influence on my life. The trip was given by my father to a girl friend and myself as twenty-first birthday presents.

We stayed up country in the Entre Rios district on a small experimental farm run by Sandy and Marion MacDougall. This was not the real prairie, we were told, this was rolling country; you could only see about thirty miles in all directions. It was entirely devoid of trees except round the homestead where there were shelter belts of eucalyptus. Sandy's pride and joy was a ramshackle aeroplane, which did not particularly interest me at first because the corral was full of horses and then my concentration was centred indivisibly on horses. The riding was unlimited and made irresistibly romantic by the addition of sheepskin saddles and rawhide reins.

The plane was a Curtiss JN, a veteran trainer of the first world-wide aggravation, and a museum piece. Nevertheless it moved my lifelong passion for horses down to second place and filled the first place with flying.

Sandy took me up one day, ostensibly on a locust hunt. There were rumours of an approaching swarm. The idea was to fly up and down alongside the swarm with the aim of persuading it to go and wreak havoc somewhere else. It sounded rather a vain hope to me, but I had no chance of seeing whether it would work or not, for although we saw the locusts, far off, like a distant dark cloud, the wind changed, and they flew elsewhere without any coercion on our part.

Sandy decided to give me a flying lesson instead.

He throttled back and shouted instructions over his shoulder, which were swept away unheard in the slipstream. Then he opened up again and waved his hands above his head to show I'd got her. I hadn't the faintest notion what to do with her. But afterwards felt a great inward glow as one who has undergone an illuminating experience. . . .

I returned to England with two convictions. One was that the world outside the British Isles was much more exciting than I had ever been led to suppose and worthy of the most extensive examination. The other was that I must learn to fly. My father, a very remarkable man, on hearing this, said, 'I see no reason why you shouldn't.'

Frank had started his career by serving his time at Vickers, Barrow-in-Furness, with the ultimate aim of becoming a naval architect, but had joined up in the first world war and become addicted to military exactitude for detail instead.

I had started my career with youthful sorties into the ill-assorted realms of veterinary science and art, without gaining very much from either, mainly because I was too busy dashing off giving riding lessons so that I could have my riding free.

Thus Frank and I exchanged life-histories – we found much in common. We found we both loved books, poetry and travel. We loved variety, excitement, adventure – danger. We found we spoke the same language and laughed at the same things.

We found we had fallen deeply, irrevocably in love.

The outcome was inevitable, but not easy.

Joy was a highly intelligent, gifted and courageous woman, a brilliant pilot, and as versatile and dominant as Frank. It is not for me to say whether the marriage was happy or not. It was certainly not a restful one. And had ceased to be – if indeed restfulness was ever a possible state between two such vibrant beings – long before this stormy petrel came on the scene.

Under the circumstances, with the three of us, of like mind, similar interests, strong wills and hot tempers, it would seem there were all the makings for a bitter triangular drama. But no: for once, possibly for the last time in all our three turbulent lives, things went smoothly.

A difficult situation was managed with delicacy throughout, and steered through the Divorce Court with entire absence of ill-feeling and recrimination.

Frank and I were married in 1939 and never regretted it.

The following year Joy was killed in a flying accident whilst having instruction on a new type of machine.

Nothing is written here for effect. But to have omitted this part of our life-story would seem to me to have dismissed it as an incident of no importance and so do less than justice to one who was above all a very gallant woman.

3

HOOTON aerodrome was situated on the Cheshire side of the River Mersey, with a road and the Manchester Ship Canal between it and the river. A thick belt of trees lined the perimeter of the landing-ground obscuring the canal, but masts and funnels of ships on their way to and from Manchester were visible above the tree-tops, giving the startling impression they were going by road.

The aerodrome had an unusual history. It had not been carved out of the agricultural solid for the specific purpose of creating a landing-ground, so to speak, but seems to have been the kind of large open space that fidgets people into doing something with it. It had once been parkland, part of the estate of Hooton Hall, a long-vanished but vast residence in its day. A marble-pillared, ornamental pile with roof statuary, where, it is said, Lady Hamilton, long before she became Lady Hamilton, once put in an appearance as a nursemaid.

I am not certain of the chronological order of events, but at one time Hooton was a race-course. The outline of the track could still be seen from the air when I was flying there. Then at another time it was a sort of horse sports-ground, where polo was played in the summer, and obstacles erected for horsemen to overcome in pursuit of hounds and a drag in winter.

It was first made into an aerodrome during world war one when the hangars were built, and it was used as a training-ground. Government interest lapsed after the war ended and the RAF moved out; then large flocks of sheep and a few head of cattle were turned out to graze on the landing-field; a polo club was formed, and eventually a civilian flying club. All pursued their particular interests amicably, if a little hazardously, together.

It was in this state of derelict indecision when Frank took over in 1934, with little more than vision, vitality and a pilot's A licence.

By the time war broke out in 1939 it was a very flourishing aerodrome. And due entirely to private enterprise, moreover; foresight, guts and ability; no lavish corporation or public expenditure here.

Nor was Frank content to rest on first achievements. He always looked beyond the horizon to rich and foreign lands. He had schemes afoot for an aerial bus-route linking the coastal towns from Barrow-in-Furness to North Wales. Towns which, though near enough as the plane flies, are separated by large bays and inlets making long roundabout journeys necessary for communication by land.

Negotiations were under way with Koolhoven in Holland for the construction of Koolhoven aircraft under licence.

And of course there was to be the continued development of present activities.

However, it was not to be.

Three days before the declaration of war, an Air Ministry order came out grounding all civilian aircraft.

Flying was finished for us. And if only we had been able to see into the future and know this for a certainty, how much time and fret and bother would have been saved. All those trips to London, all those telephone calls, letters, telegrams, all those hours waiting for appointments with 'high officials' and others not so high; all those innumerable, interminable conferences, with everyone being so charming and so evasive, but somehow contriving to give the impression that we would be so useful if we would but contain our patience for a short while. All those hopes. And nothing – nothing but talk, talk, talk.

There was the aerodrome, aircraft, personnel, management; the whole set-up in a state of suspended animation, bursting its buttons with frustration, at a time when everyone was being exhorted to 'give of their best', 'pull together' and 'go to it'.

Not that Frank had any exalted notions of being swept into the RAF, lock stock and barrel as it were. But he did think the organisation he had built up at Hooton might be of some use to the war effort. At least he expected the Army co-operation flights to continue. They had apparently been regarded as of increasing importance during the three years prior to the outbreak of war. Surely, then, in war-time they would be even more valuable. Or had we all been wasting time and effort?

The Army co-op flying did in fact continue. For how long I do not know, as it was of little interest to us. With what seemed to us a total disregard of its contract, and without any notification then or at any other time, the Air Ministry brought civilian machines and personnel from the south to carry on the work.

Then the aerodrome was requisitioned. Fair enough. But compensation was arbitrary and took no account of one or two non-flying activities pursued at Hooton and which of course were discontinued forthwith.

The house we lived in by the aerodrome entrance gates was also requisitioned, and the aircraft, together with the rest of the civilian gear and oddments, were summarily bundled out of the hangars and stored in a disused grand-stand, where the whole lot was entirely destroyed by fire. A fire caused, not by enemy action, Act of God, or any reason sufficiently cataclysmic as to be unavoidable and consequently more easily forborne, but by some irresponsible dolt starting up a machine to see if it would. The aircraft were all packed closely together in a confined space, still with petrol in their tanks. The engine started, fired back – and up she went. Wood – dope – fabric – petrol – a lovely blaze. And that was that.

The dolt got away with it. Whether he did so in the ensuing court of enquiry is a matter for conjecture. We knew there *was* a court of enquiry, as we knew the reason for the fire, but unofficially. It was not considered necessary to impart the findings, officially, to anyone connected with the property destroyed.

Altogether it seemed that we had no place in the present scheme of things.

In my own humble petty way I had made approaches to see if anyone was interested in a spare pilot – a thousand hours flying is chicken-feed today, but it took some getting then and my experience had been pretty varied. But no one was interested in spare pilots. Not female ones anyway. By the time they were I was busy with something else and couldn't care less.

Frank was deeply wounded about the whole thing. He had been all set to pitch into battle carrying the standard and crying England their England, and somehow the battle had raged off elsewhere without him and he was left, feeling foolish, without even a flag to wag.

Obviously there was no point in waiting for a nicely engraved invitation to join the fray – we were not wanted. Oddly enough, even in war-time, one has to live and find the wherewithal to do so.

We decided quickly and firmly what we were going to do and did it.

∽ ∽ ∽ ∽ ∽

In the early 1920's Frank had returned from Canada to join his father, who was a rolling-stock and railway-wagon broker and dealer in heavy plant and machinery, and he followed this comparatively sober occupation until he left it to break into commercial aviation some years later. The business entailed a great deal of travelling to inspect prospective purchases for prospective buyers, and led him down mines, and, curiously, up factory chimneys, and he exacted a certain amount of fun as well as profit out of buying and selling things like steam cranes and railway engines.

Amongst other things he got an insight into the business of quarrying, particularly in relation to the quarrying of gravel and sand.

The death of his father when Frank was established at Hooton left him as sole executor of the merchanting business, which he administered along with his aviation activities, and it was through this interest he acquired leases on two gravel quarries in Flintshire. They were worked in a somewhat perfunctory manner on the spade-and-lorry principle, Frank intending to open them up properly as soon as he was able to spare the time and capital from the flying interests. So on the abrupt and complete cessation of the flying interests he turned to the development of the larger of the two quarries with his usual dynamic energy.

An immense Air Ministry project was being mooted at Birkenhead calling for large supplies of gravel for concrete construction.

Frank interviewed the contractors and they approved the gravel samples.

But there is more to quarrying gravel than haphazardly digging at the quarry face. There is a limited amount of gravel in any one area that can be worked economically. There may be stratas of marl, etc, and the top cover removal has to be considered in opening up a quarry to best advantage. If you are not careful you may soon find yourself 'dug in' and the quarry closed with further workings impracticable or dangerous.

And in this particular instance the gravel was required to a particular specification; it was to be washed and graded, and free from impurities such as marl, clay, soil and such.

It all entailed the installation of mobile machinery – excavators, dumpers and a light-gauge railway; the erection of a washing and sorting plant; the diversion of a stream, excavation for a reservoir and the building of a dam to supply water to the plant.

In the planning of all this I witnessed, not a little impressed, an example of Frank's versatility. He seemed as much at home and as deeply interested in the extraction of stones from a hole in the ground as he had been in the launching of aeroplanes into the air. And as far as I could see he worked the whole thing out on the backs of envelopes. He was the most inveterate back-of-envelope calculator I ever knew. And what was even more extraordinary, lengthy involved arithmetic committed casually to scraps of paper produced real working things, like gravel going up the conveyor belt into the maw of juddering screens and being delivered into fore-ordained loads . . . and exactly the right amount of water being delivered to the plant, and so on. . . .

But it all cost more than it should have done, owing to the rocketing of wages, and the rise in price of machinery, which was difficult to obtain. It also cost more than there was capital available. However, there it was, eventually working, with gratifying streams of lorries bearing the product away. And there was no difficulty whatever in arranging for a mortgage.

Meantime my own energies were being absorbed in the agricultural reform of a small weed-grown wilderness.

After being driven out of Hooton we took a place called Merebrook in the heart of the Wirral, about six miles from Birkenhead and about eighteen from the quarry. The surrounding country *was* country, surprisingly rural and unspoilt considering the nearness of Birkenhead and Liverpool – towns which, whatever their standing in industry, can make no claims to beauty.

Merebrook had five acres of land and a stream as a boundary. There were woods on the other side of the stream – I saw an animal slipping through the trees there one day and called to it thinking it was my Alsatian, Biddy, then looked again and saw it was a fox.

The house was an uninspired stucco villa, the outside belying an interior of pleasantly proportioned rooms, and there was an adequate range of outbuildings and a stable-yard.

But it was the land that appealed to me when we were house-hunting.

There were two orchards, two minute paddocks, several small gardens for kitchen produce, soft fruit and flowers, leading off one another and enclosed by hedges. There were lawns and rosebeds, a sunken garden and a lily pool. And all in the most appalling tangle. Bramble, nettle, dock, sorrel and every conceivable weed rioted in extraordinary profusion. One orchard was thick with a prodigious jungle-like growth of nettles, eight feet high. We scythed them down, to discover a shed large enough to shelter a pony – it did in fact shelter a pony although it was officially designated for ducks.

And the land appealed to me because it was in such an awful mess.

I had made up my mind when the flying was finished to go in for farming in a small way. Subsistence farming with possibly a surplus for sale. Poultry, a cow maybe, and certainly a horse. All my life I had been thwarted in my desire to have a horse of my own, and by God, I was going to have one now. As a matter of fact I had two.

Like Frank I had a mania for building things up. It would have bored me to distraction to take over an established smallholding. Merebrook, desolate, neglected and overgrown, was, in truth, just my line of country: reclaiming it was the greatest fun. All sorts of odd facts and information came stealing in from forgotten corners of my mind, as though they had been waiting for the time when they would be needed. Information gathered and absorbed, quite unconscious of its having any possible future value, on my grandmother's farm where I had spent the happiest childhood holidays imaginable. And of course all my life I had been used to handling horses and dogs: and when it comes to handling different kinds of livestock, it is really attitude of mind that counts, management simply differs in detail.

We took all the technical farming papers and devoured them from cover to cover and read all the farming books we could lay hands on. Frank was drawn inexorably into the agricultural web, and we spent hours planning out crop rotations for our scrappy bit of land, with as much passionate enthusiasm as if it had been a real 200-acre job.

We had Rhode Island hens and Khaki Campbell ducks, but no cow. The land would not support a cow and two ponies, and the ponies I would not relinquish for anything or anyone. We bought a goat for household milk supplies.

If anyone had told me a year previously that goats would follow aeroplanes and become almost as obsessional an interest, I would have laughed myself silly.

But we started with one goat and before we knew what we were

20

at, we were up to the ears in genetics, blood lines, balanced rations and a herd of ten.

Petrol rationing was no hardship to me, as I had the ponies for transport and rode or drove everywhere – taking a load of apples into Birkenhead or bringing home the week's meat ration in a saddle-bag. One pony, a three-quarter-bred chestnut polo mare, had come to us in the first place as an 'evacuee', but we fell in love with her and bought her. She was a beautiful animal, a good ride and an engaging personality, but an utter fool. The other was a grey Welsh mare, highly intelligent and versatile, with an irrepressible sense of humour. She pulled the dogs' tails when they weren't looking and teased Flash unmercifully. Going to town with her in the governess car provided endless amusement. If she considered I was spending too long in one shop she would come bursting in the doorway dragging the trap after her, or else she would go off on her own to find a confectioner's where she would block the entrance and badger the assistants for cakes, which she always got – and at a time when everyone else had to go on their hands and knees and beg for them. She enjoyed being ridden but disliked harness work and often feigned lameness with embarrassing realism at the start of a drive. People with an RSPCA look in their eye used to shout menacingly at me as she hobbled along. When it was quite clear I had no intention of being brow-beaten into putting back, the lameness vanished. It was never known to occur when her head was turned towards home.

In course of time the domination of weeds was overcome and every square inch at Merebrook was urged into the production of food for ourselves and the animals. I was caught up in the remorseless rhythm of country life and made all the usual things, butter, cheese, preserves and pickles, and was pretty pleased – and a little surprised, domesticity not being my strong point – at providing a table where only items like flour and coffee were, so to speak, imported.

The small venture of Merebrook prospered quietly alongside the larger venture of the quarry, so that Frank's brief resurgence of ship-passion over the ketch *Mariana* really had not a chance. Her appearance was inopportune. She could not be moved down to the Dee or Mersey, and we could not afford to buy her for the fun of having her up at Glasson doing nothing. Nor could we afford – or for that matter, wish – to throw up everything to live aboard and look at the view.

All we could do was take a look at her, dream a little, and let her go.

Sometimes I wonder whether – but what odds – is there any more useless pastime than the speculation on what might have been . . . ?

In some ways those few years at Merebrook were the happiest in our lives: they were certainly for a short time the most contented, for living by and on the land is the most satisfying way of life there is. Of course we missed the thrill and adventure of flying, a loss that would in time have become acute and have driven us out again in search of it, because for some people the call of adventure, excitement, *wanderlust* – what you will – is absolutely irresistible; it supersedes everything else. And it is a very real thing. I have heard the suggestion that it is a survival of the migratory instinct. Be that as it may, when you feel the urge to go, go you must, and there is nothing on earth will stop you.

However, it did not come to that at Merebrook, for suddenly and for the second time in three years, the whole fabric of our lives disintegrated.

It was winter. Unprecedented frost and heavy snowfalls made the quarry inoperable, and work there was at a standstill for weeks. As long as the quarry was in production all out-goings were met without difficulty, but there was not enough working capital available to withstand the drain of weeks of idleness. Mortgage repayments fell overdue. Then the weather cleared, and once more the quarry went into production. After a period of anxious unremitting hard work back payments were made up and forwarded with present dues. To our everlasting astonishment these were returned and the mortgagees foreclosed. I am not prepared to argue this point, I am merely recounting what happened.

This hit Frank very hard indeed. He had never lacked ability nor spared himself in effort, and these had been enough to advance any project he had undertaken before the war. Then he had been thrust out of aviation, unwanted in the war effort, and now thrown out of the quarry business through no fault of his own. Clearly, ability and tenacity of purpose were no longer enough, but what else was needed he did not know. He became uncertain of himself, bitter and withdrawn; feelings only overcome after a long inward struggle, but which nevertheless left a lasting influence.

Financially it was a knockout blow. We were thrown on to the resources of Merebrook; subsistence 'farming' had to become

22

overnight the real thing. But it was a losing battle from the word go. The overheads were disproportionately high and the land unsuitable for intensive cultivation. One paddock was little more than a grass-grown rubbish dump, impossibly small and steep for working, and the other was not much better. The soil in one of the orchards was six inches off rock, as the stunted growth of trees showed only too well, and so on. Either we had to find more land to rent locally or another farm altogether.

We stuck to the agricultural line because it suited our mood.

Almost a year dragged by during which we sold the fruit crop, vegetables, milk, everything the holding produced, and subsisted on a pretty low level ourselves, and were quite unsuccessful in find-ing local land or a farm to rent.

Then we switched our lives on to another track through reading a book called *Dream Island Days* by R. M. Lockley, telling of his life on a small island off the Pembrokeshire coast. It opened up a new vista altogether.

'He's got something there, you know,' said Frank one evening, laying the book down and leaning forward to stare into the fire. 'That's what I should like to do. Get to hell and gone from all this bloody turmoil and farm one of those little islands. Only natural hazards to compete with then. No bureaucratic busybodies, no ruddy argument. Not a goddam' soul. Bliss.'

'Well,' said I, 'what's to stop us?'

And we started to look for an island.

Islands were no easier to come by than any other kind of land, but we found one eventually in Loch Lomond. At first we were in-clined to be uppish about it, we wanted a sea island and felt that one in a lake was being rather synthetic. But as it was the only one on offer we went to have a look at it.

The owner occupant of the island, a Mrs Scott, we understood to be a widow, and gathered this was a fairly recent state and the cause of her wishing to leave.

For some quite unknown reason we got into our heads the pic-ture of a lonely grey-haired soul, sternly Scotch and upright, gazing stonily through the cottage windows on to the waters of the lake, longing for the day when she would join her 'ain folk' on the main-land. Our imaginations added a subdued storm background of whining wind and low fleeting clouds.

We had to modify our views somewhat on being met at the loch-side by a stalwart, curly-headed youth of about nineteen, who grinned widely and said, 'Hello, I'm Tom Scott.' But we were completely unprepared on reaching the island for the glamorous appearance of a dark-eyed popsie in slacks and sweater who came gaily to meet us and said, 'Hullo, I'm Mrs Scott.'

. . . And the sky was blue, the loch was blue, the mountains on the mainland were blue and the island was a vivid green. Everything was bright and clear, and very beautiful. . . .

Mrs Scott had had a Cheltenham education and had married a sheep farmer. He had come home one day with the unexpected news he had bought an island and they were going to live there. Which they did, farming sheep and visitors and living happily with their two young sons, until tragedy came to the island and Mr Scott died suddenly of heart failure.

'I am uncertain what to do for the best,' said Mrs Scott. 'My husband always wanted the boys to be sheep farmers. . . . Jay is still at school but Tom's grown up now and if he is going in for sheep I think we should move to the mainland, and that means selling the island. I don't know whether to sell or not.'

The whole set-up was entirely different from what we had expected.

'That is up to you,' we said, 'we are not in a position to advise or persuade you one way or the other.'

But we had fallen madly for the island.

Inchmurrin was the largest island in the loch, about a mile and a half long, rugged, romantic and lovely. We walked some of its length and were enchanted by visions of sheltered bays, white beaches and Walt Disney woodlands and warrens.

There were one or two plantations of good straight pine.

'Hm,' said Frank, looking at them shrewdly, evoking, no doubt, lumberjack memories.

A sharp little hill rose steeply in the centre of the island to 300 feet like a miniature mountain. It was covered in rhododendron groves.

There were five bungalows scattered about the island, any one of which it would be a delight to live in.

The farmstead was exceptionally well-contained, with saw-mill, blacksmith's shop, dairy and incinerator (rubbish riddance is an island problem as we were to find), as well as the usual outbuildings. Water was laid on – spring water – and there was electricity from a home plant.

A bungalow on the foreshore by the jetty was fitted out like a

24

film-star's weekend cottage. Behind this bungalow a high rocky promontory ran out into the loch and on top of the promontory was the ivy-clad ruins of a castle, Lennox Castle, with the usual bloody history peculiar to Scottish ancient monuments.

And there were boats. . . .

Frank showed the first real enthusiasm I had seen since the quarry débâcle. He glinted at the saw-mill, so that I knew he was picturing planks coming off the saw bench like parts off a production line. From various asides I gathered he was peopling the island with opulent visitors from the South, relaxing in the peace of the charming bungalows and being supplied, of course, by us with home produce, boats and trips round the loch.

I took a few mental gallops round Inchmurrin on horseback, and thought an island would be ideal for goat-keeping; no more straying on to neighbour's land with its consequent hoo-ha.

Frank thought an island would be ideal for rearing geese in a big way – 'All this water,' he said, 'they could paddle about as much as they liked. Nae bother.' He had even begun to pick up the language.

We both thought this island ideal.

Oh dear, oh dear, we were bogged down, bewitched and be-dazzled.

Finally Mrs Scott decided to sell. An agreement was mooted and lawyers set to aggravating themselves with matters regarding deeds, documents and detail, and we hurried home to ponder the problem of raising the money.

We gave our Merebrook landlord notice. We sold the car, governess cart and gig; we intended keeping the ponies, but the traps were hardly suitable for a trackless island. An auction was fixed and advertised for the disposal of furniture and effects which would be out of place and redundant on Inchmurrin. With an eye to the future I sold off several non-pedigree goats and replaced them with high-bred Anglo-Nubians, colourful animals with long drooping ears, satin skins and milk like pure cream. Shop-window goats for the delectation and beguilement of opulent visitors.

Railway officials were consulted and arrangements made for the transport of gear and livestock to the far North.

Arrangements were complete in fact for our departure, except for the one vital one of finance.

We need not have worried, however. At the last moment a telegram arrived to say the island was not, after all, for sale.

4

'WELL, *well,*' said Frank helplessly waving the telegram, 'that puts the cat properly among the pigeons.'

We were rather in the position of a trapeze artist who has let go of his own trapeze only to find his mate has failed to lower the other and can but hope there is a net beneath to break the fall.

After an urgent passage of telegrams we confronted Mrs Scott again on the island. She said that having discussed the matter further with the boys they just could not find it in their hearts to leave Inchmurrin, and for that we could not blame them in the least; but it did not alleviate our own situation, which had become uncomfortably rugged. We talked and cast about a bit for ideas and then it was all agreeably smoothed when agreement was reached for us to go to the island as tenants: an overall rental covering the film-star bungalow, some of the outbuildings and a share of the land.

An arrangement we felt to have much to recommend it.

It meant a modification of plans, of course; we could hardly expect a share of any opulent visitors, and we decided on a modest programme of rearing geese and pedigree goats – now increasingly popular owing to the exigencies of the times – with the possibility of the sale of goat milk to a hospital on the mainland. We foresaw no difficulty in the daily transport of milk from Inchmurrin – it was not as though it was a sea island. . . .

The auction sale of furniture and effects at Merebrook realised far more than we could have hoped for in our wildest moments and gave an unexpectedly solid backing to the new venture. In the winter of 1943 we settled on Inchmurrin with our goats and geese and a comfortable optimism regarding the future.

The winter was exceptionally mild, but in spite of that the goats were kept housed to acclimatise them gradually to northern conditions. They flourished, impressing everyone who saw them, and we looked to gallons of milk and a bumper crop of kids in the Spring.

On the goose side of the venture we had two pens of fine up-standing birds, which terrified everyone who came to the island, and an incubator.

We chartered a four and a half ton sloop, feeling superiorly independent of the capricious issue of petrol coupons because, as Frank said, the wind is free.

Inspired by the novelty of our new life he wrote a few articles and sold them.

Amicable discussions were held with the Scotts and plans made for the growing of fodder crops.

Then Spring came in all its glory, and there was a wonderful burgeoning forth of flora and fauna. The goats kidded down with a splendid lot of kids and went into lavish milk production, and the weather being fine and mild they were turned out to take advantage of the new Spring grass. All round the farmstead geese were busily setting up house and hatching eggs, while the ganders kept anxious watch. We bought further goose eggs and filled the incubator.

Primroses carpeted the woods.

Fortune, we said, was a lovely lady who had come to stay with us.

We thought, before we went to Inchmurrin, we were tough. We thought we had been around and learnt a thing or two. We stayed ten months on the island and it nearly broke our hearts. Fortune, the sly bitch, silently packed her bags and slipped away, leaving us to start again at A in the alphabet of experience.

The first indication of the turn of events came just before Spring got going with her annual production.

In connection with the quarry was a charge outstanding at the Bank. In a most gentlemanly way they had agreed to leave it over until we had become established in our new venture, and we felt secure in the knowledge that our private account was substantial enough to see us through until such time as we were paying our way.

Frank opened the mail one morning and went glum.

'They've collared the lot,' he said.

'Who's collared what?'

'The Bank. We've had it . . . now that we are established etc, etc . . . interest and so forth . . . bla bla bla. Heigh-bloody-ho,' said Frank.

'But I thought – dammit they can't alter the laws of Nature, we're not in production *yet*. We're *not* established —'

'Oh, but we are. It says so here.' He tapped the letter.

'So what can we do?'

'Nothing. Pull in our belts and wait.'

The geese were fine heavy birds and trampled each gosling to death as it emerged from the egg. We managed to save some, six I think, and put them under a broody hen. The eggs in the incubator did not hatch at all, they were an odoriferous, one hundred per cent failure.

Well, well, we said, we know to keep a sharper eye on mother goose in future. We thought we knew the reasons for the failure of the incubated eggs. There were a few birds to add to the flock. We'll do better next year, we said, and hitched the metaphorical belt another notch.

The goats did not take advantage of the new Spring grass. They made a concerted attack on the rhododendron bushes and were one and all violently, elaborately, sick. I had expected this and knew from experience the experiment would not be repeated. Then with 300 acres to go at they had to pick on the Scotts' garden. An unfortunate choice. When eventually they got down to the new Spring grass they also went down in condition. Down and down they went, and the milk yield too. The kids gambolled very prettily and ate prodigiously but did not grow at all. We had never had this happen before and could not understand it.

'Och,' said Tom Scott, 'they're tender. The island's full of filth.'

'What on earth do you mean?'

'Filth,' he repeated vaguely, and said they always bought their stock from the hills, rough stuff that needed no coddling and thrived on hard treatment.

Filth? Filth? Ah – parasites. Internal parasites. Yes, the island would be full of 'filth'. Overrun with rabbits. And there were sheep too. Two animals notorious for parasitic ills. Of course, we said, coccidiæ, worms, and all the little horrors that sit invisible on blades of grass waiting to be eaten so they can go to town in someone's alimentary canal.

An extensive worming programme was carried out with the aid and advice of a local vet, whom we ferried across in the yacht and who was considerably moved thereby. He was not used to visiting farms by sail.

But we were wrong. It was not the answer. It did no good whatever. The adult animals continued to deteriorate and one by one the kids dwindled and died.

28

It was physically sickening to watch them fade and be utterly powerless to help them.

It was unfortunate too. There was an exceptional demand for pedigree kids at high prices that year, but ours were unsaleable. From a financial point of view the most sensible thing would have been to have butchered the lot and cut our losses. But we just couldn't do it, and struggled on to find the cause and cure.

The sloop *Shireen*, which might have given us a little fun, proved to be but another thorn. Too deep-draughted to lie at anchor in the shelter of the jetty bay, she had to lie outside at the mercy of whatever wind was blowing. It blew so often and so hard. The bottom was sand and gave the anchor poor hold; she was forever dragging off and we were forever dragging her back. She gave us many a wet windy battle at night keeping her off the rocks at the foot of Castle Hill, but very little sailing fun because there was always the nagging fear at the back of our minds that something was going wrong in our absence.

Yet all this might have been reasonably bearable. The misfortunes were of our own making very largely; we chose the wrong boat and the wrong live-stock for the job, and of your own mistakes you can at least say, that was a bad break, I won't do it again, and fortify yourself accordingly. But what brought us down to an almost Russian intensity of despair was the unfailing, incessant, wracking irritation of everyday life.

This had nothing to do with the island itself. We always loved the *island* aspect of the life, which made it all the more maddening that we could take so little pleasure in it.

For a long time we could not make out what was the matter. Then we saw what it was.

Nothing quite worked. It was the 'quite' that was so defeating.

There are usually two ways of doing a job: a blood-sweating manual method or a labour-saving way by machine. If the machine is available you use it. But if the machine turns out to be inoperable and the tools for repair have themselves to be repaired or made, then it is somehow more aggravating than doing the job the hard way in the first place – especially if you have to resort to blood-sweating in the end.

When this happens *every* time, with every kind of machine and implement you touch, and the articles always fool you into using them by appearing to be in working order and only break down in use, it is apt to become tiresome.

Tom Scott never minded manhandling a job. He pulled nails out of planks with his fingers and spent restful evenings putting the weight or tossing the caber after spending the day knocking fence posts in single-handed with a fourteen-pound hammer. Whether any of the machinery worked or not was a matter of indifference to him.

Frank grumbled: 'It's all very well for these Tarzan types. I'm only a hundred and forty pounds, and why should I hump things on my back now that the wheel has been invented?'

He spent an inordinate amount of time mending machinery of which Tom would say, 'Och, it's nae guid. Wants sorting.' And mending tools to mend the tools to mend the machine. A ten-minute job often ran into days of labour. It was like the old nursery rhyme, 'stick won't beat dog' – so many things 'wanted sorting' the expression passed into the family vocabulary.

This curious state of not quite working even penetrated the domestic sphere, where it reached the most exquisite degree of irritation in the kitchen.

To look at it was charming. Apple green and white, it presented a picture of an ideal kitchen as depicted in the glossier magazines for women. Visitors (for whom it was always specially burnished) used to gasp and exclaim with envy, 'How enchanting!' And we used to take a perverse sardonic delight in their pleasure because we knew it was a little hell on earth.

As a setting for week-enders content to toy with a sardine the kitchen had much to commend it; as a kitchen to live in – nothing at all.

The floor was laid with slabs of polished white granite. It shone like marble and had all the lethal properties of ice. It showed every mark, large as life and twice as dirty.

The hollow designer of that kitchen made no provision for the storage of goods, dry or otherwise. Outside, at the back of the bungalow, stood a magnificent meat-safe, as large as a henhouse, constructed of rustic timber. Very pretty it looked, quite in keeping with its surroundings. The finest fly-trap ever devised.

It is customary when living a farming, backwoods, or other form of outdoor life to use the kitchen as a general living-room. It is the hub of your little world. You have your being there because, apart from anything else, you are rarely in a fit state to loll in the parlour even if you have the time. Our kitchen was so small it was crowded if you sat down. The inevitable addition of small live-stock, such as a kid or a bunch of goslings, brought in for necessary extra care and attention, made for frantic confusion, and I am not exaggerating when I say if we squeezed something in at the back door something else had to go out of the window.

There was a dainty little sink and an even daintier little draining-board, nicely adequate for dealing with a dainty little cup and saucer. Washing-up reposed on the window-sill.

The high mark in this refined torture-chamber was the stove.

It was an elegant, glossy, green enamelled stove, as good to look at as the day it left the makers – and they were good too – but it seared my heart as surely as Calais did Bloody Mary's.

I am not a good housewife. I never pretend to be. I hate house-work. If there is a more stupefying, soul-deadening occupation I have yet to know it. But I do like cooking. And I do fancy I know my way about stoves. Or did until I met that one.

It was when we were very new chums on the island that a visitor, on learning which bungalow we lived in, said, 'Oh, yes, the Lodge. We stayed there once. Cooking by wind, eh?'

I couldn't think what she meant, but I soon found out.

There would be days when one could use all the available paraffin, dry wood and paper, only to be rewarded with clouds of black stinking smoke from the paraffin and not one flicker of a flame. There would be days when, miraculously, the fire would light and blaze merrily until the dinner was half cooked, then it would go suddenly, irrevocably, out. There would be days when it showed no signs whatever of burning, and after it had been left in despair would stoke itself into a raging furnace to carbonise everything within reach.

After Frank found from bitter experience it was not due to any lack or deficiency on my part, extensive researches were held, which disclosed that, apart from the undoubted blanketing effect of Castle Hill behind the bungalow, the chimney was led from the stove in gentle gradients round five sharp bends before finally going out, so that only a wind of gale force from one particular direction would induce sufficient draught to make the fire go.

We thought this rather depressing.

But how lucky we were to have plumbing! And how lucky we were that the lavatory only let us down once!

The valve stuck one night while we were both out doing our evening chores and we returned to find the tank energetically snort-ing out gallons of water on to the bungalow floors already six inches deep in flood. It is an amazing amount of water to mop up.

At that time we were still at the stiff-upper-lip stage with a grudge against humanity. Later we learned to laugh.

And then we were nearly at the end of the transition period: the sensitive skin of civilisation had almost peeled.

But it was all very well to laugh and grow tough. The goats were no laughing matter. And there was the future to consider. It stood before us, inescapable, staring at us with an unequivocal eye, demanding: what are you going to do now?

A question we found difficult to answer.

The herd of forty goats represented half our venture and was a failure. We hadn't the heart to kill them, we couldn't sell them, and we couldn't keep them on land which seemed to be slow death to them. As to the other half of the venture, we would just have to wait until Spring came round again to see if we had profited by our mistakes with the geese or not.

We were working very hard and getting dam-all out of it, no fun and no money. Yet it never occurred to either of us to give the whole thing up.

Being tenants made it impossible for us to exploit the island in any way, and being islanders made it impossible for us to take a job – not that it would have made much difference if we had. We shouldn't have lasted long; we were both essentially unemployable; either we were mad keen and lived our work twenty-four hours a day, or we were not interested and wouldn't touch it. But that was beside the point; mainly we felt if we couldn't get a piddling little show like this working then we had better pull the blankets over our heads for good and all.

So it was win or bust—but how?

The answer came accidentally and unsought. Frank overheard some gossip on the mainland to the effect that one of the loch islands was for sale.

'Did you hear which one it was?' I asked him.

'Inchfad. It's that green-looking one over near the Stirlingshire shore, Balmaha way. A sheep farm.'

'Hm. Fly, fluke, ticks, worms, scab and braxy . . . let's go and have a look at the condition of their sheep.'

We borrowed one of the Inchmurrin boats with an outboard one afternoon and set out for Inchfad. The motor broke down halfway and we had to row the rest, but it was only a mile or so and a nice bright day.

The sheep on Inchfad seemed in pretty good shape as far as we were able to judge, at least they were not conspicuously dying and there was a fairish crop of lambs.

As an agricultural proposition, if such an ambitious term could be applied to such super-marginal land, it was undoubtedly the best in the loch.

It was fairly flat, though not so low-lying as to be marshland, of about 120 acres and a mile long. Woodlands, alder, birch, ash and a few oak, lined the outskirts of the island to a depth inland of about fifty yards enclosing rolling grassland . . . large fields divided by stone walls straddling the breadth of the island. Grass was mainly bog and bent with patches of reed grass, but at any rate it was not rabbit moss. We saw very few rabbits. Bracken encroachment, the bane of the Highlands, was not as bad as it might be. It was bad at the south-western end of the island – the opposite end to where the farmstead was situated – but that end was very wild (and very lovely I thought) and comparatively a small portion of the whole.

A small group of stone buildings crouched at the corner of the island nearest the mainland, a mile distant, as though the occupants were marooned and were desperately keeping closest possible touch with the outside world. An impression heightened by the yearning way the jetty reached out from in front of the cottage. The cottage was stone with a wooden porch and two rooms and two attics, the latter approached by a ladder from the kitchen in which an open fire was the sole fitting.

There were two outbuildings: a combined stable and cow-shed of dry-stone construction and considerable age, and a well-built, fairly modern barn. The rest of the farmyard consisted of two disintegrating dry-stone enclosures; one had been half-heartedly converted into a pigsty, and a sheep dip which very effectively blocked entrance to the barn.

Plum, damson and crab-apple trees surrounded the cottage.

A canal led from a bay on the south shore to the farmyard, somewhat overgrown and silted, but had the makings of a useful lay-by for small boats.

We looked with a critical eye this time, weighing the snags, and there were plenty, and we were not to be blindly beguiled by the island's quiet charm – a gentle, almost pastoral loveliness in comparison with the restless rugged beauty of Inchmurrin.

But we liked Inchfad. We knew life there would not be easy, but we did not ask for that. It had no pretensions, and we did not want any, having had enough of false gods. The trappings of civilisation are for civilised settings and not for the outback. An island of our own was what we wanted, where we could put up a shed or pull down a fence and hatch our ploys beholden to none.

This island might be the answer to our problem. Maybe the change of environment would save the goats. Maybe here, we'd win. . . .

As we slowly made our way back to Inchmurrin that evening Frank said, 'Omen, Ann . . . Inchfad. FAD Frank and Ann Davison. . . .'

5

BEING broke is a relative state.

There are people who complain of being broke, and genuinely believe they are, when financially limited to the purchase of one bottle of gin in place of the usual case, who see ruin staring them in the eye when only able to afford a ten horsepower car instead of a couple of twenties, and who are convinced they have reached the ultimate in poverty and degradation when forced to do their own washing-up.

On the other hand and at the other end of the scale, there are those whose personal possessions would not fill a small hold-all canvas bag, yet who never complain of being broke because it never occurs to them that they are.

At the time we looked over Inchfad we considered ourselves pretty poor, and in comparison with 'the state to which we had been accustomed' we were. But there were still a number of personal possessions having some value, various savings and odd pieces of property extant, which we looked upon as being indispensable to our well-being, and never thought of parting with because – well – there they were, there they always had been and some day they might Come in Useful.

And after we had seen Inchfad we thought some of them might come in useful right away if exchanged for legal tender.

I said, what possible use is there for a fancy fur coat on an island in a wet climate like this? – the proceeds from a fancy fur coat would go a long way towards buying a tractor and would be far more useful. And Frank said there is something in that. So we weighed up what we had against how much we wanted the island, and the upshot was the exchange of hitherto indispensable articles for an equity on the property and various essential farm implements; and we moved to Inchfad one gusty September morning in 1944 in a northerly gale with a stirring accompaniment of water-spouts.

Other than the tractor and farm implements that we had bought and which Frank immediately overhauled so there would be no doubt of their functioning (it was his pride to challenge every visitor the Fordson would start first swing, and win every time), there were no 'cons', mod or otherwise, so there was nothing to fool us and nothing to go wrong.

There wasn't even an E.C. to start with – we instituted an entirely new line in hospitality by handing guests a spade and a page from the Sunday paper (collected on Thursday) in the morning with the cryptic advice that digging was easiest in the woods across the canal.

We drew water from the loch in bucketfuls as needed and cut down trees for firewood. In no time I developed muscles like a prizefighter and was a leading authority on the cutting and combustible qualities of the island woods. We used oil lamps for lighting, and to be perfectly honest I never missed electricity, though Frank said it would have been useful in the outbuildings, but he was prejudiced against the hurricane lamp because once in a fit of absent-mindedness at night he had plunged the lamp into the loch, and held the bucket aloft whilst drawing water. . . . The only domestic refinement I ever looked forward to was the installation of drainage for the disposal of washing-up water. Carrying water in was no hardship, but carrying it out again was rather tedious.

The island was unoccupied for some time between the departure of the shepherd and our moving in, and during this period it was visited by a gang of those jolly little morons whose peculiar delight is the slitting of railway-carriage upholstery with razor-blades and pornographic writing on lavatory walls, when not otherwise amused in carving each other up with broken bottles or worse.

They poured out from Glasgow at weekends, to descend on the surrounding countryside like a blight, for a radius of twenty miles or more. Many of them had guns or rifles and most of them had large wicked-looking knives. They used to come out to Balmaha and camp along the shores, and hire rowing boats and howl like maniacs the weekend long. They killed sheep and barbecued them over fires made from farmer's fence posts; stole poultry, eggs, fruit and vegetables – 'you gotta eat' – and broke into houses and boats at anchor in Balmaha Bay.

Police seemed powerless to control them and they were accepted as one of the natural hazards by the local inhabitants along with cloudbursts, gales, late frosts and other Acts of God. They bore no particular animosity towards anyone, but their main object in life

was destruction: uprooting young plantations, wrecking a grave-yard or demolishing a cottage.

They may have been interrupted in their depredations at Inchfad, or perhaps they thought of something else more havoc-worthy, for the buildings were not actually pulled down, but all the same we were left with a legacy of some several weeks of unnecessary work before the place was even moderately habitable.

The cottage chimneys were knocked off, every window in every building smashed even to the frames, every door battered and un-hinged, and every building filled in every compartment with rocks, boulders, paper, broken bottles, glass and a confusion of unspeakable filth – we barrowed eighteen loads away from the cottage alone.

After that bit of nonsense was put to rights, in which we discovered window glazing to be quite an art, we turned our attention to the party-wall in the cowshed-cum-stable building. It was eighteen feet high and three feet thick, dry-stone construction, with a bulge in it that foreshadowed imminent disaster. Our efforts to ease it back to the vertical with a jack and timber were not successful, and as we were discussing the next move there was a faint whisper and rush of sound. . . . We made the door and swallowed our hearts just as the whole eighteen feet of it collapsed in thunder and a cloud of dust.

It was rebuilt, a concrete floor laid, wooden pens erected and a window inserted, and the cow-byre became a goat-house.

Frank was fired with a mania for dry-stone walling for a while and reconstructed the walls round the homestead, which were mostly in a state of rubble, and disregarded by the goats as un-worthy of their attention. But as soon as the walls were re-erected they offered unparalleled opportunities for rock-climbing practice and the goats lost no time in making use of them, dancing along the top and dislodging carefully placed stones, which was rather disheartening.

It took some time to instil into the animals' heads that the island was a creature's paradise, all theirs to graze and cavort on, and extending far beyond the boundaries of the homestead itself. They were a friendly, gregarious lot, and evidently liked our company: all of them ponies, geese, and goats. They swarmed round and into the cottage, rooting through cupboards and into the bread-bin, and were shooed out only to come in again the moment my back was turned.

I lost the porridge pan one day and found the grey pony, Star, licking it out in the orchard, having lifted it off the kitchen table under the open window and borne it away like a dog.

In desperation I would drive the animals right up the island and in ten minutes they would be in the yard again, lathering and breathing hard, having been rounded up and brought back at the gallop by Star.

Island life seemed to bring out all sorts of dog-like qualities in Star. The sight of strangers approaching in a boat filled her with frenzy, and she would whinny and snort and aggravate me until I went to deal with them; then she stood at my elbow, ears pricked and nostrils distended with suspicious rage, tense and ready to cope with any emergency.

Incredible though it may seem, the other pony, Flash, was still on the mainland. All the other animals had been transported across the loch in the first place to Inchmurrin by a flat-bottomed barge, which Flash had refused to board. The combined efforts of about six of us failed to convince her it was anything but a monstrous death-trap for horses. As the wind was getting up and it was getting late we had to allow her the point, and she was left, temporarily, at a lochside farm by agreement with the farmer.

Eventually she was conveyed to Inchfad by loading her into a horsebox – horseboxes were familiar and allowable – driving her to Balmaha, where the box gangway was lowered into the barge itself and Flash led aboard before she realised what was happening. Simple enough. But it took eighteen months to get the whole-hearted co-operation of the mare, the farmer, the contractor with the horsebox, the barge owner and the weather. . . .

It hardly seems possible, but after a few months living in the Highlands you would believe anything.

There is an engaging factor in the Highland character which forbids the following of an organised plan. You can gather round a body of men, lay before them a proposition, have their full enthusiastic support and agreement down to the smallest detail, and when the time comes for the programme to go into smooth prearranged action, utmost confusion reigns, because everyone concerned has thought of a better way which he keeps to himself, and acts upon with a total disregard of anything or anyone else.

Once you realise this it adds immeasurably to the adventure of the simplest undertaking.

An interesting example occurred during our first winter on Fad.

It was, we were told, the worst winter for fifty years – fifty years being the standard lapse of time apparently between recurrence of phenomenal meteorological behaviour. (I never knew a seaman yet who did not swear a gale of wind to be the worst for fifty years.) Heavy falls of snow with drifts of eighteen to twenty feet blanketed and silenced the countryside, and were followed by severe frosts.

We kept the kitchen fire raging day and night but failed to raise the temperature above 39 degrees F., and that was close by the fire; over by the door water spilt on the stone floor froze instantly. Outside metal froze to our fingers and we began to think the Arctic Circle had slipped.

The loch froze over and we had the interesting experience of walking right round the island on ice. There was one piece of open water left between Fad and Balmaha steamer pier (fortunately for *Shireen* at moorings), but there was a stretch of ice for a hundred yards from the island shores to the water.

Food rationing at that time (1944/45) was acute and it was impossible to build up a good stock of stores. Our stores consequently gave out before the weather let up.

We were still dealing with the grocers we dealt with whilst on Inchmurrin, whose shop was in Dumbarton, and normally we sailed the six miles to Balloch at the foot of the loch and went into Dumbarton from there by bus. This was of course impossible when the loch was covered with ice.

So with the cupboard bare and a falling glass we hacked a way through the ice for the dinghy and Frank set off for Balmaha with a list of groceries, a bucket and spade and a definite air of determination, just as the hoppers of heaven opened wide to shower down a blinding blizzard of snow.

He left the boat at Balmaha pier and found road communications to the outer world cut, so rang up the grocers and arranged for them (the roads there still being open) to send the groceries by bus from Balloch to Drymen, four miles from Balmaha. An errand boy would deliver the goods to the Drymen bus.

Then he plodded through snow and drifts to Drymen and eventually met the bus.

'Och, ay,' said the driver thoughtfully, 'the parcels for Davison. They're away to Luss.'

Luss is on the other side of the loch twenty miles away.

And what, Frank wanted to know, would they be doing at Luss?

'Yon laddie gie me the parcels and said they were for Davison of

Inchmurrin, and I said ye no want the Drymen bus for Inchmurrin – it's the Luss bus ye'll be wanting, so they're away to Luss,' said the driver simply.

The errand boy had not accepted the validity of our new address apparently. After all we had only been there five months.

So Frank went on the bus back to Balloch and there met the driver of the Luss bus on his return from Luss. He had very cleverly put the parcels off at the post office at Arden, where mail and goods were usually left for inhabitants of Inchmurrin. Only we weren't inhabitants of Inchmurrin. . . . And Arden was a long snowy way from Balloch.

However, when the situation was explained to the driver – with the aid of the driver of the Drymen bus and various interested and irrelevant bystanders – he willingly undertook to bring the parcels back with him on his next journey, and Frank kicked his heels in a coffee shop in Balloch until the goods arrived just in time for him to catch the last bus to Drymen.

The going from Drymen to Balmaha was bad. It took him four hours to cover the four miles and it was just on midnight when he ploughed into the village.

He scrambled down to the shore, laid the precious groceries under a tree and found the boat sunk, having filled with the day's load of snow.

It was pitch dark and snowing all the time.

He bailed out the icy sludge and refloated the boat and went to get the parcels. They had disappeared, buried in drifts. He dug around for a time and eventually found them and then set off for home.

I, of course, knew nothing of all this. I had had to stay on the island to look after the animals, and as conditions were so bad I never expected Frank to attempt the journey home that day, and went to sleep by the kitchen fire contented that he was spending the night in the village with friends.

At four o'clock in the morning I was awakened by an ear-splitting howl of rage, and rushed out of the cottage in pyjamas, to fall flat on my face in four feet of snow.

And out on the loch was my husband tearing off an expressive strip of language that would have shaken Billingsgate into silence.

The channel we had hacked out through the ice had filled during the day with a porridge of semi-frozen snow, too thick to row through, and the ice barrier itself was too thick, and the boat too heavy, to allow of it being lifted on to the ice and dragging it ashore that way. Frank eased her through the channel by shifting his weight about, balancing on bow and stern to lift her and make her break her own way through. He had succeeded in getting her halfway when he slipped and fell in.

I gave him a hand to beach the boat and land the goods, then we beat it for the cottage. There I was horrified to see he had turned quite white, then found his head was covered in a cap of solid ice.

An ecstatic Spring followed the hard Winter, and the plum trees round the homestead were bowed down in a gorgeous drift of blossom which escaped the late frosts that devastated the mainland fruit crop, and we were able to sell the plums later to advantage. But the Spring also brought some pretty searching winds from the east, which caused *Shireen* to come ashore instead of going abroad as she was still wont to do.

We put down monumental moorings of all the scrap-iron the island could muster, including a huge old plough and a colossal iron-shod cartwheel; but she wore them like so many charms on a chain and took them with her wherever she went. One night in a northerly blow she took two anchors and the ironmongery on a trip to Balmaha and anchored herself by the steamer pier there without a scratch; bowsprit six inches off the pier and counter about a foot from an outcrop of rock.

We overcame the *wanderlust* eventually by warping her to a tree on the shore. But this did not stop her coming in in the easterlies. It was quite impossible to get her off in any normal manner; she drove in, scouring a pit for herself in the sand so that she was apparently drawing six feet in about two of water, and there were no tides to float her off; so Frank used to rig an involved series of tackles, quite beyond my powers to recapitulate, from the yacht, round trees, and finally on to the pony who was rather dispirited about the whole thing.

At a signal from Frank on the boat I would urge the pony to heave, and after a few moments of strain, in which I had visions of something going ping and Star hurtling backwards into the loch, the yacht would edge slowly, and miraculously, out into deeper waters.

There are so many islands, shallows and rocks in the loch, and the weather changes there with such lightning rapidity from calm to storm, that sailing in Loch Lomond is fraught with excitement.

Never a dull moment. We had some rip-roaring sails in *Shireen* going about our normal business, but I never learnt to sail.

Frank clung to his theory that I would be a 'natural' because of some prowess in handling horses and aircraft, and that I had only to take the tiller for nautical fervour to do the rest.

As a matter of fact I was thoroughly inhibited about the whole business. We had so much to do that whenever we went out in *Shireen* it was for some specific purpose and there was no time to play around, so I just had to 'work ship' blindly hoping I was doing the right thing, without gaining any real insight or understanding of what was happening. Frank's misplaced confidence in my supposed abilities made him impatient of my shortcomings, and I passionately envied his cheerful ease in handling the boat and worked up quite a hate for her on account of my own incompetence.

Every time we went out in her I girded on my armour so to speak and prepared for battle.

And I never could remember the names of things. I had absorbed so much technical jargon in my time there seemed no room in my head for any more, and nautical nomenclature is so steeped in tradition and obscure in origin it gives no clue to its relationships. My own names for the gear were lurid and descriptive, but, Frank said, unorthodox.

When the year's charter was up and *Shireen* had to go I expected to cheer her on her way. Now we would get a boat with a reliable engine, something any simpleton could handle, and my vanity would be soothed and confidence restored. No more black nights hove-to in tearing squalls with the headsail blown to ribbons: no more beating up between the islands against intolerable headwinds: no more hours becalmed on dead waters: no more shaming departures from the crowded anchorage at Balloch with *Shireen* screaming off on the wrong tack and Frank heaving the anchor aboard, yelling himself hoarse with unintelligible instructions. . . .

For Frank's sake I was sorry she was going; he had loved sailing her, but he knew how; for myself, I thought it would be a happy parting. But no: *Shireen* was my quarrelling focus. My friend the enemy. When she went, to my ineffable surprise, she took most of the fun of the island with her.

6

WE bought a thirty-foot double-ended lifeboat hull from the Ministry of Transport for £5. She was only about three years old and was cheap on account of severe, but not irremediable, charring along one side. She had mast, sails, sweeps, a useful collection of gear and was bored and fitted with bearers. Also from the MOT we bought a single-cylinder Acadia engine, practically new, but which had been submerged and was seized solid. It cost £25.

In the ensuing months we were able to give our 'building-up' complex full rein, and refitted, rebuilt, overhauled and reassembled the hull and engine and put them together to make a motor barge. The centre thwart was removed to make cargo space, a derrick fitted; we christened her *Phœnix* and proudly launched our working boat.

The first real working trip in her was to Balloch station, there to pick up thirty bales of hay. It was mid-January of the second Winter on Fad, not so spectacular as the previous Winter, but bitterly cold. We set off in the late afternoon and made Balloch in fine style, thinking it was all too easy now we had a good reliable engine.

The wagon-load of hay was waiting for us at the railway pier-head, but the station staff had all gone off watch and left us to help ourselves. A thick sheet of ice lay on the tarpaulin and broke like glass when we threw it off.

Phœnix was pretty low in the water when the loading was finished and looked pretty odd too, with a load of hay reaching half-way up the mast, like a floating haystack.

The wagon was twenty yards from the pier-head; and by the time we had humped each frozen bale along the slippery track and lowered it into the boat we were frozen too, and gladly accepted an invitation from the skipper of one of the loch steamers laid up nearby to go aboard for a drink and warm up before going home.

It was eight o'clock and pitch dark when we set out; not a breath of wind, a still, frosty night. Pooh, we said, it's nothing, we'll be back in no time with *Phœnix*.

About a mile on the way, in the middle of the loch, the engine blew up with a resounding report and stopped.

We had no lights of any sort on the boat: no one ever bothered about navigation lights on the loch, and we were the only folk ever to venture forth at night. Nor had we a torch aboard, and only a few matches. Frank was not at all enthusiastic about using matches to illuminate a petrol-dripping engine, and in any case they were used up, burnt out quickly and feebly, before the trouble was located.

The cold was intense, penetrating and enveloping. Our breath hung like steam on the air, and there was a film of ice on everything.

After several hours' ineffective fiddling with the invisible engine, and exhaustive swinging – it was a heavy little motor and could not be swung in the ordinary way with a starting handle, the flywheel had to be levered over – Frank suddenly gave up in panting fury, wrapped himself in the jib and curled down in the cockpit, saying tersely from the folds of his canvas cocoon, 'Grab yourself a piece of mainsail and snug down.'

Snug down indeed! Have you ever tried to snug down in the sort of storm canvas they hand out to lifeboats when that canvas is frozen stiff? You might as well make yourself comfortable with a pair of corrugated iron sheets. I crept under a corner of the mainsail covering the hay and crouched against a bale which had all the snuggable qualities of an iceberg.

For immeasurable hours we stayed like that, petrified, the slightest movement bringing great wafts of cold which was already insupportable. Then a sharp little breeze sprang up and slashed at us with its knife-edge. Frank erupted from his chrysalis, shouted, 'This is murder,' and dragging the jib with him, disappeared over the haystack for'ard.

'We've got the wind free by gosh,' he shouted. 'We'll sail her home' – and hoisted the jib.

It was an infinitesimal sail, but a very large haystack, and we got under way bobbling about the loch in a most unhandy fashion, until we reached the south-west corner of Fad with another mile to go before making home base. The wind came round then on our beam, and as it is impossible to trim a haystack *Phœnix* made determined efforts to go ashore. She went the length of the island

46

crab-wise, overhanging branches brushing against her, while we poled her off with a sweep.

It was just coming dawn and eight o'clock in the morning when we crept into the canal, having achieved six miles in twelve hours. *Shireen* at her worst had never put up a record like this.

With daylight on the problem there was no difficulty in locating and remedying the engine trouble. And *Phœnix* did not fail us again; she turned out to be the staunch island boat we expected, and worked with such efficient reliability we became ineffably bored with her.

As with the transport, the rest of our island problems settled themselves one by one.

There had been no improvement in the condition of the goats when we first went to Inchfad. They continued to waste away until we called in another vet, nearer to hand now we had moved, and he spotted the trouble at once. 'Mineral deficiency,' he said.

'But I mix minerals in their feed and they have mineral licks to go at whenever they want,' I protested.

'Nevertheless they are not getting enough. Put the mixture out so that they can help themselves,' he advised.

And I did. The goats ate it voraciously as though it was a mixture of the choicest concentrates, and from then on they picked up in condition.

There were other snags, of course. Sheep had left a legacy of ticks, and in the Spring the goats were covered and tormented with them (so were we if we didn't watch out). They had to be dipped, an unpopular proceeding all round. We found that firing the bracken, which harbours ticks, in the early Spring did much to reduce the menace.

Then entero-toxæmia made an appearance. A swift killer this. A goat would go out to graze in the morning perfectly fit and be found dead in the afternoon for no apparent reason. We were quicker off the mark with this trouble, and the answer was injections in the Spring and Summer to immunise them.

Then they started throwing inter-sex kids, popularly known as hermaphrodites, which they rarely are in fact, but in any case they are useless for breeding. This was a genetical problem; a recessive linked with the condition of hornlessness, and we had been breeding for hornlessness because hornless goats were the most popular. It was overcome, briefly, by mating naturally hornless animals with horned ones; then, although the factor was still probably carried as a recessive, it was not manifest in the appearance of thoroughly useless monsters.

On the credit side, we discovered that the Nubians could be made to breed in Summer to kid down in December; normally their breeding season is limited from September to February, but we had half the herd kidding down in Winter and half in late Spring and were able to keep the milk supply constant, more or less, throughout the year. And we found a market for the milk at a holiday camp on a neighbouring island. The warden came to collect the milk daily and paid us four shillings a gallon.

From a bad start the geese went on to prosper. We evolved a simple, foolproof method of keeping them. They were not overfed in Winter and were encouraged to fend for themselves so that they lost the gross, heavy condition so admired in the farmyard and became tough athletic types. Then the geese did not flatten the goslings as they hatched. But we also found that if the goslings were taken from the goose the moment they came out of the egg, and were raised by hand out of sight and sound of the mother goose (and the gander, who is a very responsible family man), she would, after a few days' perplexed rest, lay another clutch. These we left to her entire care. The young birds hatched out at a time when the grass was new and short, and they required no artificial feeding or attention whatever. At the end of the Summer there was no difference between the hand-reared and naturally-reared birds.

We were lucky in that there were no rats, stoats, weasels or foxes on the island: there was a pair of hawks who once intimidated me very severely, and an aggressive, enormous owl whose daylight raids wrecked an experiment with guinea-fowl chicks, but they left the goslings alone. One or two eggs were lost to crows when the geese momentarily left the nests, but we persecuted them a bit and they never became a serious problem.

Young geese were in great demand and were booked on hatching at a flat rate of £2 per head to include keep until Michaelmas.

The writing developed as a sideline, which seemed to promise no fortune but a useful contribution of real clinking money. Hitherto writing had been regarded as Frank's exclusive pigeon. I was supposed to be the artist. This was a piece of humbug we were pleased to indulge in. I was perfectly aware I had not the skill to make money out of my alleged talent, and in any case it is impossible for me to settle down to picture-making unless there are hours and hours of clear day ahead of me. I cannot abide being interrupted, and I was quite incapable of settling to work knowing that in a short time I would have to see about dinner, see about milking or separating, or the million and one inevitable, unavoidable chores clamouring to be done. This I found did not apply to writing. In a moment of irritation I wrote an article, and it sold. In a moment of even greater irritation I wrote another and that sold.

Frank said, 'If we can get you really provoked we might be able to retire.'

Unfortunately that happy stage of infuriation was unattainable, but I managed to turn out a few articles on the island goats and geese which seemed to meet with the right sort of approval. I never got any thrill out of seeing anything I had written in print. As a matter of fact it used to embarrass me so much I could not bear to read it, though Frank used to plod through my published articles, with nods of approval, whenever he could get hold of them. I found the cheques infinitely consoling.

And so, on looking round and sizing up the situation, one day we found we had to some extent mastered island life. We could anticipate difficulties and setbacks likely to occur now and get ahead of them. We had achieved a peasant standard of living at fearful cost, learnt our own limitations and an appreciation of an entirely new set of values. We had come a long way from the flying days which seemed so extravagantly carefree in retrospect, and we had a long way to go before attaining a way of life in which there would be time 'to stand and stare'. We had learnt hardly that the basics of living are food, warmth and shelter, and that everything else is just so much fancy trimming: and we had learnt to differentiate between the trimmings worth working for and those which were not.

There was a wide variety of interests in connection with working the island, touching on forestry, farming, breeding and rearing of live-stock, working on and with boats; the weather was not simply a matter for polite conversation, it was an integral part of our life. In the normal course of a day's work there was riding, sailing, and shooting—though this last we limited to rabbits; we loathed killing birds even in our most hungry early days when often mouldy bread was not only edible but relished; and the wild fowl came to look on Inchfad as a sanctuary. We could swim or fish whenever we cared to do so. Life was so full we had no need of vicarious entertainment and completely lost the taste for it. Visits to the mainland were regarded with impatience, and we never thought of taking a holiday.

But we were restless. So far we had achieved an end. And to some people achievement is in itself an end. To go on is simply a repetition, to a greater or less degree, of all that has gone before.

And there was another thing. . . .

'You know, Frank,' I said thoughtfully, 'I could do with some real gut-stirring.'

'What I like about my wife,' he replied, 'is her elegant mode of expression. So could I.'

'It was better when we had *Shireen*,' I went on, 'we never knew where we were with her. Now – everything is beginning to work – and – it's too tame. . . . There's all the world going on outside us. . . .'

' "And I shall pass this way but once . . ." I *know*,' said Frank happily. 'The high moments of blended skill and fear. The lure of the unknown. *Wanderlust* and all that nonsense. I could not agree with you more, but as to what we can do about it I don't quite see.'

Nor did I. We had known for a long time, irrefutably, we would not return to flying. We had been out of it too long, and not only had aviation grown away from us, but we had grown away from aviation. We no longer *believed* in it. And the days of starting an enterprise from scratch were over. Socialism ruled; security was the order of the day (preferably my security at your cost); the blight of bureaucracy had descended on aviation as it had done on everything else in the country to shrivel and wither all individual effort and initiative.

No; we had passed the Point of No Return.

We talked of emigrating and travelled round the world on the Atlas, but could not decide where to go. To emigrate seemed too final and irrevocable somehow.

'If only we could travel slowly and take a look at these countries before we settled,' I said.

'. . . Travel slowly and take a look at these countries. . . .' repeated Frank, looking at and through me. 'Hmm.'

The next thing was that he came back from a business trip to Glasgow with a retriever-look on his face and a sheaf of papers. Lists of yachts for sale.

'Happened to pass a yacht-broker's,' he explained casually. 'Thought it might be interesting to see what prices yachts are fetching these days.'

'Happened to pass . . . travel slowly . . . Frank, I think it's a grand idea.'

'Oh, you do, do you? Well, here's a little ship I rather like the sound of. . . .'

From then on it was an intermittent conference of ways and means.

The 'way' was comparatively simple. We should find ourselves a small ship and leisurely sail the world until we found somewhere we liked well enough to settle in. If we did not find anywhere we would keep on going – the world is a large place.

The 'means' was not so easy. There was the initial outlay and the following upkeep. We reckoned we should need £2,000 to buy and fit out a ship, then reckoned there ought to be another £1,000 at least in the kitty. Here we branched out into a frenzied argument as to how we should get the money out of the country, until Frank grinned and said we'd better get it first.

Upkeep was a problem that did not perturb us unduly. Living aboard is largely what you make it, and can be as expensive or as cheap as your tastes and pocket allow. Between us we could turn our hands to a number of things and so reckoned on being able to sing for our supper without much difficulty. Writing would be a help, there would be articles, maybe a book or two. I had already started on one of our island experiences.

Frank hit on what we considered to be a good idea in suggesting we should write a journal of our travels and adventures from the point of would-be emigrants, and post it to private subscribers from abroad – the foreign stamp would at least authenticate the job and prove we were not thinking it all up from the comfort of an arm-chair in Surrey – and apart from the monetary angle it would give our wanderings some purpose.

Outlay depended upon the sale of the island, and was the key to the whole project.

'We'll leave it in the lap of the gods,' said Frank. 'If we can sell the island well, we'll go. If we can't, then we stay.'

In short, we found we could sell the island well, and began preparations for departure with mixed feelings. Longing to go and sad at parting. Particularly with the animals; they had shared so much of our lives and struggles. The grey pony went to my sister (we sold the chestnut, and then could not bear it, bought her back and sent her with the grey). Biddy, the Alsatian, would come with us as a matter of course.

It is incredible to have got so far in this story without bringing in Biddy before. She was given to me as a six-week-old puppy by a superintendent of police, after a forced landing in a football ground in Manchester.

She flew with me at Hooton, drove with me at Merebrook, caught rabbits for us on the island, and reliably carried messages between Frank and me, with enormous self-satisfaction, when he was working at one end of the island and I at the other and we wished to communicate.

She was the most intelligent and talkative animal I ever knew, and would discourse volubly and at length, not barking, but shaping her lips round different 'words' and watching us keenly to see if we understood. Biddy was no parasitic sycophant with love-lies-bleeding eyes, she was a person in her own right, and made a trio of the Davison ménage, so that when we said 'we' Biddy was automatically included.

The goats' future did not disturb us, because people who keep pedigree goats only do so if they are genuinely interested and so good homes for the animals were almost automatically assured. But when it came to parting with my favourite kid, I baulked. I had raised her by hand and she followed me about like a dog, to Biddy's unconcealed disgust; she was of a type I had been breeding for for some time, and if and when we settled down she would be a good start for the herd I hoped to have again one day. The threads attaching me to a land life were not all severed. . . .

'Frank,' I said, 'if we got a biggish little ship – we could take Dabs with us. . . .'

'A goat?' he said. 'Aboard? I never heard of anything so crazy in my life.'

'But they used to,' I argued, determined now to eat my cake and save a few crumbs. 'They kept goats on sailing ships and large yachts for milk-supply in pre-fridge days.'

'What *size* ship do you think we intend to have?' he asked.

'It is not as though we were planning stunt voyages – out to break records or do anything epic,' I went on, ignoring his question. 'We aim to see as much of different countries as possible, and surely we'll be spending more time in port than at sea. We'll be choosing our weather and not blinding off into hurricanes if we can help it. . . . I don't see why we shouldn't take Dabs. . . .'

He laughed. 'I suppose the whole thing would sound pretty crazy to most people. We might as well put the seal on our madness. . . .

If I am to have my boat, then I don't see why you shouldn't have your goat. But she'll do better with company; if we take Dabs we had better take Black as well.'

Black was his favourite goat.

                      ◦   ◦   ◦   ◦   ◦

At the end of November, 1947, we were all ready to leave. The two goats were boarded out, a few oddments 'wanted on voyage' were put into store, and with Biddy and the rest of our belongings contained in thirteen suitcases we set out to find a ship.

7

LONG hours of discussion had been expended on our future ship; a somewhat one-sided discussion, my technical knowledge being limited to what I had seen of the *Mariana* and what I had known of *Shireen* and *Phœnix*, so my part was mainly confined to listening, with what I hoped were a few appropriate comments here and there.

But I visualised what we were after. A ship not so large as the *Mariana*; between forty-five and fifty feet overall, not more; a ketch, with diesel auxiliary. We would prefer her to be flush-decked with good headroom below, but the layout of the accommodation was immaterial. Frank had a leaning towards a working-type boat rather than a yacht, something after the style of a Bristol Channel pilot cutter or fishing boat that he could convert (the old building-up complex again!) to his own ideas, instead of taking over some-one else's notions of a dream ship. With this I entirely agreed, partly because I was as much of a builder-upper as he was, and partly because of an æsthetic preference for a 'working' model of anything.

It did not seem a lot to ask for, yet it seemed curiously unattainable, and we spent six months trailing Biddy and the baggage up and down the country in search of it.

Six months of civilisation. Six months of the frightful bonds man has imposed upon himself in the name of progress. The island years had raised an insuperable barrier between us and our urbanised fellow men, but whereas we could to some extent appreciate their aims and attainments, having once been on their side of the fence, they had not a glimmer of a clue as to what we were after, and obviously found us too brawny in outlook to be comfortable companions. This did not worry us in the least; we were merely changing trains at the station of civilisation, en route from one state of savagery to another; but it did bring home to us the impossibility of our ever being able to settle into what is regarded as a 'normal' life again.

There were very few small ships that had survived the war years in anything like reasonable condition, and our search was further hampered by our pre-war ideas of values. We had known of the rise in prices generally, but had not appreciated how much this applied to yachts and other small craft. A lack of appreciation intensified by the low price of the first vessel we looked at. She was an Admiralty-disposals craft, a fifty-foot MFV lying at Glasgow, offered at £400. If she had appeared at the right time we should not have needed to look any further, but unfortunately she came on the scene too soon, when the world cruise was first mooted, and before we had even tested the market for the island.

We had inspected her out of curiosity, because she was comparatively near at hand and thought she would give us some idea of values. . . .

Consequently when the search was really on and we went up to Fort William to look at a pilot cutter at twice the price, we were inclined to snort a bit, thinking she was too dear, and hustled off with our incredible load of luggage to the South Coast after a steel schooner which turned out to have ripe bottom plates.

Then we darted about the country chasing one chimera after another, with Frank expostulating at intervals, 'This is *fantastic*!' as we hurtled our bags from one guard's-van to the next, and carried Biddy through the London Underground in which only lap-dogs are allowed to travel. . . .

'Why don't you go into digs with Biddy and this lot,' he said, balefully eyeing our belongings, 'whilst I look . . . ?'

'All right,' I said wearily, 'but *where*?'

Half the population of the British Isles seemed to be eagerly engaged in looking for somewhere to live at the time and digs were not much easier to come by than ships. So we angrily carried on.

In South Wales the search took on some semblance of reality for the first time when we came across an old Fleetwood trawler, the *Margaret*. I fell in love with her at once, but Frank hedged. She wanted too much doing to her, he said. He didn't like the engine or the engine installation. He questioned the condition of the timbers in her counter. He thought she hadn't enough freeboard aft for our job. She was too expensive.

Then we did think we had found something in a big motor fishing vessel at Swansea. She was a huge craft powered by a colossal 100-h.p. Deutz diesel. There did not appear to be much to do to her, apart from stepping aboard and sailing away.

Frank got to talking business with the owner and did not make much headway.

'I have a man,' sang the owner, harmoniously blending the accents of North Devon and South Wales, 'coming to see her on Friday. But, if you like to give me the money, then, she is yours!'

Frank looked startled. 'Oh,' he said, 'not so fast. I want to see what's under that tingle on her stem, and I'd like to have her on the slip for survey, and I can't possibly get my surveyor here before Friday.'

'But,' lilted the owner, in protest, 'you do not want a surveyor. If there was anything wrong with her, I would tell you, man. She is a good boat. Sound, indeed.'

'Look,' said Frank, 'I do not doubt you for a moment. But purely for my own personal satisfaction I want to see her out of the water.'

He was genuinely interested in the boat and tried to get an option on her until we could have her surveyed. He took his cheque book out of his pocket and waved it invitingly—but the owner was obdurate.

'I have a man,' he persisted, 'coming to see her on Friday. . . . I would have to put him off. And if you do not buy her, I might lose him too, then where am I?'

It was a prolonged, futureless, discussion through which we missed, hopefully, one train, but not the next, and as British Railways lumbered us on to our next port of call Frank said, 'I wonder if he really thought we would fall for that old gag. There must have been something pretty phoney under that copper patch. Pity, though. . . .'

At Bristol we followed the trail of a Brixham trawler, whose particulars had been sent to us in a brief and astonishing correspondence in connection with another vessel, a pilot cutter which was advertised for £300. We had not expected the cutter to be inlaid with mother of pearl and studded with diamonds at that price, but thought she might be a possible rehabilitation job. In reply to our enquiry we learnt that she was in Eire, and all we had to do was to forward the cash and sail her away. The letter closed by saying 'It would be a nice sail back.'

(Later when we were in Ireland we saw her; it would have been a nice sail back. And a darn clever one too. She lay on her side, a stripped and battered hull, without so much as a splinter of a spar, a rag of canvas or a strand of rope belonging to her.)

One glance from the quayside told us all we needed to know of the Brixham trawler, but we allowed ourselves to be chivvied aboard by the broker because we were interested to see what heights of extravagance he would reach in his efforts to make a sale.

He found us heavy going, because we thought if we had nothing pleasant to say we had better remain silent, but we obligingly hung upside-down in the bilges to admire spiders' webs, and Frank out of politeness murmured something about 'having her out of the water', whereon the broker's hat went flying into the air and he dramatically clutched his heart crying, 'For £700! You expect too much – she's dirt cheap, I tell you. Take it or leave it!'

'Leave it,' said Frank pleasantly, and the hat came down smartly on its owner's brow and we were borne away to look at a coastal ketch. A great slab-sided beast of a thing, about a hundred feet long.

After hustling us below, the broker mumbled something about an appointment and scurried off leaving us entombed.

She had no engine, nothing, not even a bulkhead or a floorboard, though I must admit she had headroom, about ten feet of it at least. We tramped hollowly about, peering up at the great timbers, and giggling to ourselves at the absurdity of the whole thing. Then the hat appeared at the open hatch and its owner bustled down the companion ladder with an air of great importance.

'Extraordinary coincidence,' he said. 'You remember that pilot cutter? I have just this very minute received a firm offer of £200 for her. Now,' he said generously, 'if you like to put £20 on that she's yours.'

For a moment there was dead silence in the vaults of that vast ship.

'Well?' he said.

Frank said mildly, 'I am not in the habit of buying ships without seeing them first.'

'Poh!' snorted the broker. 'What's £220? She's a gift at that – you can't go wrong!'

But we thought you could, and later, waiting for the Irish boat in an hotel at Fishguard, Frank was moved to remark sententiously, that without a doubt the mantle of the horsecoper had fallen upon the shoulders of those who deal in small ships.

The huge hotel lounge was crammed with passengers for the Irish boat, and that moment a terrific roll of drums rang out, and everyone, to a man, leapt to his feet and squared his shoulders, so that we believed an unseen band for some inexplicable reason was about to strike up 'The King', and struggled to rise from our deep armchairs. But no. It was the dinner-gong. Before our astonished eyes the huge crowd swung into line, and marched, two by two, into the dining-room.

We spent Christmas in Eire. It was my first visit and I loved everything about the country. I knew I was going to like it when the steamer stole up the river to Waterford in the early morning before dawn, and a stentorian voice rang out of the darkness – 'Is that you, Mike – an' I'm glad to see ye lookin' so well.'

I loved the easy irresponsibility that pervaded everything, so that people had time to gossip and laugh: the sight of a small boy leading a calf with a rope round its neck down the middle of the main-street in Waterford on a wet night. I loved the joyous arguments with taxi drivers; the scurrying donkeys; the bright green fields; the lovely Avoca valley; the stout priest with his hat on the back of his head and a cigarette hanging on his lip haranguing a dispirited man in the middle of the road; the railway engines that unaccountably went 'off the boil' and there was nothing to do but wait for them to get up steam again; the railway porter who stared fretfully at our luggage and said: 'What would ye be wantin' to travel with all those boxes, an' it Christmas time an' all?' And the guard who looked at Biddy and said: 'Where would ye be goin' with that great big dog?' The chambermaid who forgot to call us, so that we nearly missed our train, and blamed the porter for it all. The ceaseless tramp-tramp of feet marching to Mass on Christmas Eve. The background of song – 'Silent Night', to be forever associated with Eire – swelling and dying away and growing loud again. The captivating little maid at our hotel who spoke in whispers and asked when we wished calling for Mass, and I had to tell her as delicately as I could we were heathens, and her grey eyes opened wide as she breathed, 'Oh God!'

Lovely, lovely country. 'Why haven't I been here before?' I demanded of Frank, who said, 'Yes, it *is* pretty good, isn't it?'

But alas, we could not find our boat there. We looked at a pretty little yawl which had brought a party of eight from Sweden in a great hurry through September gales in the North Sea. The owner maintained he was Swedish, but we were not so sure. The whole set-up was one of escape, and we could see no reason why a Swede should be a refugee from Sweden. I looked all over that boat to see if there was any clue as to her owner's nationality, but all the bottles, cans and things of that nature were stripped of their labels. I never saw such a de-nationalised vessel. She was too small for us anyway (how they contrived to cram eight aboard is a mystery) and when we asked the owner to have a drink with us he declined with a grave smile, and parted with a stiff bow and a smart click of the heels:

'Some day we will meet at sea, then we will drink together, yes?'

On neutral ground so to speak.

At the enchanting fishing port of Arklow we looked at a fishing boat which was no good to us, and for one wild moment we studied a large trading schooner from the quayside, then pulled ourselves together and went to Dublin where we met a family energetically fitting out a pilot cutter to sail to the Galapagos.

Then because time was getting on and there seemed no likelihood of our finding a suitable ship in Eire we retraced our steps to England and settled in an hotel in Gloucestershire, whence Frank made sorties to different parts of the coast, whilst I stayed put with Biddy and the boxes, hammering away at the island book.

When we had almost given up hope of ever finding a ship and were feeling very downcast, Frank said, 'I wonder if the old *Mariana* is still for sale.'

'After five years? Very unlikely. Besides, she's an antique by now – and she'd no engine, you remember. Anyway she's too big for us.'

'No bigger than the *Margaret* you were so keen on,' he said, and wrote to the Harbour Master at Glasson Dock. 'Even if the *Mariana* has gone he might know of something else.'

The *Mariana* had gone, of course, but the Harbour Master in his reply mentioned a fishing boat at Fleetwood which he believed was for sale. The *Reliance*, a very fine boat, he said, built on the lines of a yacht.

'More junk, no doubt,' said Frank sceptically, 'but as there's nothing else on the cards I suppose I had better take a look at this fishing "yacht".'

He returned to the hotel from Fleetwood late one wintry night and sat on the end of my bed, wrapped in his greatcoat, looking thoughtful.

'Well?' said I.

'If it hadn't been snowing, and I hadn't been half-starved, I should never have gone aboard. But the owner offered me a cup of tea and I couldn't resist, it was so bloody cold. If it hadn't been for that I would have turned on my heel and walked away. You never saw such a mess.'

'That's that, then.'

'No,' he said slowly, 'no. I've arranged to have her put on the grid for survey.'

'Now, why?'

'She's sound as far as I could see, which is more than any of the others have been. And she's magnificently built.'

Arrangements were made with Humphrey Barton at Lymington, who had surveyed another job for us, to go to Fleetwood and look over the *Reliance*.

'This looks like being it, then,' I said to Frank, thinking he would hardly bring Barton half-way across the British Isles unless he was pretty sure of himself.

'It does: if she is anything like I think she is – and oh, what a treat it will be to get cracking.'

Snow still lay in grimy little frozen heaps as we made our way along the quay at Fleetwood one mad March morning. *Reliance* was on the grid at the end of the basin with Barton in overalls already on the job. The fisherman owner in cap and blue jersey stumped about on deck looking as black as a thundercloud. Frank immediately went aboard, and I wandered about the quay taking angle-shots of the boat, which got me into trouble with the dock police. They were still war-conscious and adopted a belligerent attitude, and our ensuing altercation as to whether I could or could not take pictures of the boat we might possibly buy, brought Frank and Robbie, the owner, rushing on deck. Frank all protective, hackles up and ready to take the port apart, Robbie torn and bothered, not wishing to upset a prospective buyer nor yet the dock police.

To keep the peace I went aboard: Frank rejoined Barton in what appeared to be a systematic demolition of the ship, and Robbie disappeared moodily into the after cabin.

I wandered round listening to excited comments from Frank: 'God, look at those timbers – you'd think she had been built for the Arctic.'

And Barton, more quietly: 'When these old ships are good, they're very, very good.'

Then, 'Trenail fastened! You'll not see those again.'

'So,' I thought, 'this *is* it.' I had seen the look on Frank's face. He had indubitably found the pot of gold at the end of the rainbow.

And as I looked about I thought, oh dear, if *Margaret* wanted too much doing to her, what of this?

For *Reliance* was indeed in a mess.

She was big too, bigger than we had intended. Sixty-five to seventy feet I reckoned, beginning to judge these things. She had been a ketch, but was now shorn of her masts and spars, and a gangrenous copper funnel leaned drunkenly above a battered wooden engine coaming. Her decks were worn, rough and splintered, and soaked in oil.

Everywhere was cluttered with worn-out gear; broken boxes, bits of wood, crushed fish baskets, rope-ends, bundles of old nets, shattered blocks and tangled lines.

But underneath all the squalor was the unmistakable indefinable mark of quality. I do not know the words to describe it in a ship, but I could recognise it in the lines of her hull, just as I could in a horse, however rough it might come up from grass.

Below decks, the shambles was worse, if anything.

The forecastle was filled with rotting gear and a barrel of tar or pitch or something had been upset; I did not investigate. The fish-hold was slimy and redolent of putrescent fish.

The engine-room was enormous, the engine was enormous and the chaos was terrific.

The engine was a Gardner 26VT, slow-speed diesel with compressed-air starting, installed in 1925. The two cylinders, nearly as tall as myself, were almost lost in a plethora of pipelines whose aim appeared to be one of strangulation rather than use, after the manner of the Laocoon. Spare parts and tools in various stages of rust and disintegration were scattered about the engine-room floor, and the whole place was thick with oil.

Frank had said the engine was a bunch of scrap, but had been certain he could 'sort' it. If he said so, I knew he could, but it looked like a long job to me.

The after-cabin was dark. A small oil lamp on the table threw out a dim light, and by it stood a white-faced alarm-clock. Robbie was seated by the blazing stove and glowered at me as I entered.

'I don't know,' he said, waving his pipe towards a settee as an invitation to sit down, 'what the game is. They lads down yonder 'll have ship in pieces afore long. And, y' knaw, if there were owt wrong wi' ther, I'd tell you.'

'I'm sure you would,' I said, hoping to soothe, 'it's just a matter of form.'

'Form!' he cried. 'Who's going to pay for putting back all they tear up like? That's what I want to knaw. Happen it won't be me, if you don't buy her.'

He looked fierce.

Happen there won't be much risk of that, I thought, and changed on to another tack, saying she seemed a fine boat.

'Ay, she is that. Finest ever put out o' Fleetwood – and t' fastest.

They called 'er after America Cup winner, year she was launched. Nineteen 'undred and three... *Reliance*...

'Ay, twelve knots y' knaw....' He slowly shook his head and to my relief seemed to forget the hammering and rending noises going on for'ard, and swept off on a reminiscent stream of the old sailing days, until suddenly there was silence and Frank and Barton came into the cabin wiping their hands and looking pleased.

Robbie stopped at once and fixed them with a savage glare. 'Well,' he said. 'Are you all right? 'ave you finished riving 'er to pieces?'

Frank smiled broadly. 'Sorry to give you all this trouble....' he began.

'Trouble! It's no trouble to me so long as you put back all you've took up.'

'Don't you worry,' said Frank, 'you'll be all right.... She's a wonderful ship for her age....'

'And sound, as far as I can see,' said Barton cautiously, stooping a little; he was tall and there was not enough headroom for him, 'but of course, when they're ceiled throughout like this... it's difficult ... almost a double boat you might say,' he paused, frowning down at his feet as though contemplating the possibilities of double boats. He turned to Frank. 'I think you might make something of her.'

'There,' said Robbie, 'I told you. There's nowt wrong wi' ther. If there 'ad a been I'd a told you.'

'She's in a filthy condition,' said Barton.

Robbie was unmoved.

'Ay,' he said, 'she's bin fishing. Fished b' Danes. They're buggers on boats, but they catch fish. Pulled winch out deck wi' load o' fish they did, and brought 'er 'ome so low int water, man oo owned 'er was scared daft. He said to me, "They'll sink 'er, Robbie, the buggers," he said. That's why he got shut of 'er. Said he lied awake nights thinking of 'er and they chaps aboard 'er.

'He thought a lot o' the old *Reliance*. I bought 'er because he said if I didn't he'd break 'er up. And I wanted gear off 'er for my boat.

'I don' care,' he added, shooting a defiant glance at us, 'if I sell 'er or not.'

We bought the *Reliance*, a hull and nothing more, in 1947, for £1,450, and were glad to get her.

In 1903 she put to sea, complete down to the mustard pot, for the cost of £1,200.

For the last time, we rounded up our suitcases and Biddy, and travelled north to Fleetwood to start work on our ship.

8

FLEETWOOD lies at the southern end of Morecambe Bay. The Bay is shallow and at low water much of it dries out. A narrow buoyed channel leads into the River Wyre and the port of Fleetwood. The river mouth is narrow and a ferry plies between North End on the Fleetwood side and Knott End on the other. North End is where the Isle of Man steamers tie up, open at any state of the tide, and is a conjunction of railway terminus and pierhead. The river curves and widens to divide at a long neck of sandbank, the Tiger's Tail, upon which fishermen careen their small craft, and strangers strand their large ones if they are not careful. The river proper leaves the sandbank on its right and goes off on its own affairs, past the ICI works, into the hinterland of Lancashire.

The harbour is an inlet on the right of the sandbank with the gates to the fish docks facing you to port going in, and the basin where the smaller fishing vessels tie up and off-load their catch to starboard.

At the end of the basin is the grid and slipways.

The harbour dries out at low water, and the bottom is mud: soft turgid mud. Dredgers are constantly at work in the harbour and outer channel fighting an indecisive battle against silting-up.

A quay runs from the North End to the end of the basin. The railway terminus, between the quay and the town, broadens into a veritable network of lines making what used to be known as a goods-yard until the war, when the BBC hit on a new name and puzzled us for a long time by references to 'marshalling yards'.

We moved our clobber into apartments overlooking the Bay, and *Reliance* was moved out of the basin further down the quay towards the North End, and tied up opposite the Tiger's Tail, where it was less crowded but more exposed. If it blew up at all in the night, we leapt out of bed into oilskins and tore down to the quay to tend warps and fuss over our ship.

Nearby, on the quay, was a row of warehouses, some of which

were engaged in the fish-curing industry. We rented part of one not occupied in a kippering capacity and used it as a workshop and general store.

We liked Fleetwood; it had a pretty name, if it was not exactly a pretty town, though commendable efforts have been made on the front to create gardens and a promenade for the joy of holiday-makers. The people were homely and genuine. Surnames seem to have no part in their daily life, and specialise in the diminutive – it is always Harry or Billy or Jimmy. If they don't know you well enough for that it is 'Love'. Being foreigners, on being directly addressed we were allowed 'Mr and Mrs', but I've no doubt if we had stayed there another ten years we should have become Frankie and (oh horrors!) Annie.

From the first we were marked men. In buying *Reliance* we had also bought a piece of local history.

To set foot in the street was to be immediately accosted by jerseyed mariners, little old apple-cheeked, bright-eyed men of the sea. They stood immovable in our path and greeted us with that quick little nod that goes for a salutation in the North, and said: 'Ay, ay. Heard like as how you've bought the old *Reliance*. Eh . . . Grand boat that. Remember 'er when she was a-building. . . .' Then they were off, with the veils of reminiscence darkening their eyes. Judging by the number who remembered her 'a-building', and not only remembered but declared they had a hand in the construction, *Reliance* must have provided profitable occupation for the younger citizens of Fleetwood at the time, and it must have been a sorry day when she came off the ways.

We heard again and again, times without number, that she was named after the America Cup winner; how she had been specially designed and built to beat the fleet, and to take the sand in the Bay; of incredible sailing feats and prodigious turns of speed. They told with bitterness, as if it touched them personally, how she had been debarred from entering the Brixham Races by a regulation brought in, they swore, to prevent her competing: 'They'd seen 'er sailing and knew she'd beat 'em. . . .'

Oh, pure caviar to the generals. We lapped it up.

Frank said, 'The best of it is, they're not trying to *sell* her to us. She's *ours*.'

The only possible rivals *Reliance* ever seemed to have had were her two sister ships, the *Louie Rigby* and the *Surprise*; but there never seemed to have been any trial of strength between the three

of them. The *Louie Rigby* and the *Surprise* were later vessels, built after the *Reliance* had proved the design, and the old fishermen were disinclined to discuss them as they had deserted their calling early on in their careers and 'gone for yachts'. A fate, it would seem, for an honest fishing boat in the days of sail, to be on a par with that known as Worse than Death.

'Nay,' said the old men, 'you'll not see their like again. There's not the stuff to put in 'em today. Nor the men to build 'em neither.'

All three were built by Stoba, a Scotsman, who might have made a fortune and a name for himself if he had gone South and built yachts in a blaze of ballyhoo. But he was content to remain in the North and ruin the firms he worked for by uneconomical ideals demanding excellence in materials and workmanship.

He was exact and temperamental. And if he did not get what he wanted he went home, as he did on the day a lad brought him galvanised nails when he had ordered copper. On being told there were no copper nails in store he reached for his hat and coat, saying he might as well go home. There was no point in staying with no work to do. And he couldn't work without the right materials. . . .

An apprentice caught sharpening a pencil with a knife would receive a sharp crack over the knuckles from Stoba – 'What's your chisel for?' he would bark.

Stoba's reward in life lay in the results of his own superb craftsmanship. . . .

It pleased the old fisherman to hear we intended to put *Reliance* back to sail. At her age they did not mind her 'going for a yacht' – it was better than going to the breaker's yard – besides, engines had stolen the glory from sail and there was not the same feeling.

'Happen we'll be seeing you,' they said, 'and watch how you shape.'

Their interest was encouraging – inspiring even. They made us feel *Reliance* was quite a trust. History is heady stuff drunk from one's own cup of life.

We were longing to get to sea, and expected to be ready to sail by the Autumn. Robbie, whose own ship was then undergoing an extensive refit, and who knew therefore exactly what we were up against, pursed his lips when he heard of our hopes, and said, 'You'll have to shape.'

But we didn't see it. Plans for the refit were not elaborate: masts to be stepped; re-rigging; sails to be found from somewhere; decking to be renewed here and there; the engine overhauled; and a clean-up generally below. Frank wanted the wheelhouse strengthened and fitted with a steel baseplate, and the battered engine coaming replaced by a steel structure, and foresaw there might be a little difficulty in getting these fabricated, but on the whole we did not expect the job to take very long or to be of exorbitant cost.

Our values were still tenaciously pre-war in spite of the price we had had to pay for *Reliance*, and we still believed it was only necessary to know what to do to be able to go ahead and do it.

Very naïve we were; still arguing how to get our money out of the country. Not that we were either more or less law-abiding than the average citizen, but we were reluctant to leave our hard-earned money – and money we had was always hard-earned – to bolster a system with which we were out of sympathy, when the amount would be comparatively infinitesimal anyway and not missed, except by us who could use it.

Frank thought it would be possible to convert folding money into valuables and secrete them about the ship; an idea which had romantic appeal – my imagination seized on the picture of dark dealings with glittering stones in dark corners of the world – but I was against it in practice, if for no other reason than that I knew my tiresome give-away face would indicate plainly 'contraband hidden here' to anyone who wanted to know.

Come to think of it we must have wasted quite a bit of time in our lives discussing eventualities that never materialised.

We were disillusioned at the outset as to the practicability of doing the refit ourselves, employing direct labour, as originally planned. Material shortage, complications in connection with the employment of casual labour, multitudinous controls and obstructive officials were rocks besetting our channel and it seemed wise to have a pilot. Shipwright and engineering firms had access to a certain amount of material, second-hand and otherwise, quite out of reach of the private individual, and as there were also the steel constructions to be fabricated, contractors were engaged and work begun.

Frank was not the man to give an order and stand back to wait for it to be done. From the first he was his own designer and clerk of works, and counted every movement away from the ship as time wasted; he rushed through breakfast every morning and on to the job, and it was with the utmost difficulty he was ever persuaded to return for meals. His pockets bulged with sheaves of notes, the envelopes came into their own and multiplied; conversation was limited to calculations, costings and the details of design. He worked tirelessly, swept along on the tide of his own enthusiasm, and was maddened at the slow rate of progress.

He drove the contractors, contentedly working on a basis of time and materials; bullied manufacturers for tardy deliveries; and harried the men, who tenderly gave way to curious little outbursts of protest occasionally.

The non-arrival of certain materials, long promised and long delayed, resulted in the men dithering at nothing and finally sent Frank roaring to one of them.

'Bertie,' he said, 'go up to the shops and stay there till you get the stuff. Take your time. Stay there all day if necessary but don't come back without it.'

Bertie went. He did not come back that day or the next morning. Nor did any of the other men, except the joiner, a steady type, who remarked cryptically that they were 'all a lot of bolshies'.

On enquiry it transpired that Bertie was wounded. To his very soul. He had been told 'to take his time' and that, as he understood it, meant get off the job. Injustice! he proclaimed, and stayed off the job. Injustice! echoed the others and stayed with him.

After the misunderstanding was cleared up they trooped back to the ship full of sweetness and light, until the next morning when Bertie suddenly downed tools and swept off the job with bleating followers in train.

'Now what?' breathed Frank, going after them.

Bertie was hurt again. Frank had omitted to say good-morning.

'Good grief!' cried Frank, 'what does he want me to do – kiss him?'

But then an unshakable belief grew up, despite all denials, that settled everything. Frank was an ex-Naval type, and as such was permitted any eccentricity or display of temperament. He was endowed with Character and became a Byword. A state of affairs he found irresistible and played up to shamelessly. He went about wearing a monocle and a disgracefully shabby old blue battledress.

During the early days of the refit Dick came on the scene. He was a fisherman, a grizzled independent little man with salt water in his veins and the sky in his eyes. He sailed into life full and bye and was inseparable from his cap.

But it was no ordinary cap. It was a kneeling-pad, kettle-holder, cushion and paint-rag. When he wore it on his head it indicated his mood. Darkest gloom was notified by the peak coming hard

69

down over his eyes; then as the depression passed the cap crept farther off his brow, until at the height of good cheer it would be balanced on the back of his head.

The cap was also a universal basket. Cigarettes, stubs, matches, bits of string, twine, knives, odd fittings, shrimps, newspaper cuttings, photographs and a fry of fish, all were secreted in the crown, until at times it looked blown-up and likely to take-off any moment.

The only thing he ever brought us not in his cap as far as I remember was a long-handled broom which he said was lying about doing nobody any good.

His manner of joining the *Reliance* was characteristic.

Frank had embarked one morning on a clean-up and clear-out of the after cabin. Four built-in bunks were filled with mattresses, seven deep, all sodden; each in a progressive state of disintegration so that the bottom ones had to be shovelled out. And the rest of the cabin was in like condition.

He was digging away into the mess when Dicky came down the companionway, unexpected, unannounced, wearing his best blue suit.

Scornfully, Dicky surveyed the cabin. 'Heard as how you might be needing an 'and like,' he said. 'Eh . . . she weren't like this in my day. We 'ad t' look after boats then. These chaps now, bloody farmers, not fit t' keep pigs. . . .'

Registering deep disgust he took off his jacket and set to work.

Frank took to him at once. Dick was sound and knew his job. He was still a sailing man at heart, genuinely in love with ships and the sea. He was in love, too, with the *Reliance*. She had drawn him to us, not the prospect of a job, for Dicky was a good fisherman and could always get a boat. He had sailed as mate on *Reliance* in the old days and his knowledge of her and her sailing qualities was invaluable.

From the first he identified himself with us – she was 'our ship' – and to make the situation quite clear he arrived long after the other men in the morning and worked on late into the night. Even at weekends he could not keep away. On Sunday mornings, after we had moved aboard, he used to come down to the ship in his Sunday suit, and stamp on the deck to announce his arrival, chanting, 'If it's not done *reet* it's gotta be done again', because that was one of Frank's more notable demands, with which Dick entirely agreed, being himself a little old-fashioned in regard to work.

They never tired of talking together about the *Reliance*, though at times they would stand gazing at her, speechless with admiration, unconscious of the dilapidation, conscious only of her lines and the way she would look when the job was done. For all the world like a couple of farmers contemplating the future prospects of a good crop.

But it was one of those insidious jobs that start unambitiously and grow bigger and bigger as time goes on; each modification leading inevitably to another. Finally, *Reliance* was not being refitted so much as being rebuilt.

As the initial work of stripping progressed, revealing more of the magnificent construction, sound as the day she was launched, we began to feel nothing was too good for her. The old adage of spoiling the ship for a ha'porth of tar took on a very real significance. And our feeling towards *Reliance* was not a little influenced and intensified by the whole-hearted admiration felt for her generally. She was an exceptional ship, and our plans for her extended accordingly. She was stripped out completely above and below decks, and entirely new accommodation designed. A fascinating job and one very much a labour of love.

It is amazing the spell a ship can cast over men. No woman on earth can compare with a ship when it comes to captivating men wholesale. And it is no momentary infatuation – a ship can hold complete devotion and unquestioning loyalty for all time.

Frank delved about in scrap yards and found things for *Reliance* with the air of finding gifts for her: a Kelvin sounder, a pair of Revon ventilators, a barograph in a mahogany case, and from these searchings I, too, received a present. An aviation compass. 'There,' said Frank, 'that will make you happy.'

There was already a deckhead compass fitted in the wheelhouse which seemed to me to be the not very happy result of a cross between the ace of spades and a roulette wheel, and about as intelligible.

It was good to have something familiar in this strange nautical setting, and I took the compass back with me to the digs and looked at it for a long, long time, evoking nostalgic memories.

Scores of nameless vessels made their contribution to the completion of *Reliance*. Decking, $2\frac{1}{4}$-inch pitch-pines, came off a hopper. Decklights, doors, cabin fittings, T and G boarding, a refrigerator even, came from old trawlers. The main and mizzen masts came off a fishing boat changing to pole masts. The main boom off an old coastal ketch. The mizzen boom was originally the bowsprit of a Morecambe Bay prawner. Both booms were roller reefing, and masts and spars were all pitch-pine and looked pretty good when scraped and varnished. Whereon an outbreak of varnishing broke out among the smaller fishing boats.

Second-hand material makes twice the work and takes twice as long to fashion as new, and at that time was almost twice as expensive, but we were glad enough to get it. The condition was generally excellent, and with regard to timber, better quality than would have been obtainable new.

I have never known Frank anything but wholehearted in whatever he undertook, but never before had I seen him so supremely happy. He was unperturbed by the increasing demands of the ship and the gradual diminishing of our capital.

'What better way,' he argued, 'can we use the money? By putting it into the ship herself, we are converting it into something tangible. It isn't as though we hadn't a sound basis to build on. The value will always be there. In the unlikely event of our ever wanting to sell the *Reliance*, we would always get our money back.'

A sentiment expressed to us, earnestly, by the ubiquitous old men of the sea over and over again.

∽   ∽   ∽   ∽   ∽

At lunch time one bright morning, when the sea sparkled and the wind bowled fat round clouds across the sky, Frank and I looked out of the window of our apartment to see, very much the painted ship on a painted sea, a ketch coming out of Glasson Dock making across the Bay for the open sea. She really did look a picture with all her sails shining white in the sunlight.

'*Mariana!*' we said. And it was. *Mariana*, we discovered later, departing for the South of France, to retire there and become a houseboat. The only other time we ever saw her.

9

IN 1947 the fishing industry had just about reached its peak, fishermen were rolling in money for the first time in their lives, and those operating the smaller craft were changing engines with a prodigality of women changing their hats. They were astonished beyond measure that *Reliance* was destined to retain the old Gardner. But Frank, apart from financial considerations, had a leaning towards the old slow-speed engine – 'Good solid jobs,' he said, 'nothing much to go wrong with them, and they don't run themselves to death.' And he looked forward to the overhaul as a job right up his street.

Before dismantling he had the engine running with the aid of 'Yonny', engineer of the Danish crew who had last fished the boat.

The for'ard cylinder was seized solid, but the motor ran on one; Yonny said they had brought her down from Whitehaven like that.

Frank told me afterwards, 'You never saw anything like it. The whole bag of tricks leaping round the engine-room like a startled fawn!' Anything less like a fawn, startled or otherwise, than that great piece of machinery with its fifteen-hundredweight flywheel it would be hard to imagine, but I gathered it vibrated.

The trouble was not entirely due to one cylinder being out of commission apparently. She vibrated naturally, according to Yonny, who pointed out a long bar lying on the engine-room floor. 'In a seaway she did rrrrock,' he explained and said they used to attach the bar from engine bed to deck beam to stop it rocking. 'But in port,' he added, 'we did take it down. The Ministry of Transport would not like it. No?'

When the engine was dismantled it was discovered to be loose on the bearers, and the bearers, themselves in poor shape, were loose too. All bolts had been eaten away by rust to look like laminated pins. The concrete flooring of the engine-room, apparently sound on the surface, was found to be a crumbling mixture of cement, diesel oil and pig-iron beneath.

73

New bearers were fitted; the concrete chipped away and bilges and ballast cleaned. Frank and Dicky did this with a grim eye on one another one day when the wind came sweeping across the Tiger's Tail at high water and caused a considerable lop. . . . Eventually the flooring was relaid with steel checkerplate, and until this was done and the engine reassembled there was constant battle to keep the bilges free of wood waste.

There was no place for me aboard in the early days of the refit. I stayed at the digs flogging the island book until I hated the sight of it, then Biddy and I would fling ourselves out of the house and go for long walks along the shore to where the town dwindled to a house or two and it was a desolate haunt of curlew which made me homesick for the island.

Frank and I had always worked together on our previous ventures; it was a new experience to be shut out, as it were, and I did not like it. I was impatient to get to work on the ship myself and learn something about her.

Then at last the forepeak and the forecastle were ready for painting, which gave me a chance to take an active part in the refit.

I used to go down in the evenings after the men had gone and enjoy myself hugely. I had a lot to learn even about this; any previous experience was mainly confined to slapping a bit of creosote on a barn door, so I had a lovely time with scrapers, sandpaper, putty and undercoating. Frank and Dicky were too busily occupied on a much higher level to give more than cursory advice, but it was fun finding out, and having once achieved a walking-on part there was no getting me off the stage.

I was used to working amongst men. In the days when my interest was in horses it was far more a man's game than it is now; when I was flying, the number of women B licence pilots in the country was probably not more than a dozen all told, but I had found no difficulty in penetrating and being accepted in either sphere of interest. Not so this time. A fishing port is almost monastic in its exclusive masculinity; a woman's place is in the home, in the net-making shops, in the fish-curers' possibly, but certainly not aboard.

There was a skipper fitting out his boat alongside us. At least sometimes he was alongside us; he was forever moving his craft and when he warped her about Frank used to give him a hand, and I would join in too, because I wanted to learn how you managed these things.

74

My presence as a hand used to have the most peculiar effect on this man.

'Now,' he would say, 'if *father* will take hold of this rope, and *mother* will take the end of this one. . . .' And mother, convulsed, assiduously avoiding father's eye, would oblige, feeling exactly like mother taking one end of the rope and not in the least like Ann Davison learning a job of work.

Dicky was the only one who ever really accepted my interest in the ship as genuine, and who did not look upon me as a wife who had inexplicably strayed out of the kitchen. And even he was inclined to be suspicious at first; then he got used to the idea and said I reminded him of his mother, which shook me a bit, Dick being in his sixties. 'She was like you,' he added, and went on to explain that in the old days they mixed business and pleasure rather more than they do now; fishermen held regattas and the rivalry was pretty keen.

Dick's father, having entered his boat in the big race on one of these occasions, retired to the local on the morning of the race to explain to one and all exactly how he intended wiping everyone's eye. Crafty rivals saw to it his glass was never empty, and by the time the race was due to start, Dick's father was unrevivably unconscious.

But Dick's mother rose to the occasion.

Gathering her skirts about her and seizing the young Dick, then aged about eight, by the arm, she swept aboard the boat, saying, 'Come on, lad – we'll make it go!'

And they did. They made it go to such effect they won the race.

For Dicky, then, to say I was like his mother was no end of a compliment, but one I knew very well I could not live up to. Had I been called upon to skipper a boat suddenly – never mind race it – the resultant sound and fury would have simply provided a spectacle for onlookers but no honour for me.

I used to think horesmen were the most critical race in the world, until I got mixed up with seafaring types, then I knew the seamen had it. Fishermen seem particularly jealous. Even Dicky, who was good enough in his own line to be able to afford generosity in this respect, was heard to say – 'Who, 'im? Huh. He's no fisherman – apprenticed cabinet-maker, that's what he is' – which considering the man in question had been at sea and fishing his own boat for over thirty years seemed to stretch criticism rather far.

But then blame is so much easier to apportion than praise. We are all so fallible, and subconsciously at any rate, are well aware of the fact. The sea offers such tremendous opportunities for the making of mistakes; and a mistake at sea *can* be the last. . . . Criticism of one another's follies and foibles is fundamentally sympathetic, I think – 'There but for the grace of God' – though you would never think so to hear the talk sometimes.

My own base reaction to the sight of groups of trawlers stranded high and dry all over Morecambe Bay one morning was one of unrestrained delight. They had gone out on the night tide in thick fog, confident of knowing the channel as well as the backs of their hands – and there they were, looking foolish.

Closer observation of local seamanship brought the consoling, though slightly surprising, conclusion that apart from a few who really knew their job, a very large number of fishermen were stupendously bogus. Their seamanship was imitative, not based on solid knowledge at all. They played follow-my-leader getting to and from the fishing grounds, and simply pointed their noses at wherever they wanted to go with the hope of getting there.

It made me feel that perhaps, after all, 'mother's' shortcomings might not be outstandingly noticeable when the time came for us to get under way. And confidence was further restored after the conquest of The Ladder.

There are big tides at Fleetwood, thirty foot and more at springs. To get on and off *Reliance* at low water meant the negotiation of a twenty-foot ladder. A long, thin, melancholy ladder, which figured largely in our lives. During our two-year stay at Fleetwood, I suppose I ascended and descended this ladder on an average four times a day.

And *Reliance* did not always settle in exactly the same place at low water. Sometimes she lay well out from the quay, and the ladder would stretch upwards from the deck across an expanse of glistening mud, and the flimsy structure would sag and give as one mounted. Then at other times, the ship would lie close to the quay wall and the ladder seemed to be leaning almost over the vertical.

An exciting feature was the presence of dry-rot in the woodwork which caused the rungs to snap without warning. And then they were replaced by slats nailed irregularly across the ladder, which effectively destroyed the rhythm of climbing, but added immeasurably to the interest of the operation.

If I seem to dwell on this unduly, it is because I have no head for heights, and anyone who has ever teetered, sweating, On the Brink, will appreciate the control necessary to overcome this disability.

Frank said he could not stand heights either, which was absurd, for he shinned up and down the ladder, and later up and down the masts and rigging, with a sort of crag-to-crag nonchalance which I envied with all my heart and soul but could never hope to emulate.

But I *did* overcome the horrors of height. And after a few practice runs could even look down from the ladder on to the waiting mud beneath with comparative equanimity.

After that I felt capable of tackling – almost – anything.

On reaching deck one night and looking up with my usual satisfied triumph at the quay above, I remarked to Dick it would be a tidy way to fall. . . .

'Ay,' he said. 'It is that. I did once.'

'What?'

'Ay. I fell in.'

'How come?' said Frank, appearing through a hatch with ears akimbo.

'Low tide and all,' said Dick with some relish, extracting a cigarette from his cap.

We trooped below into the fish hold to put a kettle on the stove (there awaiting installation in a galley not yet in existence) and seated ourselves on upturned boxes.

'It's a while back now,' Dick began. 'One Christmas. I'd bent on a new suit to go Christmassing. And as I were going out door Missus says, "Now mind you bring cat home with you tonight. Don't leave it on boat while holidays, pore liddle thing."

'Fond o' cats my Missus.

'Well. Christmas were a bit long like that night, understand my meaning, and it were nearer nor three int' morning when I started for home. And I were thinking Missus weren't like to be too pleased.'

Dick searched the recesses of his cap for another cigarette and lit it, smiling to himself at the recollection of the long Christmas.

'I were near half-way home when suddenly I remembers cat,' he went on. 'Ah, I says to meself, *that*'ll please her, so I goes about and makes for boat I were on then, down b' quay.

'Eh . . . y' knaw . . . there were powerful headwind that night . . . I were making little short tacks . . .' Dicky's blue eyes twinkled, 'all along quay . . . when suddenly, right ont' edge . . . I misses stays. . . .'

He stopped to let us appreciate the picture of him that dark

Christmas night lurching on the edge of a forty-foot drop. Then he leaned forward and said solemnly, 'Y' knaw, I could feel meself going – and there were nowt I could do about it!

'Over I went!' he said, 'and landed in mud up to me neck. Lucky I were little chap and lucky to go in feet first.'

'I bet that sobered you up,' said Frank.

'It did that,' said Dick with a quick grin.

'What did you do then?' I asked, shovelling tea into the pot to make the hideous fishermen's brew both Frank and Dicky liked.

'I stayed quiet like – thinking,' he said, 'and saying here's a rum do to meself. Y' see, there were nowt to catch hold on, and I'd to be careful how I moved, you understand.'

We did, vividly.

'Then I thought as if I could get me coat off and spread it on mud like it'd give me summat to lean on.'

'I see,' said Frank, 'on the principle of putting straw under a slipping wheel to give it a grip.'

'Ay, that's it,' said Dick, 'and I lifted me arms careful like and wriggled ... wriggled. ...' He raised his arms cautiously and wriggled to show how he got his coat off.

'It worked,' said Dick. 'I edged me way to quay. But t'were no use; lower landing stage were way up out o' reach; I'd still nowt to catch hold on ... barnacles on piles were that sharp. ...

'I'd to wait for tide,' he said, 'to come and float me up.'

'Why didn't you shout for help?' I asked, handing out cups of tea.

'I did,' he said patiently, 'but t'were Christmas you understand, everyone'd gone home. There weren't even watchmen on boats. Nay, I'd to wait for tide.'

'That must have been a cold job,' said Frank.

'Ay, it was and all. B' time tide carried me to lower staging I were fair starved. And me new suit! Me new suit! I squeezed mud out edges like and put coat on when I got ashore because I couldn't be much worse, and I set course for home.

'Then ... oh ... cat. Well, I'd come for cat and cat I'd have, so I comes about again, and goes aboard boat and finds cat. She didn't seem to want to come wi' me, but I buttoned her inside coat like and that was her fixed.'

'And you too,' murmured Frank.

Dick laughed. 'Ay. 'Twere daylight b' time I got home. I crept int' kitchen quiet like but Missus were awake. She heard me.

' "That you, Dick?" ' said Dick, falsetto. ' "It is that," said I.

"Have you got cat?" she said. "I have that," said I. And I pulls cat out from me coat and puts it ont' floor. There it stood, a bundle of mud, with its tail stuck up like a marlin spike.

'Missus comes in kitchen and screams, "Eh . . . Dick. . . . What have you been doing to that pore little cat?"'

'And y' knaw,' finished Dick, 'me new suit . . . it never did me no good after.'

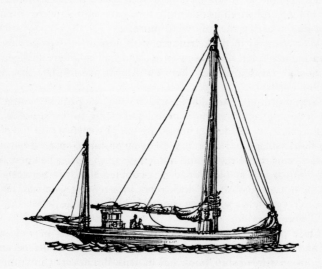

10

WE had planned out a nice little deckhouse for the goats, but it was still on paper when they joined us suddenly a couple of months after we started the refit.

The people with whom they were boarded got sick of them or something and wired us one night to say the animals were entrained and due to arrive the following morning.

We were still in digs, frothing with despair at ever getting the ship habitable let alone seaworthy, and had nowhere to keep the goats and nothing to feed them on. And it was too late that night to find either.

Next morning (it would be early-closing) we panicked round the town buying cabbages and oatmeal and trying to find a stable. We found plenty of stables, as horses are used extensively on the docks for short haulage work, but none with any room to spare. Eventually Dicky came to the rescue and influenced a fish carrier he knew, who kept horses in a stable hidden in a cobbled alleyway between two public houses just off the dock road, into renting us a stall. Willie was reluctant to do so at first, saying he'd had donkeys last time and they were no good.

Once the goats were safely installed, on a deep bed of straw behind a gate made of spare wood off the ship, my life became a curious mixture of ship, book and animals. But never at any time had I kept animals so easily as those two goats in the middle of a town.

They were in very bad condition when they arrived, pitifully thin and shabby, and I feared the change-over from freedom to confinement might set them back even more. Not a bit of it. They thrived and were soon fat and glossy again.

Corn merchants called weekly for orders, which were delivered into the stable the following day. A patch of waste ground on the railway, near the ship, grew from apparently a mixture of cement and sand a really first-class crop of clover which we gathered nightly

80

for the goats, and if ever I had need of veterinary goods I had only to walk fifty yards down the road to the chemist's which had a veterinary department.

I used to visit the stables twice a day to feed them both and milk Black.

The stable had a small yard in which was a walled-in midden. Sometimes I let the goats out, and they promptly climbed the wall, to dance on top, to the huge delight of passers-by and the street bookie who conducted his business in the alleyway.

'Hullo, haven't you gone *yet?*' was his daily greeting, and when business was slack he would recount his experiences fishing out of Newfoundland. I gather he preferred his present occupation.

News of the goats spread like wildfire through the town. Frank, at first uncertain whether they were in character or not, basely excused their presence on the ground I had refused to sail without them. But they excited far less comment among the fishermen than one might have supposed, mainly because a goat had been kept aboard one of the local steam trawlers for many years. She was chiefly notable for having eaten a potful of white lead without suffering any dire consequences.

Children found the goats an irresistible attraction. Hordes of them used to wait for me in the morning and surged into and all over the stable as soon as I unlocked the doors, tussling, shouting, clamouring with glee, until I started to milk, when they crowded round to watch in awed silence.

They asked what I did with the milk and were conservatively aghast to learn we drank it in the usual way. One small golden-haired Gretchen of about four had no such prejudices and used to bring a mug with her as well as a baby brother that spoke like Donald Duck whenever he uttered, which was not often.

Gretchen was pretty loquacious for her age, and offered the somewhat irrelevant information at one milking that she had gone all the way to heaven when she was a baby and came all the way back again. A small boy ceased tormenting one of the stable cats long enought to deny the possibility of such an excursion. 'You didn't,' he said. Gretchen, outraged, said, 'I did.' The boy said, 'You didn't.' 'I did then.' 'No,' said the small boy flatly, 'you couldn't. It's too far.'

Black was the favourite. She was hornless and gentle. Dabs was young and lusty and threatened strangers with her horns if they dared approach. She was eminently teasable and probably got more than her fair share when my back was turned, for goats are pretty fighters and Dabs always rose to a challenge. She would back away, rear gracefully on her hind legs to take the measure of her opponent, and then swoop down. She loved a mock battle with me, pulling her punches at the last so that her horns missed by a hair's breadth. But with anyone else she meant it, and visitors learned to give her a wide berth and teased her from the other side of the gate.

For two years the goats dwelt in those stables and the novelty of them wore off for most of the youngsters round about, but there was one young admirer faithful to the end. A thin little elf with straight dark hair and bright blue eyes who never missed a morning milking if she could help it. As there was no particular reason to keep to a rigid time-table my visits to the stables were erratic, but Kitty would be waiting, and as I entered the alleyway, pounced with her ecstatic cry of 'Oh, Mrs DAY-vison!' which was the beginning of a lively chatter that only ceased when I left.

Kitty had a passionate interest in everything. She kept up a rapid fire of questions and never forgot anything I told her, as I realised – with misgivings – when she compèred the show of milking and feeding for any strange audience that happened to appear.

She loved Biddy, the goats, the horses (of whom she was a little afraid), strange babies and stray cats, with an all-embracing indiscriminate affection, and when in due course Dabs kidded she was enraptured by the kids.

Her family relationships were complicated and widespread. I never got the hang of them at all. She came bursting along one morning with the news her sister had just had a baby. Imagining a twelve-year-old to be pretty thrilled at the notion of becoming an aunt, and her sister to be a young woman, I supposed it to be a first baby.

'Oh, *no*!' cried Kitty. 'It's her thirteenth,' adding reflectively, 'but she don't keep 'em all herself. She *couldn't*.'

At a loss for a proper comment on this, being immediately obsessed by irrepressible visions of a queen bee, I switched to the subject of birthdays in general, and we found ours both fell in June, which was a satisfying coincidence.

Mine happened to come first and I was very touched by the breathless arrival of Kitty on the morning to present me with a brooch in the shape of a white-sailed yacht. She then asked how old I was, and on learning I had achieved the ripeness of thirty-five years, shrieked, and said she thought I was *much* older. Age was not one of my vanities. If one lives one is bound to grow older, there is no logical reason for self-congratulation for happening to be born at a particular time. (Though there was a time when to be told I was old for my age would have brought forth a self-satisfied smirk – horrid child that I was.) Now I smugly maintained one was as old as one felt. That morning I tottered along to the goats, quite grey round the muzzle, feeling like Methuselah's aunt. . . .

Coming out of the stable yard one evening I ran into a drunk, who glared glassily at Biddy and said, 'Dangerous brute.' I took no notice and locked the gates.

'Take 'im round with you for pro-protectshun – I suppose.'

'Her,' I said, picking up the milk-can.

He reeled forward an inch. 'If,' he said, waving a forefinger round the compass, 'Ah sees bloody dog about be isself, Ah'll . . . Ah'll . . . kick 'im t' death.'

Biddy stared into the middle distance to show that she dis-associated herself from the whole affair.

'If you lay a finger on her,' I said, 'I will personally cut your throat.'

To my surprise he shambled off.

When Frank heard of this episode he insisted on coming with me to the stables in the evenings. We encountered drunks as a matter of course, and sometimes stepped over sober bodies lying on the pavement with kitbags for pillows for want of anywhere better to go. Police usually chivvied them out of it at night, but during the day people sat about in the street as they pleased. At first I was disconcerted at the sight of a man sound asleep against a wall, or gossipy groups of men seated on the pavement with their feet in the gutter enjoying the sunshine. But after all, why not? When there are no fields or gardens what else could you use but the street?

When the pubs were shut at night there were sporadic outbreaks of fights and brawling along the dock road, but we managed to keep clear. The nearest we ever got to both being involved was coming out of a café near the station late one night. The front shutters were almost down and one had to go on hands and knees to get out. Frank went first, and just as I was half-way through someone hauled me back by the scruff of the neck, hissing, 'Don't go out – there's a scrap on!'

I got to my feet and turned round. 'I won't stop it,' I promised, and a discomfited stranger apologised saying he thought I was someone else.

'Then you wouldn't mind if I joined in . . .?'

He grinned sheepishly and I crawled out under the shutters to find a tense circle blocking the way. Inside the circle were two tall Danes squaring up to one another.

Frank took my arm.

One of the antagonists moved up close to the other, lifted his hand – and shook his finger vigorously in the other man's face. 'Foolish!' he thundered, 'Foolish!'

And that was all there was to it.

Frank and I laughed and went home to add 'foolish' to our list of family sayings.

Then one night I was laid up and Frank went milking on his own. Coming back he was accosted by a besotted mariner who insisted the milk-can was full of beer. . . . 'Cum on, mate, gi' us a sup,' and utterly refused to be shaken off. It became one of those things and finally Frank clocked him.

'A beauty,' he told me later with intense satisfaction, 'he went clean out.'

I was sorry I missed that.

Willie, the haulier, found our goats more congenial than their predecessors, the donkeys. There would be traces of horse-feed in their buckets every morning, which Willie explained away by saying they used to look at him so and he couldn't feed horses like without giving 'em a bit of summat.

We used to return the compliment at nights when the horses were in by giving them some of our hay, which they received with friendly whickers, regarding our late visits to the stables as being solely for their benefit. They were two Irish horses: Tommy, an aged, disillusioned gelding, one of Life's plodders, grateful for small mercies; and Peggy, a fine-looking mare, meant surely for better things than dragging loads of fish through fish slime. She expressed her hatred for the bonds that held her wild spirit in thrall by an exhibition of unwonted ferocity. With flattened ears and threatening hoof, she seized the manger in her teeth and worried it, to show what she would do if only she was free.

When she found we were not intimidated in the least she would turn round in the stall with pricked, expectant ears and an expression of, 'Have you got anything *nice* for me?'

Willie, who drove her, never looked as if he had the substance to cope with so much strength and spirit, but he was one of the few

84

townsmen I ever met who handled horses as a livelihood and understood them.

He was a likeable kindly grey wraith of a man with melancholy moustaches and a sudden illuminating smile, who used to bring fish for the miaowling multicoloured stable cats and never seemed to eat himself. Nor drink either. Not for Willie the solace of a pint. 'Me stomach,' he said resignedly, 'Ulcers. But beer ain't worth drinking today, nor food worth eating. Time was when a man could sit down to a bit of steak like and feel he'd had summat. Now – what they give you don't seem no good to you. You're best without.' When there was not much fish in port he would come back to the stables early and spend the afternoon studying form, his sole relaxation and interest in life. Something was amiss with his home life, what, I was too shy to ask and Willie did not explain, but he used to say wistfully it was *no use* going home till tea, so there he would sit amid the dust-laden accumulation of years, peering through steel spectacles, absently rolling thin cigarettes and sorting out tomorrow's winners.

His younger brother drove the gelding and was the very antithesis of Willie. A big burly man in his forties, Stevie was an overgrown schoolboy, and always referred to with affectionate head-shaking on the part of Willie as 'That Lad'.

Stevie came barging into the stable one day and roared at his brother: 'Ah bin all round bloody town and can't find bloody —— cow any road.'

Hopping with embarrassment Willie shouted, 'Hush!' and Stevie looked at him in astonishment. 'What the bloody 'ell's eating you?' At which I laughed and he saw me. He blushed to the roots of his hair and danced out of the stable on tip-toe, biting his lip for all the world like a big bothered schoolboy.

Willie collapsed weakly on to the stable broom, 'Eh, that lad,' he said, 'e's a terror.'

The brothers were the practical men of the haulage business, the fountain-head being their father, a stern old man in the eighties, who kept a tight rein on the finances and 'the boys', as I discovered on giving Willie a cheque for the rent.

'Best make it out to me Dad,' he said with his engaging smile, 'e'll tak' care o' yon. Don't trust us lads yet – not old enough like.'

Poor Willie, he died suddenly in his sleep one Sunday morning, and the onus of the business fell on the broad shoulders of the Lad. The stable wasn't the same without him. Peggy lost much of her verve. Maybe Stevie had not the same patience with her. Or it could be she pined?

By the time Autumn came round our hopes of getting away that year had transferred themselves to the spring of '48, and I sent Dabs away to be mated so that she would get the kidding over and come into profit before we sailed.

I discovered a breeder of pedigree Nubians near Manchester and Dabs was packed off by rail.

In due course she returned, looking very dashing in borrowed finery, rugged up like a racehorse, and accompanied by the breeder himself, a cheerful little old man, who had been utterly unable to resist coming out to see this curious set-up of goats and boats.

By that time Frank and I were living aboard *Reliance*, but the goats were still in the stables. The old man came with me to reinstate Dabs, to whose reappearance Black took perverse exception, having noisily bewailed her loss throughout Dabs's absence. We left them to sort things out for themselves and went back to the ship, where we all talked goat and lunched together in the new saloon. But the old man could not concentrate. He was intrigued beyond measure by the home we had made for ourselves aboard, and by the idea of sailing with a dog and a couple of goats as crew.

We showed him round the ship, explaining what this was for and what that was going to be, and he was so thrilled he climbed the ladder ashore without turning a hair. All part of a novel day's outing.

Whilst on the island I had written a few articles of our experiences for a farming paper, and although our interests had now, as it were, been transferred from Ag. to Fish., I still made an occasional contribution, the goats and milk production in unusual surroundings providing the required 'farming' angle.

Some weeks after Dabs's return, I opened this paper at breakfast, and there under my latest effusion was an account of his visit by the little goatkeeper.

I began to read it aloud to Frank.

He had read my articles, he said, and it was all quite true about the goats and the ship. He had seen it all for himself. He described *Reliance*, the goats, Biddy and ourselves . . . and closed his rather charming and quite breathless account with the remark that it was 'surprising what a male goatkeeper meets in the mating season'.

We hadn't enjoyed breakfast so much since bacon rationing.

11

BY June 1947 exasperation at the slowness of the refitting of *Reliance* had given way to resignation, and we had sunk into the rut which seems at times inescapable whatever way of life one may choose. Frank spent his time on *Reliance* and I divided mine between the book, the animals and the boat.

I am handicapped by a narrowness of mind which permits of only one aim at a time, and concentrates upon the achievement of that aim to the exclusion of all else. At that time my mental energies were centred on the book. I had no literary aspirations, but I thought that if it was possible to write an acceptable story of our island experiences, the book and our eventual sea wanderings might have a reciprocal publicity value, and I would then have contributed something useful towards our venture.

But it was much harder to write a book than I had ever imagined. Progress on writing was as slow as the work on the ship, and the output of waste-paper was extraordinary. And the harder it got, the more my bulldog brain held on, so that when Frank breezed back into the digs one morning and asked for the plans of the galley, I was abashed. They had been left to me to draw up and I had forgotten all about them.

Frank, frowning down at the MS paper strewn all over the floor, said, 'You are holding up the whole job now. We'll never get aboard at this rate.'

It was true enough. The forepeak and forecastle were completed; the construction of the galley was the only thing wanted for us to be able to move on board. A move eagerly awaited by us, and no less eagerly by our landlady, who, good soul, had given us winter rates and not raised them on the approach of the holiday season. But those whose living depends on holidays have to make the most of a short season. Ours was a large room capable of containing a number of Lancashire holiday-makers for whom doubling-up is one of the vacation's joys. Our room therefore was wanted.

But the kindly landlady, loath to throw us out, simply hoped we would go of our own accord.

'Oh dear,' said I, deeply guilt-stricken, 'I'll do it for you now,' and down I went on the floor, which is the best place for working out such things, and drew out a rough sketch of the galley.

From then on the Galley was All, and my single-track mind was switched to that end. As soon as the joiner was out I was in with sandpaper and pots of paint.

Then Frank flew off at a tangent and decided to salvage a smack.

She was a stranger to Fleetwood. The skipper with the owner and his wife had brought her round from the East Coast to work her out of Fleetwood. Coming up the Fleetwood Channel on one of those low, hard-blowing grey days, which moves everyone to remark it is not a bit like summer, the engine failed and the boat was swept out of the channel on to the Pilling Sands, where she took the ground good and hard.

Failing either to get the engine going or the boat off, they lit paraffin flares for assistance, nearly firing the ship in doing so, and were taken off by the local lifeboat. There was some fuss about finding the ship's cat at the last moment.

Further attempts at saving the ship were unsuccessful, and finally she was declared a total loss and abandoned. There she lay on the sands with every tide going through her.

It was the talk of the town, of course. Every fisherman knew just what he would have done and how he could have got her off, but none of them attempted to prove their point.

It was too much for Frank. 'Let's have a crack at salvage,' he said, and Dicky grinned assent. Seeing they were set on it there was nothing for me to do but agree. If there was going to be some fun I did not see why I should miss it, but I laid down my paint-brushes feeling as if I had been brought smartly up against a buffer-stop. That is the worst of a one-track mind.

The wreck owner's agent, Gosforth, was a local smacksman, whose boat was moored astern of *Reliance*. Gosforth, having served his time at engineering some ten years before Frank, joined him in a glorious mutual snorting at modern engineering practice. He was a large, anxious man who used to refer somewhat cumbrously to his own father as Charlie's grand-dad, Charlie being his son, an elegant youth, known to us in consequence as Charlie's grand-dad's grandson.

Gosforth confirmed that the vessel was abandoned, but when

Frank suggested he should join our little salvage syndicate he was thrown into an awful fever of uncertainty. To have to make a decision and follow a plan of action was agonising for him. First he thought he would, then he thought he wouldn't. He spent most of an afternoon trotting back and forth between his own boat, the *Millway*, and the *Reliance*, to tell of his latest and final decision. When brought almost to the brink of breakdown he decided not to join in with us, but agreed to hire us his thirty-foot motorless pinnace for the job.

Then, before committing ourselves any further, Frank, Dicky and I went to have a look at the wreck at low tide. We crossed over to Knott End on the ferry and walked three miles out across the sands to where she lay.

She had been a week on the sands by then, and without seeing it I should never have believed it possible for a boat to have broken up the way she had in that time. There had been a bit of wind, but nothing more than what I should have called a good stiff breeze, a bit of sea, and this was the result. A wreck indeed.

She had scoured a deep hole in the sand, and lay on her side in a deep pool of water, her hull holed and battered, the decks sprung away from the hull to point upwards and leave a huge gaping wound – as if giant hands had torn her apart. Everything below decks had broken away, and lay hidden at the bottom of the pool, an invisible, inextricable tangle of nets, gear and engine.

Dicky, who had a private line on all the grape-vines in town, said she had been a Dutch yacht before being converted for fishing. He compared her unfavourably with 'our' ship who according to him could bang about on sand like this for years on end and never turn a splinter. In view of later events I am inclined to think he was not exaggerating.

The two men toured round the wreck and agreed that salvage of the vessel was out of the question, but they glinted at her and said she was worth stripping.

Arrangements were made to have the pinnace towed out by a pleasure-boat on the early morning tide, and as soon as our intentions were known the fishermen changed their tune. We hadn't a chance, they said, the weather would reduce her to matchwood before we'd get a fairlead off her. They pointed to dark silhouettes of past wrecks, sticking up out of the sands like the ribs of long-forgotten, long-dead monsters, and said that once on the Pilling Sands a boat was no good to anyone.

Still, we thought it was a gamble worth having, and notified the Receiver of Wrecks, who received the information with enigmatic calm, and everyone stood back to watch the fun.

We spent four days on the job and got everything off the wreck worth having. The weather was kind and the tides were right. We had four days in which the sun beat down and the sands burnt hot.

Our syndicate finally numbered five. Gosforth, at the last moment, threw in his lot with us, having probably spent a sleepless night deciding, as he heroically put it, to burn his boots. And we were also joined by Ernest, a tall easy-going young yachtsman, then living aboard his cutter, which was tied up alongside *Reliance*. She was reputed to be an American craft and to have made an Atlantic crossing. Ernest had thrown up electrical engineering to contemplate the dubious pleasures of living aboard without visible means of support. A salvage gamble had a certain financial appeal if nothing else.

We used to go out on the morning tides with the pinnace loaded with demolition gear, and the pleasure launch *Queen Mary* acting as our tug streaming ahead, with Big Harry at the helm, steering the boat with his bottom, which always struck me as a masterly exhibition of casual assurance, and Billy, his mate, heaving the lead and making nonsense of the depths. They had a horror of being stranded on the sands and missing a day's joy-riding.

At the wreck, whose curved topsides were just visible at high water, the *Q.M.* cast off and left us at anchor to wait for the tide to recede. When it did we leapt overside and went at the remains of the *Wyvern* like a flock of vultures, gleefully demonstrating the lamentable but irrefutable fact that destruction is a prominent trait in human nature.

When the tide came flowing in again in the evening we loaded our well-gotten gains into the pinnace and waited for the launch to pick us up. Things such as masts or sampson post, too large to heave aboard, were towed into port.

Work went very well considering we were such a diversity of creatures, though occasional signs of friction were discernible between Gosforth and Dicky. A growth of feeling of which Gosforth was entirely unaware. With the obstinacy of a good-humoured bear he was incapable of recognising any viewpoint or method of working other than his own, which invariably differed from the general opinion. He argued every move and when overborne by weight of numbers kept up a constant nattering which amused all but Dick, who was incensed.

Gosforth fished out of the pool a new, unused coil of rope.

'By!' he said, calling us to look. 'That's not half a coil!'

'Ay,' said Dicky walking past. 'It's not, it's a coil.'

'Ay, not half,' said Gosforth.

Dicky stopped. 'It's a coil,' he repeated with fire in his eye.

We all laughed and someone started to explain that 'not half' was an expression. Dicky turned on us like a wounded tiger, pulling his cap down over his eyes so that he had to throw his head back to see from under the peak.

'Bugger that,' he roared, blowing off his suppressed irritation in one, 'they's coils and they's half coils. That's not half a coil. It's a COIL!'

'Not half!' yelled Gosforth laughing. 'What I said!'

We all propped ourselves against convenient portions of wreck and howled with laughter. Dicky, incoherent with frustration, would have flounced off the job if it had not entailed the impossibility of flouncing three miles across flat sand. He flounced round to the other side of the wreck instead and proceeded to knock hell out of it.

Two things showed up in the first day's working. We lacked certain minor items of equipment and had not taken nearly enough food with us, so the following morning, Ernest and I, being the two most easily spared, somewhat to our chagrin, were left behind to remedy matters, and to make our own way out to the wreck at low water.

We divided the duties between us and met at the ferry, sweating under our loads and the blazing sun, and boarded the ferryboat amid overt, wondering glances from our fellow-passengers, mostly holiday-makers. Ernest in heavy seaboots and yachting cap was fairly convincing as one about to do business in deep waters, but I struck an obviously dissonant note in this theme by wearing khaki drill slacks rolled to the knee, off-white sneakers, a bush shirt, and leading a large Alsatian. We were laden down with bags of nails, tacks, and oddments, loaves of bread and parcels of food, and hung about with a formidable array of knives, axes, hatchets and wrenches, and supported parlously between us was a six-foot cross-cut saw.

One of the passengers after studying the set-up for quite a time made the enlightening remark that he could see we were off for a spot of yachting.

Those three miles across the burning sands that morning were the longest I have ever walked. The image of the wreck danced ahead of us in the heat haze, seemingly as unattainable as any mirage. Even Biddy lost her usual bounce and trailed her paws beside us, drooping her ears and displaying a yard of weary tongue.

The rest of that day, as far as I was concerned, was spent brewing up on a temperamental Primus.

Our salvage activities rivalled piers and slot-machines as a holiday attraction and a stream of visitors plodded out to watch us work, causing no little anxiety by the tardy way some of them strolled back across the sands as the tide started to make. This appeared first as a luminous white line far away on the horizon, and to anyone who did not know there would seem no need for haste. But the tide sweeps in across those sands faster than a man can run. A woman with a party of small children were all that remained of the crowd one afternoon. The tide was then about a couple of hundred yards from the wreck; the children were still scattered about treasure-hunting in the sand with Mamma fondly watching, oblivious of swiftly approaching danger and ignoring our warning shouts as the vulgar badinage of the mob. Finally Frank yelled in his parade ground voice, 'Run, woman—or you'll all bloody-well drown!'

She clucked up her brood and ran, more from fear of the rough sailors than of the incoming tide.

Biddy was never quite sure whether crowds were strangers to be warned off or guests to be welcomed. And our reactions were nothing to go by for they varied from *Good* Afternoon, gabber, gabber, gabber, to Hi! Put That Down. When the crowd became too pressingly curious I heaved Biddy aboard the pinnace with instructions to 'guard the house' – our private guard order – in the hope of keeping souvenir-hunters away. Biddy, who had an extensive vocabulary, regarded this as a singularly idiotic piece of whimsy. So then I would make myself clear by giving the barking signal 'Boh!', at which she would bounce up the boat and gaze sternly seawards giving an unconvincing buff of a bark, and after looking keenly alert at nothing for a second or two, would turn to me with a wave of her tail, 'Well, Boh! if you like, but honestly I see nothing to Boh! about.'

She liked being with us because she thought we were a nice couple though not quite bright and she felt responsible for our safe conduct. And we were given to doing jolly things at times, possibly entailing a ride. Biddy would give her dew-claws for a ride in anything, from an aeroplane to a wheelbarrow.

We had touched bottom in her estimation these past few days, not only because of our irrational behaviour in choosing to waste time on a heap of wood in a worthless desert, but on account of the extraordinary behaviour of the desert itself, which would suddenly become water. Water you couldn't even drink. As we ordained most things in her life we were probably responsible for this state of affairs as well. There was no sense to it, the whole world had gone mad, and we had gone mad with it. Of this Biddy was quite convinced the night we elected to stay with the wreck to 'see the engine down'.

The engine was the plum in the pie, the *pièce de résistance*, the very central diamond in the crown of our undertaking. It lay on its broken bearers at the bottom of the pool, all fankled up with nets, gear and coils (not half) of rope. With the aid of chain blocks and tackle it was raised sufficiently for the attachment of forty-gallon oil drums and floated up on the rising tide. But when the *Q.M.* put a tow-rope on it and tried to draw it clear that night it only came so far and no farther, held fast by invisible gear tangled round the broken bearers. There was nothing for it but to leave the job until the following day.

Frank said, 'I am going to stay with it and see it down. I don't want it to drop back into the pit if it can be helped. Any volunteers?'

Ernest and I said yes at once, though for the life of me I could not see what we could do to prevent the engine slipping back into the pit if it had a mind to do so. The *Q.M.* laid out a kedge in the hope of preventing this eventuality, Frank climbed out of the pinnace aboard the incongruously floating engine, and Ernest and I, accompanied unwillingly by a deeply disturbed hound, clambered out on to the wreck. Dicky, muttering darkly that he didn't like it at all, heaved the anchor aboard, signalled the *Queen Mary* and away they went.

The engine was floating about fifteen feet from the wreck. Frank sat down on it in comparative comfort. We had standing-room only on our wreck with dappled summer waves washing across our feet.

Across the water came the sound of angry voices as Gosforth and Dicky violently disagreed.

Biddy, with one agonised glance after the fast disappearing boats, turned her back on Ernest and me and sat gazing out to sea with eloquent ears half-mast.

Slowly the voices died away. A blood-red sun sank into a blood-red sea. Then colour drained away as twilight deepened. Little twinkling lights sprang up landwards. Night fell and we were alone.

It was cold and time was slow. Biddy shivered and made to move her position, slipped and went straight into the sea. We hauled her out panting with fury.

Then as the tide turned and the water sank we had a little more room to stand on.

Suddenly there was a lurch, the wreck shuddered. It swayed and groaned beneath our feet. Ernest and I looked at one another, startled, vividly aware that demolition work had paid little attention to structure. . . . Frank laughed. 'Come on in, the water's fine,' he called, 'if that breaks up you're due for a swim.'

'It might, you know,' said Ernest.

'It might roll over,' I offered, thinking of the possibilities when the water sank to such a level that it no longer supported the main-mast upon which the wreck was leaning. The disquieting fact being that the mast had been freed in preparation for withdrawal. I rather wished I had not thought of this aspect, or had thought of it earlier on.

We discussed which way to jump, amid unfeeling comments from Frank who shouted, 'You'd better make up your minds. If it goes over it won't wait for you! How many cigarettes have you got?'

'Three.'

'Well, let me have mine before you go in.'

'For that you don't deserve one at all.'

Nevertheless, we tore a long strip of wood off the ship's side, stuck the cigarette packet on a nail at one end, lit the cigarette, put it in the packet and handed it across.

Frank had no sooner taken the cigarette than there was a loud crack, the engine heaved and before our astonished eyes he came hurtling through the air to land plop in the water by the wreck.

We heaved him aboard.

'A judgment upon you for mocking our predicament,' I said severely.

But Frank, dripping, waved his cigarette in triumph. 'Look, look, still going – not even damp!'

And so it was, but why I cannot think.

'What was all that in aid of?' I asked.

'Must be settling – I left it because I didn't want to be trapped underneath if it rolled over.'

'Ah, you see what comes of laughing at others.'

'That's all right. I've had my baptism, yours is still to come.'

But nothing untoward happened. The tide hurried away on its own affairs into the dark, and the wreck settled down into her pool once more. Biddy leapt down with relief as soon as she saw the wet sand, and Frank followed her. I started to make the descent, my rubber-soled sneakers slipped on the wet hull, and I shot straight down into the pool, up to my neck in water.

'Ah,' said Frank, 'that comes of laughing at others.'

'Your turn now, Ernest,' I shouted, crawling out of the pit. But forewarned by my effort he came down backwards in safety and spoiled the set.

The engine had not rolled over, and the kedge had held it from dropping back into the pit. It was now silently at work digging a new one for itself. We could see the tangled line of gear stretching back into the pool and which had prevented the engine from coming clear.

'The simplest method of getting all this and the mainmast away would be by dragging them clear with a breakdown van,' said Frank after inspection. 'I'll see if I can get hold of one tomorrow.'

Midnight struck faintly in the distance as we set out on our three-mile trek across the sands, and we were fascinated all the way by our giant phosphorescent footprints.

The ferry had long ceased running, but Dicky had left the dinghy for us and we rowed over the river to Fleetwood just in time to make Ernest's cutter before the tide left her on the mud. Ernest went aboard, and Frank, Biddy and I squelched back to the digs.

The following was the last day of working. Only the larger items remained for salvage. Daniel's grand-dad's grandson joined in and undulated round the job. A breakdown van from Knott End was persuaded to brave the sands and a great carfuffle of activity took place.

It was very hot again and everyone moaned for tea, which I was not being successful in producing, the Primus having broken down, apparently irreparably.

'Never mind,' said Frank, hurrying past as I struggled vainly with the stove, 'make a fire.'

I looked after him darkly. Make a fire. In the middle of this vast marine desert where the only combustible materials were part of a wreck. And wet.

Under the leeward side of the pinnace I built a fireplace out of a sheet of metal and four good baulks of timber. I took an axe to some of the drier planking, and soaked the bits in paraffin and somewhat to my surprise made a most effective blaze, upon which the kettle was soon boiling merrily.

This little boy-scout act attracted a good deal of chaffering attention.

By the time tea was over and the fire dying down, Frank came nosing round looking for some heavy timbers to lay in front of the engine to prevent it digging in the sand when the breakdown van started to pull it clear.

He seized on the four I had used for my fireplace and laid them still smouldering in front of the engine. The tow-rope was made fast and Frank was about to signal the driver away when Gosforth came huffling on to the scene and saw a thin wisp of smoke rising from in front of the engine.

'Stop!' Dramatically he pointed to the smoke. 'Fire!' he shouted.

'That's right,' said Frank, and nodded to the driver.

'Stop!' yelled Gosforth agonised. 'Fire!'

'Yes,' we chorused, 'there's been a fire. It's all right.'

Smoke continued to rise inexplicably from the engine and Gosforth looked aghast. Frank signalled the driver to go ahead.

'Stop! Stop!' shrieked Gosforth, appalled at our indifference, but the driver settled the matter by driving off in spite of Gosforth's protests.

The engine was dragged free. The mast hauled clear of the wreckage, and endless miles of warps and netting pulled clear of the pool. Then the breakdown van departed. Oil drums were reattached to the engine, and gear loaded into the pinnace. The *Queen Mary* brought out a case of beer for celebration that night. Big Harry looked at me as he handed the bottles across to the pinnace.

'Who fell int' water last night? Y' great gaup! Y' don't deserve no beer y' don't.' Frank's involuntary bathe did not count apparently.

The engine and masts were towed into harbour and our salvage party was at an end.

All that remained of the *Wyvern* was a few battered fragments of hull. Next day the weather broke and they were swept away. Nothing remained on the sands to tell of her ever being there.

We had salved the engine, a Thornycroft diesel, the main and mizzen masts, spars, capstan, sampson post, steering-wheel and engine, hatches, fairleads, fittings of all sorts, warps, ropes, fishing gear, in fact everything down to the kitchen sink. A professional valuation for insurance gave the worth as being between £800 and £900. We did not get anything like that, of course. I forget just what we did get. There was a lot of argument involving local politics which our little syndicate was not nearly fly enough to rebut, and we took with mixed feelings the grudging pittance doled out to us a year after the event.

But it had been well worth while if only for having jerked us out of the rut. The next month we moved aboard *Reliance* to start a new life – and fall into a new rut.

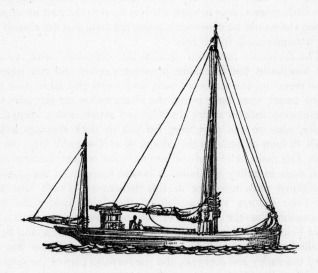

12

WE moved aboard amid the frightful conglomeration inseparable from a refit. A multitudinous assortment of cans and pots inter-mingled with chests and bags of miscellaneous tools: boxes of nails, tacks and screws of all sizes, boarding, fittings and the all-pervading woodwaste – sawdust, chippings, shavings and blocks – littered the ship, which, still minus masts, spars and wheelhouse, bore little resemblance to what she had been in the past or what we hoped she would be when the job was finished. But life aboard was not uncomfortable for all that.

The forecastle had been divided into forepeak, with lavatory and washbasin, and forecabin, in which a settee and two pipecots were tiered on the starboard side, and a seat and table with cup-board under were built round the chain locker on the port side. There were lockers under the seat and settee, and a companion ladder, also on the port side, led out to deck through a steel hatch. A door aft led into the saloon, or as it was still then, the fish hold. The main hatch and companion were erected, leading down from deck to galley and hold. A hoarse voice from the quayside proclaimed with reference to this structure – 'That's wur they 'ave their dinners and teas – down that 'ole.' Under the main companion was the smaller of the two fresh-water tanks, the other being in the engine-room. Both tanks were new and newly installed and together held 350 gallons of water. Water was laid on to the galley and forepeak and the forward part of the ship was wired for electricity.

I had a nightmare the first night we spent aboard and Biddy fell into the dock.

Biddy's immersion was entirely her own fault, though as usual she did not look on it in that light and held us to blame.

It was high water; and just before turning in, filled with pride of possession, we were having a look round on deck to see that all was in order. Frank stepped on to the rail aft to see if the dinghy, tied to a web of mooring warps, had ridden up under the counter as it had a habit of doing, and Biddy thought he was going ashore. Misjudging the whole situation she leapt lightly after him. *Reliance* was lying at the full length of her warps some distance from the quay. Biddy realised her mistake in mid-air. She realised that not only was Frank not going ashore, but that she was not going to make it. She scrabbled helplessly, appearing to be suspended by an invisible wire, for an interminable time before she dropped into the water.

Frank hopped over into the dinghy and picked her up, and together we heaved her back aboard.

After that she grumbled round the deck with us, so busily occupied in shaking herself free of water she did not look where she was going, and almost went straight through an open hatch. To save herself she flung herself flat on deck, clutching at it with rigid claws. And there she lay, fuming, and glaring at us with impotent fury. 'You two lead me into some scrapes – but THIS is the bottom.'

We turned in on our pipecots that night, warmed by the golden pleasure of a little achievement – the first night aboard our own ship. And the next thing I knew was waking up, struggling for air, with water pouring in through a gigantic hole in the side – a tumultuous welter of water, sweeping, rushing, roaring. As the ship filled, and water swirled over me, I fought and tried to shout for Frank, reaching wildly out for him. . . .

Then I really woke up, with Frank leaning over from the upper berth saying, 'What on earth is all the fuss about?' Bewildered, I had to tell of my nightmare, but could not explain it. We went to sleep again untroubled further, that night.

But the curious thing was that I had the dream again and again. It never varied. Always the terrible rush and roar of water – the sinking – the struggles and vain shouts for Frank. Sometimes I would wake with hammering heart getting out of the cot. Once I was actually opening the hatch doors leading on to the deck. Escaping, I suppose.

As I have the digestion of a horse and am not prone to nightmares there seemed no logical explanation for this.

If due to a deep-seated fear of the sea, the subconscious had shown a nice sense of the dramatic in waiting for our first night aboard before demonstrating its hidden terrors. At any rate I had no conscious fear of the sea. Not because I was courageous or unaware of what the sea can do – a winter gale or two in North Atlantic had left me with no illusions on that score – but fear, with me, is like pain, impossible to evoke because for some things I have no imagination, so it did not occur to me to be afraid of the sea and there is nothing heroic in that.

Nor did it occur to either of us to look on the dream as premonition of disaster. Long after, when our fortunes went agley and it seemed inevitable that *Reliance* would be lost to us on the rocks of finance, I could not help wondering then if the dream had a symbolical significance. But at first we looked on it as an unaccountable disability, as one might a persistent cough, an inconvenience out of one's control that would eventually pass. We were jointly concerned lest my sleepwalking efforts to escape would land me in the dock one night!

However, it never came to that. Instead of going in myself I pulled a stray dog out one night coming back from the stables and got bitten for my pains. A week or so later Frank and a couple of fishermen rescued the dredger nightwatchman, who, going aboard the dredger for duty after a party, missed his footing and went in, and was carried away up-river on the incoming tide. They went after him in the dinghy and got to him just in time. Frank said he was as tight as an owl, which probably saved him as he was rigid with cold and they had an awful job getting him into the boat. He did not actually bite his rescuers but seemed about as grateful as the dog.

Life aboard was many things, exasperating, tantalising, invigorating and amusing, and never for one moment was it dull. Most of the excitements seemed to happen at night.

Gales in conjunction with spring tides usually gave us a bit of action. During one strenuous night the dinghy broke away and surged up between *Reliance* and the fishing boat outside her and was crushed before we could prevent it. Not, we thought, irreparably, when we hoisted her ashore next day. But whilst lying on the quay awaiting repair, she was turned over by unknown passers-by evidently curious to see what she looked like the other way up. She was sixteen-foot and a heavy boat. They let her drop pretty smartly on to a railway line and it finished her. When we went to patch her we found she was matchwood, worthless as a ship's boat. Which was a pity.

Another night blow with the wind offshore gave us quite a party. *Reliance* was lying next the quay; outside her was a Brixham trawler, the *Fernleaf*, also being converted to a yacht, and outside the trawler were a prawner and a couple of small boats. At the top of the tide it was blowing great guns. *Reliance*, throwing her head like a horse getting behind its bit, reared and plunged at the furthest extent of her warps. The two quarter ropes parted with loud bangs and the strain came on to the head and stern ropes, fat grass lines pinched to half their normal circumference. Frank said, 'My God, they'll never stand it,' and we scuffled about on deck amid the clutter to find spare warps. The *Fernleaf's* stern rope to shore parted, she ripped her lines off *Reliance* with a roar of thunder and swung out amidstream hanging on to her head rope with the small boats still alongside.

The owner was aboard single-handed, but he had an engine. We hadn't. If our lines went, we were for it. Up the river and into the trees! The ladder with its foot on the bulwarks just reached the quay and hovered horizontally. Frank scuttled across this parlous bridge with a rope. 'Hi!' he shouted to a couple of chaps plodding by, 'can you give us and the *Fernleaf* there a hand?'

They halted and pondered. They looked at *Reliance*. They looked at *Fernleaf*. Then, 'No,' they said, 'we're pilots. And we're going home.' And they went.

Still, we managed. The *Fernleaf* got her engine going, cast off and came ploughing back alongside us. Frank shooed her away. Our warps were at breaking strain. If the *Fernleaf* tied up to us we would all go up-river together. After making a couple of circuits of the harbour with her litter of small boats, she managed to tie up at the jetty by the fish dock entrance. And we got various ropes, warps and bits of string ashore to hold *Reliance* captive until the tide left her and she settled in the mud.

One of the more joyous night escapades did not concern us at all. We were merely spectators, and brought from our bunks by blood-curdling howls and the roar of an engine like an aero job running up on a test bench. Concluding it could be nothing less than invasion from Mars we shot on deck, to find a fishing boat, known to us as the *Peril*, running amok in the harbour. She was on her way down to the dredger at a rate of knots when we first saw her, apparently intent on ramming it head-on. At the last moment she came round with a destroyer bow-wave and flashed up to the quay-wall, grazed round that, and tore off at a tangent towards the dock entrance. There she momentarily disappeared and we had visions of her hurtling through the steam trawlers in the dock. But no: in a few seconds she reappeared, having spun round in the entrance itself as neatly as any cab in London's back-streets. Then she went all out for the dredger again, missed it and went on a smart cruise of the harbour. The fishing fleet was just going out. Boats scattered in all directions as she buzzed among them as frenziedly as a bee in a bottle. They took exception to her behaviour through their loud-hailers. The owner, distraught and impotent, added his quota to the opprobrious advice filling the air, as he hopped along the quay, where a large delighted crowd had gathered.

Finally the *Peril* fetched up, still with her engine screaming, on a sandbank, where the tide left her.

A voice chuckled down from the quayside. 'Poor old Waller.'

But poor old Waller had had, quite accidentally, the night of his life.

The *Peril* had just completed an extensive refit and her owner – new, ex-merchant navy – had wanted to run her out in hand, as it were, that tide. POW was giving him a hand to get under way. The *Peril* was berthed outside the *Millway*, Caldy's boat, and while the owner was aboard *Millway* casting off, POW got mixed up with the controls. Before he, or the owner, realised what had happened, he had slammed her in gear, opened the throttle wide and the *Peril* was off like a rocket.

POW was short-sighted; a slow-thinking equable man. The windows of the wheelhouse were large, of the unfortunate type that reflects everything twice. It was necessary for him (so we heard afterwards) to take a stroll on deck now and again to see what was really happening – and then dodge back to take evasive action. In this he appears to have been entirely successful, but he did not seem to be able to come to terms with the controls, particularly the throttle.

But he said he quite enjoyed it all. Made a change like. He said all the lights round the dock entrance were beautiful. He had never seen anything that luvly – just like fairyland.

Poor old Waller used to find time hang heavily on his hands; he told me he went to the pictures every night to get taken out of himself. That was one night anyway he did not need to spend in vicarious enjoyment. . . .

Occasional outbursts of fun and games at midnight were good for us. Helped to keep us Young in Spirit at a time when we were in danger of brooding ourselves grey over the work on *Reliance*, which dragged on and on like a monstrous python over obstacle after obstacle. This was due to no fault of the men, who were taking an encouraging interest in the job now, but to interminable delays and inexcusable set-backs in deliveries of various materials.

It was not until the masts were stepped that we began to take heart. Half the town turned out that morning and took heart with us.

Reliance was moved up to the end of the quay under the crane, and action was cracking, for as well as the masts there was the wheelhouse, steel engine coaming, and four new steel fuel tanks to be got aboard. A carnival spirit pervaded that little corner of the port, not untinged with anxiety as to whether both masts could be stepped on that tide. *Reliance* was due on the grid the following morning and Frank wanted the masts in for that. Moreover it was the last of the suitable tides; if we missed it, it meant waiting for another fortnight.

I scampered about from point to point taking pictures of the whole proceedings – stepping the fifty-five-foot main, a ton of pitch-pine, was quite a job – while old shellbacks, young fishermen and all, came pounding up to tell me what a fine boat the *Reliance* was and what fine boats the *Reliance*, *Louie Rigby* and the *Surprise* were.

Robbie bequeathed the shilling to go back under the main for luck and Dicky had found a sixpenny bit in the bilges which went under the mizzen, and everyone said that of course in the old days they would have been golden guineas, and Frank said, My God, and I would have had to unstep these every time I was broke. And the masts were both stepped on that tide.

The lightest apprentice was sent up to fix the temporary rigging, and a woman on the quay seeing him draped round the hounds screamed, 'Look at what they are doing to that poor child.'

As *Reliance* was going on the grid in the morning we did not move back to our usual berth that night, and as she had settled comfortably enough on the morning tide we did not wait to see her down on the night tide, but turned in, with the result that we were awakened by a series of crashes. Our automatic reaction to leap from our cots was somewhat hampered by the fact that *Reliance* was lying out from the quay at a shocking angle, having rolled over at low water, and we were not lying on our pipecots at all but on the side of the ship.

We scrambled on deck and moved with extreme delicacy, for everything there was unattached and on the point of slide: the fifteen-hundredweight flywheel, the steel engine coaming, the wheelhouse and an enormous chest of tools, all very difficult to lash down under the circumstances, and if any of them had started to go, nothing on earth would have stopped them. They would have gone smack into the mud and taken the bulwarks with them. We worked on the upper side of them, which entailed some pretty tricky balancing feats on the bulwarks at times. We did what we could and got another line to shore, aided by the dock police, who illuminated the deck by shining their torches down from the quay.

Then, keeping our fingers crossed, we crept below, where oddments intermittently went zip, and shot across the ship.

Fortunately none of the big stuff on deck moved.

Only after we had turned in again and I was almost asleep the thought occurred to me that perhaps a silk nightdress – pink – was not customary wear for messing about with boats. Even at night.

Although heartened by the shippy appearance of *Reliance* with her masts we began to lose faith again as the usual hiatus between beginning and completing a job developed over the rigging. This was being done by a local firm of riggers and sailmakers who had all the fixings.

Week after week after week went by. No riggers, no rigging. Every time Frank went up to the shops he was greeted with plausible excuses about priority rush jobs on trawlers. The fact was that the sudden arrival of a sailing vessel, to be rigged the old-fashioned – the proper – way, deadeyes, lanyards, and all, presented them with a problem to which, unwilling as they were to admit it, they had scarcely a clue. Whether the idea was that after months of frustration we would give up altogether and go in for steam, I do not know, but in the end a man was found who could tackle the job, and very well he did it too.

One of the more amusing aspects of living aboard was provided by the quayside commentators, who made their remarks irrespective of whether we were visible and within hearing or not. The general assumption seemed to be that anyone aboard was either deaf or daft. The smallest details of daily life roused abnormal interest. I overheard one woman say to another, 'Eh, look, love, turnips!', as one might say giraffes or golden-crested eagles. A string of washing blowing in the shrouds would collect an admiring throng. ' 'E knows it's washday all right.' The possibility of a woman aboard not being considered, of course, in spite of the markedly feminine appearance of some of the garments. If I came on deck with a bunch of scrapers and a can of varnish the crowd positively surged forward. Mothers called to their children, 'Look – thur's a woman down thur!' I felt it was up to me to justify their excitement by turning cartwheels or hanging upside down in the rigging, and only refrained from doing so because I can neither turn cartwheels nor hang upside down anywhere.

After the Press got on our track and printed some stirring write-ups the attentions of holiday-makers grew even more pressing, much to Frank's amusement; he was ever a showman, and to my secret dismay, for no one as unphotogenic as I can ever enjoy publicity. They stopped us in the street and asked about our plans – where we were going – 'You're never going to sail that little thing all that way be yourselves?' and the more knowledgeable, 'Eh, but you want a big crew for 'er.' The most unlikely and out-size Lancashire matrons remarked, 'Eh, but Ah wish Ah were coming wi' thee.' To which Frank always gallantly replied, 'Come on then, Ma. Plenty of room.' And brought down the house.

As they could not visualise a life of wandering at sea we gave up trying to explain the fluidity of our cruising plans, and gave instead a definite destination, which was more understandable and satisfactory to their way of thinking. But as we both said the first place name that entered our heads, considerable confusion existed as to where we were going. Small boys, sticklers for exactitude, tried to get this cleared up. 'Hey, Missus, you're going to America ain't you? Harry here says you're going to Africa.' And I would say, 'Nonsense, you're both wrong. We're going to Easter Island.' That foxed them. But I must say I warmed to the small boy who stopped his big brother on the quay and pointed out the ship – 'Look, Jimmy, that's the *Reliance*. The ship that's going to Shangri-La.'

13

THE trouble with doing (and being on) a slow job is that, as you see it in your mind's eye from the beginning the way it will look at the end, you do not appreciate progress as it is made. But gradually the craftsmen worked their way down the ship until they were fabricating lockers in the counter, and were, so to speak, on their way out. The old dark after-cabin had passed through the transition of being a forest of two-by-fours and become an alley-way, with chartroom, bathroom, store-room and two sleeping cabins on either side. There was still an enormous amount of work to do – engine reassembly (two words and how much they mean!), plumbing aft, wiring aft; rubbing, stopping, painting, polishing, scraping, varnishing; wheelhouse fittings; steering gear; oh, a myriad details. But we felt at last we were getting to the top of the hill and would soon be coasting down the other side on to the plains of fortune.

Always a jump or two ahead in our plans, we began to discuss sailing seriously.

Frank said, 'I've been thinking. We really need an extra hand on this job. When we sail, I mean. It is going to be pretty arduous at sea for a crew of two. And it means in port one of us will always have to stay with the ship. Which is going to be a considerable bind.'

We had been through all this before. And concluded that the risk of introducing a third party, who might turn out to be in-compatible, was too great to run for the sake of – problematical – convenience. I am not gregarious by nature. I love solitude, and would choose it. Not because of a failure to get along with my fellow men; on the contrary, I get on with most pretty well. But generally speaking there are too many of them! And we all talk too much, having nothing to say. I am as bad as the rest. Heaven knows I can bore myself to death. But privacy is a most important factor in life. For some people it is an absolute necessity, and privacy aboard is hard enough to get and keep, even on a ship the size of *Reliance*. With Frank and me this did not count, we had become so perfectly attuned to one another. We had shared isolation and still preferred one another's company to anyone else's. We could be silent together, and had learnt that differences, however violently expressed, meant exactly nothing – between us. But I knew myself well enough to recognise the dangers of intrusion by a third party . . . as my grandmother used to say, there isn't a house big enough to hold more than one family. And I felt this to go for a ship as well. Particularly a ship with me in it. I thought then, as I do now, either one should be single-handed (or with someone with whom you are on such terms that it amounts to the same thing), or there should be a crew large enough to prevent petty differences from assuming undue proportions.

But there was something in what Frank said. Especially with regard to the necessity for someone to remain aboard when the ship was in a strange port. One of the greatest pleasures we looked forward to was the exploration of the fringes of strange countries. And pleasure loses so much of its lustre if not shared with one who understands and appreciates things in the way you do.

Besides, Frank had a grasp of the realities of sailing, and if he thought we should have an extra hand it was not for me to quarrel.

I said, 'Have you anyone in mind?' And he said, 'Ernest.'

Ernest, the young yachtsman, who had worked with us on the wreck. He had given us a measure of himself then, and he seemed the right type. Keen on the sea, undemanding, unassuming, not the sort of person to get in one's hair.

We all had lunch together one day, and Frank asked if he would care to come along with us. He said without hesitation, 'Nothing I would like better.' Which was the right sort of reply too. No ifs and ands and buts.

So Ernest threw his lot in with us and moved aboard into the spare cabin and set to work on the electrical wiring of the ship. . . . He made a thundering good job of it.

But after all Ernest did not stay with us.

We were too long in port. Which has been the undoing of more than one crew. Ernest was an enthusiastic yachtsman. Dicky was a genuine dyed-in-the-wool sailor. They talked together for hours of ships and the sea. Ernest in his capacity of an amateur metaphorically sat at the feet of the master, a situation which naturally pleased Dicky enormously. They went off for drinks together, and parties together, still talking ships, Dicky laying down nautical law and Ernest lapping it up.

Insidiously an afterguard-foreguard atmosphere developed, for Frank and I had no time now for the party spirit. The trouble that had been growing quietly had now become serious financial dissolution. Urgently we pressed forward with the completion of the ship, fighting our money troubles underground, knowing that once it was public knowledge we were done. For it is strangely permissible to kick a man if he is down – financially.

So jollification was not in our line. We had neither the cash nor the inclination. A mistake. The only real regret I have in life is the opportunities let slide. 'Gather ye rosebuds whilst ye may' should be written in capital letters in everyone's notebook of life. For, by God, once the petals have fallen, those flowers are dead. And there is no way of bringing them back.

However.

Dicky undertook the job of rattling-down, the fitting of those transverse lines across the shrouds like ladder rungs, and having completed it, stood back, as it were, to receive medals.

Frank said, 'Good-oh. But, Dick, those bottom four aren't level.'

Dicky bristled. 'They's straight.'

'No,' said Frank, 'they can come up a bit.'

Dicky, his authority challenged, said if he didn't know how to rattle-down, no one else did. And it all came of listening to quayside talk.

'Nonsense,' said Frank with an irritability arising from other matters altogether. 'But if that's the way you feel about it, we'll have them the wrong way. My way.'

At which Dicky downed tools without a word and walked off the ship.

Ernest, mildly defensive, said that in his opinion there was something to be said for Dicky's point of view. Frank, now thoroughly exasperated, said there was only room for one opinion aboard. So Ernest took his ashore.

With Ernest we were soon on amicable terms again, though there was no question of reinstatement. He went fishing for a time, and then, I believe, returned to electrical engineering.

But with Dicky it was a different matter. We saw nothing of him for a time, then Frank ran into him accidentally one day and they tentatively buried the hatchet. But I was bitterly disappointed. I felt, unjustly, it was a case of 'et tu Brute', and I was incensed at his petty behaviour. In return I behaved even more pettishly and refused to have anything to do with him.

All this happened about the end of February or March 1948. January 1949 we were still in port. Dicky came aboard and held out his hand, 'Come to wish you happy new year like.' My resentment dissolved as we gravely shook hands. We were friends again and I was glad. But it was not quite the same. Some of the old careless confidence was missing, and would always be.

Nursing a grievance is one of the most futile forms of self-indulgence.

The contractors were already off the ship by the time Ernest and Dicky departed, so we had the job to ourselves. To be perfectly candid this suited me very well as I had a chance to partake in, and learn something about, more constructive work than the eternal painting and scraping which had hitherto fallen to my lot, and of which I was heartily sick.

Although my role was that of 'boy', the reassembling of the massive Gardner engine was one of the most interesting things I have ever had a hand in. I do not take to spanners naturally and mine is not the precise mind of the engineer, but I do find with mechanics it is like being out in the rain – good fun, once you are reconciled to taking what's coming to you. If you play about with engines it is oil. Buckets of it from head to foot.

Swinging the great flywheel, all fifteen hundredweight of it, into position, with less than a quarter of an inch clearance either side of the pit, was an intensely satisfying achievement. To do this we used a gadget called a Hi-Lift jack, a modification and advance on the usual chain blocks and tackle. It simplified the handling of all the colossal engine parts, and was a veritable godsend to us, then and later, in all our engine-room work.

We pored over blue-prints, which became as exciting to me as an atlas, and Frank explained the set-up and workings as we went along, and the old engine grew in personality as well as stature as it went together. These old-fashioned motors may lose out on efficiency (one of the most overworked words in the English language, as well as being one of the most overworked beliefs of today) but they certainly gain on character. When it was completed, green-painted, and with all its brass fittings and copper piping gleaming and winking, the two tall cylinders were curiously reminiscent of ancient drawings depicting Chinese war-lords, and we christened the Gardner, Tuo-Lung-Bong.

At the aft end of the aft cylinder was a fuel panel with all sorts of cranks and levers and one thing and another to go round and round and up and down, highly pleasing for those who like to see the 'works'. And it gave the impression this was a proper ship's engine.

It was a proper ship's engine-room too. Proportionately it occupied the largest part of the ship. The engine was off centre with the propeller on the starboard quarter. On the port side of the for'ard bulkhead was a door leading into the saloon. On the starboard side of the door, but between it and the engine, was a large refrigerator. A thoroughly unsatisfactory siting, but there was absolutely nowhere else on the ship to put it. On the port side of the engine-room were two fuel tanks and a 320-gallon fresh-water tank. On the starboard side, forward, was a workbench with vice, and tool drawers under, and then two more fuel tanks. Fuel tanks contained a total of 800 gallons of diesel oil which gave a range of 2,000 miles under power alone. Nevertheless Frank maintained that Tuo-Lung was an auxiliary. . . .

The engine was compressed air, hot-bulb start. The air bottle was strapped on the engine-room flooring under the fuel tanks on the starboard side. Fitting the pipelines from air-bottle to engine was a fascinating bit of plumbing. To lead the piping from A to B so that it was adequately supported, so that it did not get in the way, and so that best use was made of available piping and joints, was a practical application of one of the more involved picture-puzzles. In spite of particular care in sealing the joints the first test sounded like a factory whistle blowing for knock-off, and we had to break the joints and start again. When the leaks were reduced to one slow one, then the game became really difficult, for in sealing that one you would inevitably disturb a good joint. But eventually the pipeline was proof.

On the starboard side of the aft bulkhead was the Norman petrol auxiliary engine which charged the batteries, the compressor for the air-bottle and operated a pump, which either emptied the bilges at the rate of 300 gallons *a minute*, or sucked up sea water for the deck fire-hose. The whole of this outfit was contained in a steel frame and could be removed *en bloc* if desired. Frank designed it thus, thinking it would be useful to be able to take it ashore on occasions. Whilst undergoing construction it was known as Mr Davison's Flying Machine.

A companion ladder aft led to deck through a sliding hatch in the steel coaming, and a door on the port side of the aft bulkhead led into the alleyway and aft compartments.

In the engine-room were also the header tanks for hot and cold water laid on to galley, bathroom and forepeak.

With our usual incurable optimism we expected the engine to go first crack off and felt personally affronted when it refused to do so. But it was too much to expect of Tuo-Lung; the engine was stiff after reassembling and needed the several minor adjustments – nothing in themselves, one would think (this one at any rate), but collectively enough to prevent a start. We saw several tides go out with our hopes of making the engine operate that day, but we got plenty of useful experience working up a team-spirit for the ritual of starting, for this was no press-button job. And it wasn't an engine you could swing either. Theoretically, it was only necessary to heat the cylinder heads with blow torches for fifteen minutes, lever the flywheel round to starting position (marked by a white-painted section), and press the air lever on the aft cylinder, to have the engine going. But in practice it was necessary to start up the auxiliary motor at the same time as the torches were lit, for these blowers used so much compressed air that by the time the cylinder heads were hot enough there was not enough pressure in the bottle to give the main engine its initial boost. Frank looked after the blowers, standing over them with an ordinary blow-lamp, which saved innumerable boxes of matches (the torches were themselves a bit temperamental starting), and needed nice adjustment of the mixture of air and diesel oil, otherwise they would go out or burn with a 'cold' orange flame and fill the engine-room with clouds of impenetrable black smoke which almost suffocated us.

I took care of the Norman motor and the air compressor. When the pressure in the air-bottle was over 180 lb. the auxiliary engine laboured and was inclined to stop altogether, so I had to keep a finger on the compressor release valve to stop it momentarily and allow the engine to build up its revolutions again. The compressor gained slightly on the blowers and by the time the cylinder heads were hot enough there would be 200 lb. pressure in the bottle. Then we were ready for off. I would hop across the bridge over the shaft between engine and gear box, to open the compression taps on the port side of the cylinders, so that Frank could lever the flywheel round to starting position. He would give a few turns on the lubricator box handle, a few jerks on the fuel levers, and if the atomisers were doing their stuff, smoke would stream down from the compression taps. If no smoke appeared the atomisers or sprayers would have to be whipped out and the jets cleaned. But all being well Frank would signal me to close the compression taps, and then he, on the other side of the engine, pressed the starting lever. If we were lucky the engine started. If not, he went on pressing the lever until there was no more useful pressure in the bottle – under 120 lb. we found it a waste of time trying – and if the engine still sulked we had to begin at the beginning again . . . if there was enough water, but usually by this time the tide would be well down and we would have to wait for another day.

The noise accompanying the starting ritual was enough to waken the dead. The auxiliary screamed, the compressor stuttered with a hard, peculiarly penetrating beat, and the torches blared – and how they blared! They roared with such heady urgency one was impelled to do everything at a hard gallop, with the overhanging fear that if one didn't then something awful would happen. And when at last Tuo-Lung consented to go the comparative silence of his intoxicating tom-tom beat was as the sweet peace of sleep. And in fact TLB was a remarkably quiet engine with hardly any vibration – Frank took a cup of coffee all round the ship and stood it on various shelving to gloat over the unrippled surface of the coffee.

We went into the wheelhouse to try out the controls and had *Reliance* ranging back and forth along the quay within the confines of her warps. The usual crowd of quayside watchers collected and shared our excitement. They listened to the bonk-bonk of the exhaust with as rapt an expression as if the functioning of Tuo-Lung-Bong concerned them personally.

Then at last the refit was at an end. A moment which arrived and passed almost imperceptibly, for work on a ship never comes to an end; maintenance goes on as long as she is afloat, and with a vessel the size of *Reliance*, if you are maintaining her yourself, the work has a Forth-Bridge aspect. When you've worked down the ship with a paint-brush you have to begin at the beginning again. But construction work was now over, and conducted tours were the order of the day. Living on a show-ship has certain disadvantages. People take it for granted you are delighted to show them over any time of day or night, and no matter where you are or what you are doing there is always the likelihood of an admiring, pop-eyed stranger appearing round a doorway. Frank, of course, loved showing visitors over *Reliance*; it was the only thing for which he would willingly interrupt any work he was doing. But *Reliance* was his brain-child, the product of his skill and planning, a product of which he had every reason to be proud, and I never knew anyone to see *Reliance* and fail to be impressed.

The Press were very much in evidence these days, and I remember a reporter saying, after spending the afternoon aboard, 'It is a pleasure to write-up a genuine job like this' – which made us feel pretty good.

One of our most charming unexpected visitors was Alan Villiers, who happened to be in the district and dropped aboard to see what was going on on this *Reliance*.

We had both read his books avidly and I thought Frank was fooling when he said who was aboard.

Alan Villiers surprised me in not looking in the least as I had imagined him, having the appearance more of a countryman than a sailor.

Frank and he talked ship and took pictures of one another, and Villiers kindly offered advice regarding markets for articles, photographs and such, as one who has urged ships about the seven seas and known the financial hazards of doing so. He told us when he would be next in New York, suggested meeting there and generously offered introductions. . . .

Villiers sailed the *Joseph Conrad*, a full-rigged ship, round the world, possibly the last man to do so in a ship (in the true sense of the word) and for this he will always be remembered. But actually the voyage was remarkable for his unshakable faith and tenacity of purpose, for Villiers met with every conceivable difficulty, any single one of which would have defeated a lesser man.

In connection with this voyage Villiers made a remark that my mind seized on and docketed.

'I did it,' he said simply. 'I got her round. And whatever happens to me now it is something I have done, and can never be taken away from me.'

⌒　　　⌒　　　⌒　　　⌒　　　⌒

Reliance was built in 1903 and the Gardner two-cylinder 48/60 h.p. semi-diesel engine was installed in 1925.

She was 70 feet OA, 64 feet LBP, with a beam of 18·1 feet and draught of 9 feet 6 inches. She was built of pitch-pine on oak frames, with a sheer strake of greenheart and garboard of English elm. Deck beams were pitch-pine, except in the saloon (erstwhile fish hold), where they were oak. She was ceiled throughout with $2\frac{1}{2}$-inch pitch-pine. From the inside of the ceiling to outside the hull was a depth of 13 inches. The frames were doubled and so closely spaced she might have been built for Arctic exploration – and there was no room for a porthole anywhere in the ship. The shelf was pitch-pine and decking $2\frac{1}{2}$-inch pitch-pine.

It was a good basis to build on, seeing that in 1947 she was practically as sound as ever.

Frank dreamed of putting her back to her old gaff rig if and when sails, spars and hands were available, but was temporarily contented with a jib-headed main and Bermudan mizzen, which was, he philosophically remarked, as much as the two of us could handle anyway. Sails were very difficult to get at the time we were fitting out, but we were lucky in being able to get, through a friend, an unused suit (no. 1 canvas), jib, main and mizzen, intended originally as steadying sails for a large steam yacht. The mizzen was too big and Frank was torn whether he should have it cut down, or make a spare main out of it and have a new mizzen made, so took no action at all for some time and the sails remained in store. The only sail bent was the forestaysail, a tanned fisherman job. There was also a silk balloon jib, but where these two sails came from I cannot for the life of me remember.

Below deck the finished accommodation from for'ard to aft was forepeak, forecastle, then saloon. This was approximately 14 feet by 11 feet, which made a sizable cabin. Before the joiners got to work and while it was still a hold 2,000 gallons of fresh water was pumped through to clear out the accumulation of years of fish filth. We prepared the woodwork for painting ourselves and laboriously scraped forty-odd years of fish paint off the oak deck-beams, which were then simply oiled and looked magnificent. The saloon was panelled out in a composite material, and painted ivory. Fittings included sideboard, wine-bin, table, bookshelves (every fisherman who came aboard goggled at the number of our books) and settees. There were lockers under the settees, behind the settees, under the bottom step of the companionway, beside the water-tank under the companionway, and on top of the tank itself (which made a useful cold larder). 'Cor,' said the joiner as he worked, 'bleeden bloody lockers everywhere. What th' 'ell are you going to put in 'em all?'

As this was to be our reception room, so to speak, we wanted it to be specially sonsy and employed professionals for the painting, and staining and french-polishing of the woodwork. The french-polisher made an excellent job. He stained the raw wood walnut and gave it a mirror-like finish. His masterpiece, though, was the renovation of the table, which was the original old deal table from the main cabin aft. After he had finished with it it was unrecognisable. Many a visitor tapped it knowingly and remarked, 'Nice bit of stuff that. The real thing' – which always made us giggle more than somewhat. But it was a good job of work, and his charges were the most reasonable we ever had for any work done on the ship. The painter also made a good job, but to this day I cannot see how his firm justified the bill they sent in. Frank said when it came in, 'Good grief! I don't want to buy the bloody firm.' It was not as if the painter had had all the preparing to do even. . . . We did the rest of the painting ourselves, and it was every bit as good as professional work.

Double doors in the saloon, starboard aft, opened out to the main companion leading to deck, port, and a doorway into the galley, starboard. On the port side, aft, of the saloon was another door leading into the engine-room.

The galley was our pride. I shall never know a better galley to work in as it was exactly what I wanted. Possibly the only time in my life I shall ever attain just that. It was a compartment 6 feet by 5 feet 6 inches, and strictly utilitarian. There was no room for any of those superannuated, lidless, handleless, bottomless, useless, to-be-mended-one-day utensils which inevitably clutter a kitchen ashore. Pots and pans were kept to a minimum – I wanted but little there below and got that little good!

The cooking stove was a paraffin, pressure type, and looked like an electric cooker, in grey and white vitreous enamel with two hotplates on top, a hot cupboard and oven beneath. It was extremely satisfactory and Frank extended its capabilities by making and fitting in the hot cupboard an electric grill. This was by way of being a bit of an amp eater, so it was intended for use only when the batteries were being charged. As charging was a daily routine matter this was no hardship. Another burner, fed from the same paraffin tank as the stove, in a bracket fixed to the for'ard bulkhead above and between the stove and draining-board, heated a two-gallon copper urn. Water in this would keep warm for four hours after boiling without further heating, and was a most useful accessory.

The sink and draining-board were made of a metal which polished to shine like brass – and like brass, tarnished as quickly. But it looked pretty good on the occasions I was overwhelmed by house-pride. There had been some difficulty in getting the sink fitted at the height I wanted. One of the unnecessary exasperations in life is backaching over a too-low sink, and this I was determined to avoid. But when the joiner first put up the sink, he padded off to Frank in horror, insisting there was some mistake. It was far too high. Frank took a look at it and panicked. He thought it was too high. Freddie nosed in and asserted it was definitely too high – 'Eh – water'd run up your arms like!'

I took a look at it and said it was just right, and was prepared to defend it with all my might. I won my point amid much head-shaking, but it was right in practice, and the water did not run up my arms. . . . It would have been as perfect as any sink can be if it hadn't needed so much polishing to keep it bright.

Hot and cold sea water was laid on to the galley, and the sink drained into a forty-gallon sludge tank in the bilges. The sludge tank was emptied overside when necessary by a charge of compressed air. In port we filled the sea-water tanks with fresh water, but at sea fresh water was to be obtainable only from the one tap on a pump in the galley. This was an extremely simple self-priming pump. Above the draining-board were crockery racks, and on the other side of the sink was a work-table with a cupboard above, and drawer, built-in pastry-board (*that* shook the fishermen) and cupboard under. On the aft bulkhead were shelves to hold tins, bottles and working supplies of tea, sugar, coffee, flour, etc. An electric air-extractor with vents over the stove and sink kept the galley well ventilated in hot weather.

Aft of the engine-room the accommodation was entirely new, and where there had once been one dark cabin was now a complete little home from home. The engine-room door opened on to an alleyway which ran right aft to the wheelhouse companion ladder. Immediately to port, coming out of the engine-room, was a large wardrobe locker – big enough to stand up in. Frank made a small electric heater to fit in the light socket for airing our clothes. Next came our stateroom. This had a double bunk with a locker at the foot, and two enormous drawers under, a seat locker and a dressing-table. It was a comfortable cabin, but we were both reluctant to leave our 'suite' in the forecastle. Aft of our cabin on the port side was a small spare cabin, with a bunk which could be double or single as needed, with lockers and drawers, etc. Then lastly was a locker containing a 60-gallon paraffin tank and space for paints and bosun's stores.

To starboard of the alleyway, moving aft from the engine-room, was first a chartroom, which was also the office. In it was a large flat-topped desk over the 24-volt accumulators, and above the desk were shelves for files and technical books, charts, tide-tables, sailing directions and so forth. The type-writer was fitted on a small shelf at right-angles to the desk, and there was a large cupboard against the aft bulkhead for navigation and photographic gear. The switchboard was on the forward bulkhead in the chartroom. Next to the chartroom was the bathroom with handbasin, lavatory and full-size bath. We were rather proud of this big bath – 'None of your sitz baths aboard this ship,' said Frank to visitors.

Then came the store-room, designed and shelved to hold seven or four-and-a-half-pound biscuit tins, which are easy to handle, and easily discarded and replaced when too rusty for use. There was also a built-in locker for the storage of canned goods. Lastly on the starboard side was a small locker for bonded stores.

At the end of the alleyway, aft of the mizzen step and companion ladder to wheelhouse, was an emergency door to the sail locker in the counter (which also had a steel hatch on deck).

We reckoned that our tankage and storage space for fuel, water and food would allow us to be independent of land for three months at a time.

As port-holes were out of the question, decklights were let in the deck to provide light during the day below. In the smaller compartments, bathroom, alleyway and such, these were small, either oblong prisms or inverted 'lemon squeezer' types, but in the saloon, stateroom, chartroom and galley the decklights were twelve-inch diameter and gave remarkable light below. We pondered many a scheme for the protection of these in heavy weather, but they never gave us a moment's anxiety in practice, and were the least of our troubles in days to come.

The whole layout was planned for ease of working at sea and comfort in port. Nothing was left to chance. For instance, there were three bilge pumps: an automatic bilge pump on the main engine; the pump operated by the auxiliary motor; and a hand bilge pump on deck – a hell of a thing with a six-foot lever – on the port side of the steel engine coaming. The main engine also charged the batteries when running; a dynamo was fitted on the starboard side of the for'ard cylinder and run off the flywheel. And there were two sets of batteries. There was a mains plug so that in port where it was available lighting could be run off the town supply. One could move from one end of the ship to the other without going on deck, an invaluable asset in bad weather, and there were plenty of exits and entrances so to speak – the forecastle hatch just for'ard of the windlass, the main hatch just aft of the main mast, the engine hatch and the hatch in the wheelhouse, so that one could get on deck in rough stuff more or less where one wanted to be without groping for lifelines in heavy seas. The wheelhouse was strengthened by steel uprights and a steel baseplate. It was a roomy deckhouse and had good visibility, yet the windows were not dangerously large. For'ard of the wheel was a mahogany chart-shelf (made from a couple of mantel shelves we had carted round with us since Hooton days with the idea they might Come in Useful), and fixed on the port side of this shelf was my pride and joy, the aviation compass. Its nautical equivalent was a deckhead fitting. Navigation lights were electric and there were two decklamps on the front of the wheelhouse. Light switches and fuse panels were fixed on the aft bulkhead inside. Throttle and gear controls were operated through a system of wheels, chains and shafts to the engine.

There was a mast winch on the deck by the main hatch. Three anchors, two heavy fisherman type and a kedge, were stowed in the bows, and an anchor davit was fitted on the port side of the stem head. The davit was removable and could be used as a boat davit. We were still trying to replace the small boat and had not yet succeeded. Dinghies were as scarce as hens' teeth and prohibitively expensive. A Carley float was lashed to the starboard side of the wheelhouse. We thought it would be rather fun for bathing in tropical waters.

And I forgot to mention the two life-jackets suspended under the wheelhouse shelf. A couple of Mae Wests – relics of our flying days. Life-jackets were a compulsory part of equipment for flying over sea and five were kept stowed in the Monospar for trips to Ireland or the Isle of Man. I remember once being infuriated whilst flying the Monospar on a co-op job over Liverpool, when both motors packed up; due to icing conditions, which was a new thing then and we didn't know much about it. Anyway I was slap over the middle of Liverpool with no height to speak of and it was either the river or the town. I chose the river. And it looked like being a wet party. The Mae Wests were right in the tail of the machine and she was an awkward craft and would not trim for level flight, you had to fly her all the time. Even with the trimmer right forward you could not let go of the stick or she would stand on her tail. We were gliding now, of course, but even so she couldn't be left to herself. There was no height for any fun and games. I couldn't go aft and get the jackets and they wouldn't come to me. However, I had a lot of fret for nothing. In the warmer air down near the water one motor de-iced and picked up. We hobbled home to Hooton skating up the river and over the trees – with me spitting out bits of chewed heart all the way. But I could never look at those Mae Wests without thinking of how I had nearly wanted one.

Reliance in the Summer of 1948 was all but ready for sea. The ball was at our feet and . . . we were told we must not kick it.

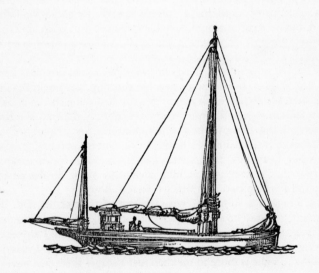

14

WHEN at last we had reached the stage of being almost ready for sea, when we should have been planning shakedown cruises, ordering stores, studying charts and generally enjoying the fruits of our labours, we were tied to the quayside by a misplaced honesty and a horrible tangle of financial complications. If only we had sailed early on before matters got out of hand, we should have been at the other side of the Atlantic, pounding out journals, articles, books, and working the ship, gathering in pieces of eight to clear off the dead wood, before anyone would have been the wiser or been able to do anything about it. If only we had sold *Reliance* at the top of the market. . . . If, if, if . . .

We could not do these things anyway. We could not clear out in the early days of our troubles because the ship was not ready, nor were we ready to take such a step. We still had some shreds of belief in law and order, and that all would come right in the end. We could not sell the ship because she was not complete, and to part with her would have broken Frank's heart. I did suggest something of the sort when I saw how things were going – we were by no means in the red – but money was melting away like snow on the desert's face, and I recognised the path we were following.

But Frank was so in love with the ship. 'Sell her?' he said. 'For why? It's going to be a tight squeeze. But we'll make out. We must.

'Look, Ann,' he went on slowly, 'I can't start again. I am sick of starting things. This is the last. I have put everything of myself into *Reliance* . . . she is more to me than just a ship – there will never be another.'

And I knew that if I harped on selling her, and nagged him into doing so perhaps by resorting to the abominable dramatics women are wont to do – 'choose between the ship and me' sort of thing – for ever afterwards the spectre of *Reliance* would come between us. I would be the one who had failed, the one who had not the patience or guts to see the thing through to the end. Our relationship was far too precious to be squandered thus or haunted by the ghost of a ship. Besides we were not completely broke, there was still a chance we could pull through. I could see his point of view only too well. And – I had grown feelings for *Reliance* too.

It is so easy to be wise after the event. To criticise each other's mistakes. We, being inviolable of course, would never do this, that, or the other. But we have not the faintest notion of what we would do in any given circumstances until they are upon us.

At the beginning of the refit it seemed we had plenty of cash for the job and in fact we were more concerned as to how to be able to use it abroad. At the end of the job we were broke, with a pack of creditors snapping at our heels, and Frank, drawing on reserves of wry philosophy, said, 'Well, we've one worry less now – how to get our money out of the country.'

We had made a good job of *Reliance*, but she was not a luxury conversion. There was no chromium-plated nonsense about her – she had no silver coins inset for step treads as in one conversion we knew of – she was simply a sound working ship and we had paid through the nose for her so to be. It was impossible to wring an estimate out of a firm in those days, for they were still under the giddy influence of costing on a war-time basis of time and materials. It was no secret that we planned to go abroad and from contractors' points of view we were lemons to be squeezed but once. They made the most of their opportunity. They knew we could not get materials without them. We did not quarrel with high prices. Nor blame anyone for sticking out for the highest they could get, that is simply normal business practice after all. For the value of an article largely depends on how much you want it and what you are prepared to give for it.

We paid a considerable sum for *Reliance* in the first place because we wanted her, that was the price, the seller would not take less and we could afford to pay it. We did not *have* to have her. But we did take exception to what struck us as a series of altogether excessive overcharges and scamped jobs. For instance, the mast showed signs of softness above the hounds and instructions were given for the decaying timber to be removed and a graving piece inserted; but we found that the workman had merely slammed on a bit of putty and called it a day. Frank rioted over this and eventually after further attempts at evasive action the job was done properly. But it was all charged for.

We took a firm stand over the questionable items and refused to pay, which resulted in writs being hurled at the ship, a form of blackmail, hallowed by time and long usage, for a ship cannot move with a writ on her. If one's livelihood depends upon the working of the vessel one is expected to pay up and go quietly to avoid legal proceedings. For the Admiralty Court is a mill that grinds very slowly indeed: proceedings are long-drawn-out and excessively expensive. It is therefore often cheaper to meet excessive demands rather than fight, with the ship lying idle for months. But we fought. A legal wrestle with no holds barred on either side. We were so infuriated we made no secret of what was going on, and many a fisherman agreed it was time someone took a stand against this sort of thing. But for themselves they never dared to. 'It's all right for you,' they said, 'you don't have to live here, we do.' But it was not all right for us. True, it was all eventually settled out of court, and we won our point, but the delays and expenses cleaned us out, taking not only all we had got but what we had not got besides. There was a mortgage on *Reliance* and this was eaten away too.

About half-way through the refit, calculations clearly indicated we were not going to be able to complete with our remaining capital, so, without any difficulty, we raised a mortgage on the vessel. We altered our future plans accordingly and were unperturbed, for fishing at that time was a profitable undertaking, and we thought a season or two fishing would put us on the right side, build up reserve funds and give us plenty of experience working ship and getting the 'bugs' out of her. Then afterwards we could carry on with our original programme. Frank went into the matter very carefully and it did not seem possible to lose out. Dicky backed the idea enthusiastically and I was very keen. Fishing had always interested me and I thought it would not only provide valuable copy but invaluable experience in seamanship. There is nothing like *having* to do a job to learn something about it. An ounce of practice is worth a ton of theory.

We pressed on with the refit, having no reason to believe other than that we should soon be at sea and paying our way. The mortgage and our remaining funds would see us through and provide sufficient working capital to start with. However, it was not to be.

The interminable delays in deliveries, in getting jobs done, like the rigging already mentioned, and the winch on which modifications took nine months to complete. And many, many other items.

Finally there were the frightful quarrels over accounts, which did not happen in a day or two but dragged on over weeks and months, using up time and money until there was none left.

Meantime we had come up against a snag in the fishing project, which at first sight did not appear to be insuperable. For inshore fishing it is not necessary for a boat to be skippered by a certificated man, but fishing inshore is limited (or was, regulations may be altered by now) to vessels with engines under 40 h.p. *Reliance* with a 48 h.p. engine did not qualify, and therefore we had to find a certificated man. Dicky had gone by now, but in any case he did not have a 'fishing ticket', having failed in a sight test on account of colour-blindness, which was one of his grievances against life. There were many fishermen who would have come with us, but none of them had tickets. And extensive search could not produce a certificated skipper. The shortage was largely due to the prosperous state of the industry and demand exceeded supply. Skippers of big trawlers were then earning between £3,000 and £5,000 a year and were not to be lured away to a comparatively twopenny-halfpenny proposition like ours. It was a bad time for intermediate-sized vessels such as *Reliance* – there were five boats in port held up then for similar reasons, which was no comfort at all.

When the difficulty became apparent, without ceasing our search for a skipper or giving up the fishing project, we followed other schemes for making the ship pay, with the intention of pursuing the first practical proposition that presented itself, and promptly came up against further unlooked-for snags.

We advertised for partners to share the cruising or working of the ship and 'paying guests' whom we were prepared to sail to any destination. There were thousands of people then bitten by the idea of emigrating. People unable to settle into peacetime niches; people tired of the bonds of socialism; people tired of the bonds of any civilisation, all turning their eyes to distant lands across the sea, but thwarted because shipping space was so short after the war and waiting-lists were so long. Many had to give up the notion altogether or face the prospect of waiting a year or more before their names came out of the hat and they could sail. It seemed to add up to something for us. We would fill the ship with emigrants and take them to South Africa, New Zealand, Australia or anywhere they wished.

We were not wildly excited about taking either partners or passengers – 'he that hath a partner hath a master' – fishing was far more to our liking, but we were not in a position to choose. Our main object was to get *Reliance* to sea, and earning. How, was immaterial.

It was disconcerting to find it took at least six months for an advertisement to appear in a newspaper, after surmounting obstacle number one – getting the effusion accepted in the first place. Some papers would not consider advertisements appertaining to small-ship voyages under any circumstances. We were not the first to light on the notion of running an unofficial passenger service. Others had been before us. Others with ill-found vessels and scratch crews who had sobbed into the nearest port in dire distress. Others who perceived in the shortage of shipping space yet another opportunity for fleecing a gullible public. Many an unfortunate put up and lost money for a passage to the Antipodes that was never intended to take place. Private ventures as a whole were in bad odour in a socialist State and private sailing ventures simply stank to high heaven. Newspaper editors, moved to an unwonted concern for their readers, were chary of being in any way party to such things and looked askance at our alluring ads. We produced the right references on demand – we still happened to know some acceptable types then – and our advertisements appeared in due course. But by that time the public were not interested. They had given up the idea of the outback or become resigned to a long-delayed sailing date, and one and all were shy of making passage in a little ship, regarding them all as suicide ships or floating bucket shops.

No one was interested in a cruising partnership from a practical viewpoint. I got so sick of hearing people say, 'Gad, if only I was ten years younger,' or, 'If I wasn't married I'd join you like a shot,' that I rudely answered, 'Rubbish – if you were ten years younger you still wouldn't have the guts to join us.'

Most of the answers to our advertisements were from impoverished types hankering after adventure, eager, so they said, to work their fingers to the bone for us if only we would take them along.

We worked out a scheme for commercial travelling on a big scale, turning *Reliance* into a floating showroom to exhibit Britain's wares abroad. As everyone was busy yapping about the supreme importance of the export trade we thought we were on to something good. It was an original idea, and indeed the project excited quite a lively interest. Levers' overseas sales-manager kept us on the hop for six weeks; such hopeful weeks they were, with Frank going to London and Liverpool for conferences and returning with encouraging reports. But in the end it was decided that Levers could not afford the luxury of a sailing showroom, seeing they could easily sell the limited amount they were able to produce at that time. An attitude adopted by all manufacturers we approached. It was a sellers' market then and nobody gave a damn for the future – why should they? But they were all so interested and were most earnest in their well-wishing. If wishes were horses . . . Ah me. We followed trail after abortive trail. Enquiries even reached us from abroad – travelling in French brandy suggested appealing possibilities – but the various offers made were not enough in themselves to cover our liabilities and it was impossible to negotiate by remote control.

Newspaper articles, the inevitable peg for itinerant adventurers to hang their hats on, was snapped off short by the paper shortage. We contacted all the leading daily and Sunday papers, whose editors cocked a faintly keen eyebrow and told us to submit articles when we had got going but would not commission any to help us to do so.

We tried to charter *Reliance*, willing to let her go without us even, so that we might keep her in the end, but failed even in that.

Thwarted at every turn it was clearly apparent that whereas nothing may succeed like success, certainly nothing exceeds like failure. If we could have but landed one little fish it would have made bait for bigger catches. . . .

The island book, my humble offering at the altar of Fate, was completed and sent off on its rounds of the publishers through an agent. It was eventually returned with a request for a further 10,000 words. The agent said he had interested a publisher, who might consider it with this addition, but not without. Having purposely kept the story short under the impression it would be more acceptable thus whilst paper scarcity existed, this was maddening to a degree. Until I re-read the MS, which depressed me beyond measure; and I concluded any publisher must be pretty hard up for material to consider it under any circumstances. I started to rewrite the story from the beginning.

I do not think I have written so much for so little result in all my life. Apart from the book which ended up as fish food, I hammered out articles, some of which were accepted and right glad we were to get the cheques for them, and wrote advertisements for skippers, partners, passengers, charters, and reams and reams and reams of correspondence for Frank in connection with our numerous schemes.

Hard-luck stories are a bore. They are all the same really, for once you start on that downward spiral you gather momentum until there is nothing to stop you from landing crash at the bottom. But you never can believe this and grab vainly at hope after hope as you flash on your way down. That was one of the reasons why neither of us attempted to take a job. It would have been impossible for us in any case to find employment lucrative enough to settle the mortgage within the time-limit laid down. And we were always just on the edge of something which seemed to hold the answer to our problems.

When, for instance, the Preston pilots approached us (or we approached them, I forget which) with a view to using *Reliance* as a pilot boat, we thought the ship was saved, literally. It was for a twelve-month contract at a rate which would have put us into the clear, but they wanted her then and there, at once, immediately, and with the best will in the world we could not comply. Certain work absolutely essential for seaworthiness was not complete, the pilots could not wait and that was that.

There was the Jew who got in touch with us, wanting a ship for an undisclosed purpose in the Mediterranean. He kept asking us for facts and figures. Facts and figures. But it is impossible to lay down facts and figures at random. You must know what they are for. As he refused to commit himself it was a deadlock.

That mysterious plant withered and died without so much as shooting a bud.

Then a Dutchman contacted us from Holland. He was a master mariner. Had been trading in the South Seas for the past nine years and was in Europe looking out for a ship and a partner to take back to the Pacific. Romance and finance. What a combination! Lagoons and swaying palms – coconuts, copra – and cockroaches – dizzied our imaginations. It was an exciting correspondence. But faded to nothing.

An ex-squadron-leader left his market garden in Sussex to visit us aboard and discuss the possibilities of a partnership in fishing.

He had been in Burma during the war and liked it. He liked the jungle. He used to look at it and say, 'My God, I'm being paid for all this.' Post-war conditions, spurious security, and market-gardening depressed him. 'No future,' he pronounced gloomily, 'no justice, and, I am beginning to think, no hope.'

By God, how right he was.

But unfortunately the squadron-leader was unable to put up the necessary capital, the skipper problem was still unsolved, so away winged yet another hope.

Lewis was a picturesque figure optimistically embarking on a round-the-world tour for the purpose of amassing material for a book he proposed on the prospects of a World State. Seeing that round-the-world tours were right up our street we arranged a meeting to see if we could work out a plan for our mutual benefit. Lewis arrived from London with a somewhat grander manner than we had become used to, a faintly amused smile lurking behind a heavy black moustache. In his grip was a turtle-necked sweater in keeping with the guttering candles and general atmosphere of Long John Silver he envisaged. But we never saw the sweater. We were not sufficiently piratical, or perhaps it was the electric light. Lewis confessed he dare not wear it, afraid of appearing to us as a poseur. But something in the atmosphere influenced him. He wore his cap at a decidedly more dashing angle on departure and boarded the south-bound train minus collar and tie.

We spent the weekend discussing ways and means, progress, art, politics, Scotland and God. Lewis had tried to interview H. G. Wells on the subjects of a World State and World Peace. But Wells had not much faith in either, 'which showed how he had lost his grip,' said Lewis. 'Or how much he had gained in wisdom,' commented Frank.

But the partnership failed to mature for want of sufficient capital, which we regretted. It might have worked out well. Lewis made no pretensions of being a sailor, but he was a most stimulating companion.

Early on in the refit when our hearts were young and gay we had tentatively launched the Journal by inserting a few advertisements in the personal columns of the more pompous dailies. The idea of a personal newsletter relating the adventures of a couple of sea-wanderers caught on quite well, but we were unable to follow it up then as vigorously as we would have liked, owing to the unexpected and lengthy delays in getting the ship ready for sea. But the response had been gratifying enough to encourage us to try again. We embarked on as extensive an advertising campaign as we could afford, scraping the bottom of the old oak chest and pawning the sextant to do so. We held a Press conference aboard, bringing on the goats at high tide for local colour – Dabs with her kids was eminently photogenic – and laid on the beer. The Press gave us good write-ups, generously stressing the Journal angle. Over sixty applications descended on us from people wanting to join the crew of *Reliance*. They had wanted to do this sort of thing all their lives. They could not contribute towards expenses, of course, but they would stop us going mad from loneliness at sea and would work their fingers to the bone if we would only take them on. They were adaptable, personable, adventurous at heart, they told us modestly. But not one of them mentioned the Journal.

The advertisements were more productive. But there were not enough subscribers to give us a start. The frustrating part of it all was that those who subscribed were wildly enthusiastic and we knew the Journal would grow like a snowball if only we could get going. If only – but we were just the wrong people with the wrong ideas, the wrong boat at the wrong time.

The constant raising and dashing of our hopes had the most demoralising effect. And in the welter of anxiety Biddy picked up rat poison in the stables one night and died after a frightful illness lasting three months. We did everything we could to save her. The Vet visited her every week. On his advice we fed her beaten white of egg and brandy, which she loathed, buying eggs on the black market and using Napoleon brandy – our last bottle cherished for a celebration. We gave her our meat ration, which she could not digest. We would have tried to give her the moon if it would have done any good. The poison rotted her system and she faded to a pathetic helpless bundle of fur resigned to death and resentful of treatment. Until at last the agony was too great to be borne and the Vet put an end to her misery.

Her going made a breach in the wall of our lives which was impossible to mend. The Chinese rug in the saloon where she used to lie, watching us at work on our ploys with screeds of paper spread before us on the table, was poignantly empty. We missed her immeasurably.

      ◇   ◇   ◇   ◇   ◇

By the Summer of 1948 the situation had grown pretty desperate. No longer able to meet mortgage repayments, we borrowed £250 on a promissory note, to keep up to date, determined to shanghai a skipper and get fishing. But it was no use. Time went on until the mortgagees suggested something must be done. They were mild and very fair, even suggesting if we cared to remortgage elsewhere they would speak kindly of us. We hawked *Reliance* round every finance house in the country, whilst still pursuing elusive skippers, partners and passenger. But markets were closed, money was tight, times were hard. Suddenly, without warning. We could not believe it. Reduced to the lowest ebb of living we had not enough money to buy food, and were driven to sorting over the sack of greengrocer's waste given us for the goats to find something edible for ourselves. Our cigarette ends were jealously guarded to reroll into needle-slim smokes. Sly periodic visits to the pawnbrokers reduced our stock of personal treasures, but enabled us to continue advertising, letter-writing, telephoning, and to keep up a spurious appearance of wellbeing.

We racked our brains frenziedly for articles, some of which brought in cheques. But payment was slow and the amounts about as useful a contribution as a tumblerful of water thrown over Niagara Falls.

Finally the mortgagees, having exercised more patience than we could ever have hoped for, said they must foreclose. We begged one last boon. If *Reliance* had to go, we asked if we might sell her ourselves, a private sale being more hopeful of profit than a forced one. To this they agreed and the ship was placed in the hands of agents.

For six months she was on the market and we did not get so much as a bid. No one had ever doubted the value of the vessel. The manager of one of the biggest trawling companies had given his opinion that she was worth between £10,000 and £12,000. He had no axe to grind and we had no reason to disbelieve him. We had spent over £6,000 on her. And of this only a total of £2,000 was outstanding. And we were eating rotten tomatoes.

Frank, stricken at the thought of losing the ship without even having had a sail out of her, kept murmuring, 'It's fantastic . . . there *must* be some way. . . .'

The goats living entirely on greengrocer's waste started to lose condition. I did not see why they should be involved in our troubles and said we would have to sell them, but Frank said, 'No, no, hang on a bit longer, something may turn up yet.'

We could not sleep. All day we pursued possible and impossible propositions. All night we discussed them, until our minds were befogged and we turned to heated abstract arguments to give them a rest, tumbling into bed at four or five in the morning, to awaken a few hours later, unrested, leaden-spirited, bleary-eyed. 'God, another bloody day.'

There were still a number of odd jobs to be done about *Reliance*. But we could not bring ourselves to do them. Not that we had lost interest, but we had lost heart. If she was to pass out of our hands, then the next man could do them. Damn his eyes.

On Christmas Eve, 1948, we received notice of foreclosure.

That same evening young Basil came down to the ship full of the party spirit, bearing bottles of beer and a determination to make Christmas merry with us. He found us unaccountably depressed and heavy-going, for though he may have had his suspicions that all was not well with us, he knew nothing of the latest development, and we had no intention of making our situation known until it was unavoidable. Basil was the keenest member of Frank's 'dear, dear public', a gang of sea-hungry youngsters who haunted the ship and Frank with offers to help with the work. Usually they quickly tired of any job they were given to do, preferring to talk about ships to working on them, and they were really more nuisance than use, but it is only the most heartless that can wilfully discourage the young.

We seemed pretty heartless that night. Our merry-making was undisguisedly hollow. We drank beer and pulled crackers as if it was a funeral feast. My cracker contained three motto slips. Each one said unequivocally, 'He will Not take you to America', which I thought very unfunny, and made instinctively to get rid of them. But Frank, evoking a false heartiness, saw me and put out a hand. 'Come on, what's the joke?' Silently I handed them across. With a fixed grin he read each one, crumpled them in his hand and said, 'Well, they seem pretty definite about it.'

Legal formalities regarding foreclosure went through the courts in London some time early in the New Year. We were given ten days in which to make a complete settlement. We did our desperate best, but of course, were unable to do anything of the sort. And inexplicably nothing happened. The ten days dragged on into weeks and even months without our hearing anything more from the mortgagees. We did not know where we stood. They were no doubt generously giving us every chance, but the uncertainty was killing.

Then at last we found a fishing skipper. Too late. We had given an undertaking not to move the vessel until the mortgage was settled, and as we could not raise the money, could not get fishing. The secretary of the mortgage company paid us a surprise visit in April 1949. He was a kindly, helpful young man, not at all in the traditional manner of a mortgagee. Frank put up one or two propositions, which he listened to sympathetically and promised to lay before his directors. But we heard nothing more, and realised the end had come and we would hear nothing more. That same morning, after the secretary had gone, a ship-broker arrived saying *Reliance* had been placed in his hands for auction. The agent went over the ship taking down details and surlily crabbing her after the manner of his kind, which incensed us. Frank swore at him so that he shut up, and I do not think he realised how close he was to being flung overboard.

We resigned ourselves to the inevitable and made plans for starting at the beginning again. From scratch with nothing but our wits for capital. As the market stood it was clear that *Reliance* would probably just make enough to cover our engagements. There was no joy in our planning, we were just good generals preparing lines of retreat. We would gipsy our way to the South Coast, picking up odd jobs on farms as we went, find work in a boatyard in the South and scrape together somehow enough money for a minute sailing boat. Something to take us away from England.

Then the people from whom we had borrowed the £250 brought out a summons against us. Heaven knows they too had waited long enough for their money, but they had gambled on an exceedingly high rate of interest. Their action was precipitate. And it was our undoing. The case would obviously go against us. It would mean a writ on the ship and ruination to any chances of an auction sale successful enough to meet all our debts. For to have a sale at that time was bad enough, but with a writ on the ship as well ... We hadn't a chance.

It needed just this to push us over into the abyss from which there is no return.

15

TO gain time we fought a rearguard action, on the principle of believing whilst there is life there is hope. So long as the ship was still in our hands, so long as the issue of the writ was delayed, there was still hope of recovery, remote though it seemed. Hope was a habit with us then rather than a belief. We quarrelled fiercely with the writ, got an adjournment to May 17th, and the interest on the loan voluntarily reduced to five per cent. Which latter point was unimportant. It was time, time, we wanted. Not that it did us the least bit of good when we got it. The agony was simply being prolonged. Our efforts at getting out of the financial snare continued to be singularly ineffective.

By the beginning of May we had still heard nothing from the auctioneers, no date for sale, so far as we knew, was fixed, and it seemed that our dismal affairs were to be dragged through the courts first.

One morning, sitting in the saloon working half-heartedly on a new outline of the island book, more with the intention of keeping my mind off present anxieties than of achieving much in the way of rewriting, I paused to watch Frank pacing to and fro like a caged tiger. Suddenly he stopped:

'Ann. I cannot stand any more of this. Let's clear out.'

It was as if life – our life together – turned a swift somersault and landed up on its feet facing the other way. Because I knew he meant it. There is a limit to what anyone can stand. You did not have to look very searchingly at Frank's strained and haggard face to realise he had reached that limit. I thought of all that lay ahead. The grubby misery of the law courts. Writs on the mast. Brokers in the ship. Ignominies of a forced sale. Vultures swarming over *Reliance*. Losing her to someone to whom she would be just another ship. Someone else's bargain ('Silly beggar overspent himself'). All Frank's efforts, the culmination of his hopes and aims, to come to nothing. All the years that had gone before, years of struggle and endeavour, valueless.

'No future. No justice. No hope.'

'... Not even to have had a sail out of her,' he was saying savagely.

'At least we can have that,' said I, putting down my pen to roll a couple of cigarettes. He took the shaggy little cigarette automatically, looking at me narrowly.

'Do you mean that?'

He slumped into the swivel chair on the other side of the table and lit up. 'No,' he said slowly. 'No, I can't drag you into that. I'll take her myself. . . .'

'You bloody won't,' it was my turn to be savage, 'the rough *and* the smooth. I've had quite enough of the rough – and you needn't think you can keep the fun to yourself. *Reliance* goes to sea and I go with her. . . .'

'It is not as though we've spent our all on riotous living,' he said irrelevantly. 'Christ, I'm beginning to wish we had. . . . We've sweated and worked and believed for years. . . . One bad break after another. Hooton, the quarry, Merebrook, the islands. Now this. It's too much. From now on the game is going to be played my way. To my rules. And if anything goes adrift it will be entirely my fault. And that will be a change. – We will sail *Reliance* across to the States, or Cuba . . .'

'Cuba,' I said. 'I've always wanted to learn Spanish.'

'. . . or somewhere, and we will have a chance to sell her for something like her value. She'll have an Atlantic crossing to her credit. That should be worth something.'

'And a story that will make the headlines,' said I with an eye to the main chance. 'That should be worth something too.'

'It's our only chance as I see it, of meeting these liabilities. You never know, we might be able to work it to keep the ship. Get a job for her that will pay off our debts, which certainly won't happen here. And I'm damned if I am going to wait like a chicken for the axe. But if the worst happens and we have to part with her, at least we will have the advantage of starting again in the sunshine. Somewhere where it is not accounted anti-social to be an individual. Somewhere where private enterprise is not regarded as a crime.'

'And we will have had a sail,' said I, gathering up the MS.

So the decision was made, and jettisoning the weary burden of anxiety, relieved of the uncertainty and confusion of mixed issues, no longer dependent upon the will of others, we plunged into preparations for departure. The relief of being in action, on our own, was enormous. I could only regret we had not taken this step months and months ago. Had we done so, I do believe we could have been across the Atlantic, pounding out Journals, articles, books, and working the ship to some advantage, clearing away the deadwood before anyone would have been the wiser. And knowing what I know now I doubt very much whether there would have been any tumult. People are not fussy how they get their money, what it may cost in others' health, sanity or lives, so long as they get it.

For the benefit of quayside watchers – the 'key men' as Ernest used to call them – we presented our usual appearance of plodding along with the detailed work on *Reliance*. To anyone who enquired, we said with the resigned air of having counted our chickens once too often, we hoped to be away by the Summer. This was all perfectly reasonable. There was no public announcement as yet of the auction, no broadcasting of the summons. The mortgagees were in London and we had not much to fear from them, but the lesser lenders were local, less trusting and more dangerous. Though even they would hardly expect us to publicise our misfortunes and forthcoming quarrel in court. Whatever may have been suspected or known generally we had no means of telling. The necessary secrecy of our preparations lent them such an atmosphere of cloak-and-dagger dramatics that they seemed hard to believe and quite remote from real life.

Time was short. Less than a fortnight remained before the 17th. We had to get away before the writ, certain to be issued as a result of the proceedings, was clamped on the ship. To get away after would be pretty well impossible, and to attempt to do so would invite really serious trouble. Contempt of Court on top of everything else would be just about the end.

We picked Havana for our destination. We realised the ship would probably be seized on arrival, but Havana seemed to be as good a spot as anywhere to be held, and we figured we stood as good a chance there as anywhere, the Latins being generally less hidebound than the English-speaking races. We made plans for a straight run through to Cuba, allowing eight weeks for the voyage, which would, we thought, give a margin for storms and delays, as we would not be able to pick our weather and would have to take what came. Sailing date was fixed for Sunday, May 15th. The tide was right then, around midday, when the quay would be deserted – nothing short of an earthquake will keep a Lancashireman from his Sunday dinner – and we could make our departure unnoticed. A night departure, though more in keeping with the project, would entail too much risk. We wanted everything on our side and day-light was more to our advantage than darkness. We were taking an untried vessel out by an unknown – to us – and admittedly difficult channel. It would be an ignominious end to the venture if, through faulty navigation in the dark or engine failure, we fetched up on a sandbank in the Bay. Interested parties would hardly be impressed, we felt, by our stubborn hopes that a long sea voyage would be to the ultimate benefit of one and all. . . .

Our plans for the voyage were briefly to 'steam' (full speed ahead) down the Irish Sea, keeping over to the Irish side, until well into the Atlantic, where we would blow down the boilers so to speak, hoist sail, and amble southwards to about the 23rd parallel, pick up the trade winds and turn our flight westwards to Cuba.

Frank had a leaning to put in at Las Palmas in the Canary Islands, arguing that as no one would have the faintest notion where we were heading we could be in and out of port before any action could be taken. Our passports and papers were in order, it would be a chance to extend meagre stores. In spite of the fact that the com-missariat *was* going to be difficult, England still being in the throes of pretty severe rationing, I was not keen on the idea. The risk was too great in these days of radio. A runaway ship was bound to be news at home, and how far that news might spread we could not tell. We would have no Customs clearance, which might cause sufficient delay for havoc to catch up on us. However, we agreed as a safety measure to make for the vicinity of the Canaries, so that we could put in in case of dire need. One never knows. . . .

There was a lot to do in the short time available. Spare sail to be cut down for a mizzen. Tanks to be filled. Diesel oil, paraffin, petrol, water; methylated spirits for the stove. Lubricating oil, gear oil, grease. Oddments of tools, bosun's stores. Stores, edible and medi-cinal. Charts, sailing directions, light lists to be sorted out and ordered. Signalling flags. What should we do about a small boat? Lifebelts. Radios to be collected from the shop where they had been for goodness knows how long undergoing repairs. Sextant and deck watch to be redeemed from 'Uncle's'. A mass of multitudinous detail. And money to be raised. We compiled list upon list. Cut them by half and by half again. Even so we found it would need at least £80 to get under way. Certain essential items, such as sail and fuel, could not be obtained before outstanding accounts were met first, which heightened the cost of departure. We had not eighty pence.

Two things we agreed on. To abandon the venture if unable to raise the money – there could hardly be two ways about that – and secondly, should any workable alternative present itself, such as an offer for the ship, provided it covered our engagements, we were bound to take it up. Actually, even at this stage, it seemed more probable to us that something would arise to prevent our going than that we should sail off out into the blue. We were not surprised, therefore, when a somewhat peculiar letter arrived asking particulars of *Reliance* – was she thus and thus, suitable for a world cruise? It was peculiar in that it was written, not too well, by one person for another, at the instigation, it appeared, of the mortgagees. We replied with pages of particulars, suspected a trap, continued with our preparations and heard no more.

Everything saleable in our possession which made no contribution to the working of the ship we sold. Articles, hitherto regarded as indispensable, such as the typewriter, or of irreplaceable sentimental value (Biddy's Chinese rug with the cavorting dragons and halcyon memories), all went. Memories need no tangible reminder and one can write with a pen. Pressure was brought to bear on those who had borrowed from us in our more prosperous moments in the past. Thus, unpleasantly, money was acquired to make departure possible. Obstructive accounts were settled. The mizzen sail was put on order. We began to lay in stores.

Frank brought back the mizzen sail and made to bend it on. 'Must see how it fits,' he said, meticulous as ever. 'The less said the better,' I warned. 'No need to attract attention. It will fit near enough.' He looked at me appalled ('if it's not done right it's gotta be done again'). 'Near enough!' he grinned wryly. 'Suffering catfish! What are we doing' – and he flung the sail down on the others lying on the for'ard part of the engine coaming.

He went to the radio shop to collect the radios, one good one that belonged to *Reliance*, and one not so good which had been used for DF on the Monospar, and found someone had been before him. The old aviation model was still extant, but irreparable and useless. The other had gone.

'Eh. That went months ago,' said the shop man. 'Chap came in, said he was working for you and took it. Said you'd be in later to pay for job. Looks like we've both been done. You've lost wireless, and I've lost job.'

Frank bought a secondhand portable for £7 10s. We hid it in the chartroom cupboard along with the frightfully give-away charts of the Irish Sea, Atlantic and West Indies.

It was essential *Reliance* did not appear in any respect ready for sea. Tailings of the refit, rope ends, bits of matchboarding, holoplast and oddments, littered the deck. Sails were left casually dumped on the engine coaming. Below, bookshelves were left unfidded, and ornaments bestrewed the saloon, houseboat fashion. Hoping for a continuance of the prevailing fine weather, we intended to get ship-shape at sea and watched the barograph keenly, listened daily to weather reports. Stores were brought aboard in penny numbers and hidden away immediately. But there was no secret method of filling up with diesel oil. This meant notifying the oil company and moving *Reliance* down the quay to the end of the basin. An opera-tion that would undoubtedly attract a lot of attention. Because of this and possible repercussions I wanted to leave taking on oil to the last moment, but Frank said, 'Let's get it aboard,' and made arrange-ments for tanking up on the morning tide of Monday, May 9th. And pretending the engine was out of commission, fixed for a fish-ing boat to tow her into the basin. As the whole operation had to be done in the open it seemed best to bluff it out. And it was as well we did. Old-timers halted on the quay as the oil pipes were slung aboard. 'This looks more like it,' they approved. 'Happen you'll be going soon.'

'Aye, one of these days,' said we, cheerfully.

On our way back to our berth the fishermen cast off too soon, *Reliance* was swept off on the outgoing tide and fetched up on the dredger-chain stretching across from the quay to the dredger. Pan-demonium. People danced on the quay and threw lines. The little fishing boat dashed up and down like a distraught bumble bee. Lines went hurtling through the air to land from all directions. Amidst the shouting and the hooha, silly with laughter, we got a line out to a boat by the quay, whose fisherman started up the capstan and hauled us back out of trouble. Secure in our berth we leant against the wheelhouse, mopped our brows and wiped our eyes.

'Good job we didn't try to make a secret of this,' said Frank.

A few days later I blundered down the companionway with a load of provisions, to find Frank entertaining in the saloon. I pitched the purchases into the galley and went in.

'This is Mr Blank,' said Frank without so much as a warning flicker, 'from the Ministry of Transport.'

A tall grizzled stranger rose from the settee at the end of the table, holding out his hand and keeping his head down, as one who has learnt the decapitating properties of small ships the hard way. 'We heard you were leaving soon,' he said genially, 'and I have just come round to see what you are up to.'

'Piracy and contraband,' I said, hoping my expression was not as aghast as I felt, and wondering what was going on. Frank was wearing his party face, and talking in his party voice. With monocle and disreputable battledress for props he was playing his character part – with considerable dash.

Mr Blank smiled. 'I have been meaning to visit you for some time,' he said, 'your name has been lying on my desk – you see, we are . . . er . . . interested in all craft preparing to go abroad. Then we heard you were ready for sea. I had to visit another boat here this morning and I thought I would take the opportunity to drop in on you.'

He turned to Frank. 'You promised to let us know when you were going,' he added a little reproachfully.

'So I did. But I am not ready yet. What makes you think so?'

Very daring this, I thought, controlling my eyebrows, which had a tendency to fly up, with difficulty.

'When you fill up with oil, the company serving you notify Customs and Customs tell us.'

'Oh,' said Frank, legitimately surprised.

Mr Blank from the Ministry of Transport studied the deckhead. 'Oh yes,' he said, 'you cannot do anything these days without its being notified, checked and indexed.'

We laughed. Not hollowly; nor yet too heartily. I wished he would go. I wanted to ask Frank if he too read a warning in those words. Or was I getting jumpy?

'What I am mainly concerned with,' went on Mr Blank smoothly, 'is whether your navigation lights conform with regulations. If you want to sink yourselves, that is your affair, but we cannot have you sinking other people.'

'Quite so,' said Frank pompously, on firmer ground. 'Come and have a look round.' Together they plodded off on a tour of the ship, affably discussing details of MOT requirements. I went into the galley, ostensibly to see about lunch, in reality to relax my face and brood.

Frank bounded into the galley a little while later. We looked at each other questioningly.

'What do you make of that?' he said.

I shook my head. I didn't know.

It was all very disturbing. We felt as if we were walking blindfolded along the edge of a precipice.

I sold the goats to someone I knew would give them a good home, and volunteered the information at the stables that they were going away for a few days, implying that they were being sent away for mating, to allay any rumours their departure might arouse. We saw them off on the evening train, southward bound, on the Friday night, and returned to *Reliance* silent and heavy-hearted, haunted by visions of their comic, worried little faces when we had tied them up in the guard's-van. They were the last link with the old life, and now they too were gone, but there was no point in dragging them half-way across the world to face a very problematical future.

On the way back we were met by a fisherman off the boat lying alongside *Reliance*.

'Customs been down asking for you,' he said.

'Say what they wanted?' asked Frank.

'Nah. Asked where you were. I told 'em you'd gone away for weekend. I seen you go ashore wi' thyer suitcases this afternoon, and I thought you 'ad.'

. . . One cannot do anything these days without its being notified, checked and indexed. . . . That afternoon we *had* gone ashore with suitcases. Full of articles for disposal in the secondhand shops in Blackpool.

'Thanks,' said Frank easily. 'I guess if it's important they'll come again.'

Later aboard, when we were alone he said, 'Scent's getting hot. What do they want, I wonder?'

'Better get your blow in first and see them in the morning.'

'No,' he considered, 'that might look anxious. Let them come to us. Remember, we haven't done anything yet.'

'But the ship is full of the evidence of our intentions.'

'There is nothing illegal in having a full store-cupboard. And what else would you expect to find aboard but a few charts?' he retorted.

But for all that he was as worried as I was. A visit from the Customs following on one from the Ministry of Transport showed how strong the rumour was we were getting ready to sail. In spite of all our precautions. How much was actually known? How much was suspected? Working blind on our side, teetering on the edge of that drop, we had the feeling of being watched by unseen eyes. Unfriendly eyes.

Preparations reached a climax on Saturday, the day before we planned to sail. Frank and I rushed on separate tasks to and from the town, bringing back loads of gear and goods. Time after time we sallied forth. Time after time we staggered back to dump our loads aboard: then off again to collect the next batch.

Shopping for stores for an eight-week voyage was fatiguing. The purchases had to be spread over several different shops. To buy 40 lb. of flour from one grocer's would disrupt the whole organisation and clinch any rumours going. We were tired, and ready to start at our own shadows. Strangers seemed unnecessarily inquisitive.

One in particular, felt-hatted, fawn-mackintoshed, loitered on the quay in the vicinity of *Reliance* with what seemed to us sinister significance. In the ordinary way we should never have noticed him, but then in the ordinary way would he have been there? We cast caution aside and speeded up operations. All morning the mackintoshed one hung around, eyeing our loads as we brought them aboard; then at lunch-time he went away and did not reappear.

At last we were finished. On my last trip back from town I ran into Frank, resting inexpressibly weary on a large tin box parked on the quay, talking to a Polish fisherman. They were discussing our mythical summer cruise, arguing hotly the number of souls needed to sail *Reliance*.

'. . . It is not as though I shall be single-handed,' Frank was saying as I came up. The fisherman looked at me with nettling scorn, showing what he thought of my capabilities as a hand.

'You can go without food,' he said. 'But you can't go without sleep. That's what gets you. You are like drunk. . . .'

He staggered a bit to show how like drunk you are without sleep. I felt rather like drunk at that moment.

We spent the rest of the day, listing and stowing stores, working with pricked ears all the time, listening. Danny, foreman of a nearby smokehouse, kept hens. Unwittingly, he proffered a most timely offering of four dozen eggs 'to put down'. I dipped them in

140

preservative: wrapping and packing them carefully in boxes in the store-room, wondering what Danny would have thought if he had known where his eggs were bound for on the morrow.

The commissariat had been a headache. One had to consider food value, cash value, and monotony. Food rationing was still acute. We had lived on bits and pieces for the past fortnight to save basic rations, fats, sugar, cheese, bacon and meat. I lumped the meat together and made a stew on Saturday night. It would give us something to go at. Basic rations were small, totally inadequate. I eked out fats with unrationed sweetened fat, peanut butter and tea-seed oil. The only canned goods available then were tinned herrings and whale-steak. I looked to the sharpening effect of sea air to offset the monotony. Points were expended on canned milk, rice, dried beans and peas and dates. We had 40 lb. of wholemeal flour and 7 lb. of rice, a bag of potatoes, some fresh fruit and vegetables and vitamin tablets for when these ran out. Frank was very susceptible to vitamin deficiency.

We were neither of us particularly fond of tea, rarely used our ration and had enough in hand to see us twice round the world. We hoped we had enough coffee to see us to Cuba. A half-bottle of rum reposed in solitary confinement in the wine-bin as emergency ration. Six ounces of tobacco was not going to be enough to ease our strained frame of mind but we could not afford any more. We were left with £4. Various items of equipment had been unobtainable. A small boat, lifebelts and signalling flags. But we had the Carley float, life jackets and an Aldis lamp – which needed 'sorting'.

Last thing on Saturday night we wrote letters. Frank wrote to the mortgagees:

> As I have not as yet been able to find a private buyer, or suitable charter, and as the financial position prevents me using the ship as a working fishing smack for profit, it seems that I cannot but look forward to a 'forced sale' auction, and with today's buying market it is obvious that the price realised will be a poor one and leave me little or nothing after meeting your requirements.
>
> I have made the most exhaustive efforts to avoid this becoming necessary, for *everything* we have is in the ship and two years' work and worry.
>
> My only alternative is to sail the ship to a destination where she will bring her value, and this is the course I am taking today. I

will get in touch with you in due course, and advise you as to how funds will be passed to you to meet my liability.

I deeply regret the trouble that I am putting you to and assure you that I would not have taken this action if there had been any other alternative available. . . .

'We'll post these just before we sail,' he said.

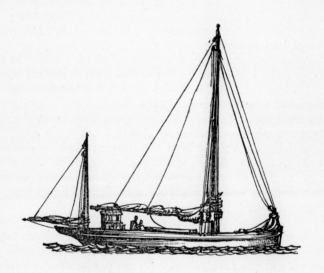

Book II
LAST VOYAGE

16

'WELL,' said Frank with a yawn, 'this is The Day. Wake up, you.'

The Day. I opened my eyes and stared up at the narrow beam of sunshine streaming down through the decklight overhead. The Day. 'First stop, Cuba,' I thought incredulously. Despite the hectic preparations of the past fortnight there had been little of the substance of reality in our project. It had been something to do to keep our minds off the mental merry-go-round. A dress-rehearsal for something that might happen one day. A challenge to Fate to show to what lengths we were prepared to go. And all the time at the back of our minds was the assurance that something would happen to prevent our going or make it unnecessary.

But nothing *had* happened. The situation was unchanged. Fate had called the bluff. Today was Sunday, the day we set sail for Cuba.

Sunday morning lapped round the ship peaceably as a summer lake on the shores of an island. Seagulls wheeled overhead, wings glinting in the spring sunshine, crying and mewing as they soared on the updraughts, mocking the earthbound with their hideous laughter. Fishermen and trippers in dark off-day garb strolled the quay accompanied by satin-bosomed wives and scampering children. Some stopped to look down at *Reliance*. I heard their comments from below: 'Ay, that's 'er, the *Reliance*. Going round world, they say.' And was tempted to shout back, 'And sailing today. First stop, Cuba!'

First stop, Cuba! The preposterous phrase hammered in my head like a stuck gramophone record, until I was forced to believe in it and my very finger-tips tingled in response.

Silently, rapidly we worked below, sorting, stowing and battening down, bundling the jib and silk balloon sails through the steel hatch into the forecastle. The main and mizzen sails were too big to bundle about and were left lying on the engine coaming where they would be handy when needed. Which would be soon enough we reckoned and thrilled at the thought.

Frank, doubling the roles of navigator and engineer, sped from chartroom to engine-room, making ready for departure with unfeigned abstracted delight. With a certain grave significance I moved the barograph from its houseboat site in the saloon to its duty station in the chartroom, affixing it on the typewriter shelf by broad bands of webbing to the bulkhead. We tuned in to weather reports. The weather had been pretty good up to now, but there were signs of it breaking. We pored over charts, Frank explaining the course we should follow. 'We shall be here by nightfall,' he said, pointing confidently to the Skerries. 'Monday night we shall get a check on the Tuskar light. . . .'

Bereft of ornaments, now securely packed in seat-lockers, the saloon looked austerely workmanlike, though the shelves were still full of books. There were no fids for them as yet, but we would soon rig something to keep them in place once we got to sea.

The morning wore on, gathering momentum as it slipped by. Excitement mounted like the seagulls on a gusty upcurrent, until at last, ready for starting with the tide on the make, we were shivering with prickly anticipation.

Slowly the water came creeping in, swirling silently past the ship. Restlessly waiting for enough water to begin starting the engine, we took turns darting on deck to watch for those we had no wish to see. But the strollers were thinning out as Sunday dinner-time advanced. There were no signs of a watch on our movements. Suspicion seemed in abeyance.

Then – one last look round – and down to action stations in the engine-room. Torches were lit and the auxiliary started; blaring, screaming, stuttering, the barrage of sound filled the engine-room and battered our giddy senses.

Two hundred pounds registered on the air-pressure gauge. Twenty minutes, five extra for luck, head heating, were up. The preliminaries over. The moment had arrived.

A push on the starting lever . . . the flywheel flew over and came to a standstill.

I leapt across to the compression taps and opened them as Frank barred the flywheel over, and tried again. Once more the flywheel flew over with a bonk and came to an abrupt standstill. I sped up the ladder to look out through the engine hatch. No one in sight. Then down again to the compression taps. Frank to

146

the flywheel. Feverishly we worked. The engine-room was stifling. Heat and anguished excitement spangled our faces with sweat. It ran in rivulets down our temples, into our eyes. We went over the fuel lines, dismantled the atomisers. Fitted new ones. But with all we did the engine would not start. We used all the air in the bottle. The heads grew cold. The tide turned.

We stood back and looked at one another helplessly.

Frank shook his head. 'No time to go through all that again,' he said, 'there won't be enough water soon – Hell, it's months since she ran. Nothing for it, we will have to go tomorrow.'

(He will not take you to America. He will NOT take you to America. He will **NOT** take you to America.)

We lunched off the stew we should have been eating at sea and put the stowing operations into reverse, bringing out ornaments and hiding charts, getting things into place, just as a fisherman friend climbed aboard for a chat. We laughed at his jokes and listened to his politics and wished him away so that we could tear the guts out of the engine. As soon as he went ('Must you go? Stay and have a cup of tea . . . if you dare!') we dived into the engine-room and worked there far into the night. There was nothing radically wrong with Tuo-Lung. Just stiff, as Frank said. We took it to pieces and put it together again, making the minor adjustments that, unattended, had collectively prevented it in its stiffness from starting, and were sorely tempted to give it a run on the night tide. But we resisted this, and on the following morning, Monday, the engine started first bang off, without any trouble. Frank immediately stopped it.

I stared at him blankly. 'Now what?'

'No oil pressure,' he said briefly, pointing to the gauge.

Methodically he took down the oil pump, found a vital part cracked into two pieces. I nodded as though expecting this. We looked at the two bits of metal lying in the palm of his hand. A few ounces of broken scrap and – he will not take you to America.

'A choke . . . incredible what pressure can do,' he mused, turning the pieces over in his hand. 'Well, if it *had* to happen, better now than later. . . .'

Impatiently I said, 'What do we do now?'

After a moment's thought he said he would ring the makers – 'Just possible they might have a spare. They could put it on the train; we'd get it tonight or tomorrow morning and be away on the afternoon tide.'

Tomorrow.

'Cutting it fine,' I fretted. 'Tomorrow is the day we go to the block, by proxy. What time is the execution?'

'Eleven o'clock,' he said absently; then turning up the local tide-tables. 'High tide three-thirty. They'll not be able to shoot a writ at us before that. We can make it – with luck.'

'And supposing there isn't a spare available?' I asked.

'Might be able to get it welded,' said Frank without conviction.

Hastily we stuffed charts back under the desk and into the cupboard in the chartroom, bestrewed the saloon with brass and bronze oddments, fluffed up the seat cushions. Made it look homey again. Then having nothing in particular to do and unable to bear the suspense of waiting, I decided to go along with Frank to the phone box.

Two men stood by the ship's long ladder to shore as we stepped on deck. Square-shouldered, gimlet-eyed, they were staring intently at *Reliance*, a grim uncompromising pair. My instinct was to stay behind, but to do so would look too obvious if my suspicions were right, and would almost certainly start an untimely explanatory argument on my change of plan with Frank, who, deeply concerned with the oil-pump problem, seemed entirely oblivious of the stern watchers. They stood back as we climbed the ladder and did not speak. A silence which seemed to me oppressive.

We were going into town to telephone and as we crossed the footbridge over the railway I had a chance to glance back discreetly, and was relieved to see they were following slowly. *Reliance* looked much as usual on deck, but the irrefutable evidence of our intentions below – I did not care to have anyone with a suspicious mind look her over just then.

Frank had an enormous stride, he always walked as though catching a train without any time margin. I had to trot occasionally to keep up with him.

'Those men,' I said quickly, 'should I double back to the ship?'

'Eh – what men?' he said, absorbed in other matters, 'what of them?'

'Two men on the quay, as we came ashore. Plain clothes,' I said. 'Detectives.'

'Nerves. You're getting windy.'

'Maybe; but they looked uncommonly like detectives to me.'

'How do you know what detectives look like?'

'No one could look like that and not be a detective. Should I go back? I can nip down the Dock road and back across the level crossing.' I took another look round. 'They're not following any more. Supposing they've gone back to *Reliance* – and no one aboard?'

'Ann, you're getting overwrought. Why should detectives be watching us? And if they were, they would not go aboard in broad daylight and poke round in our absence. They wouldn't dare.'

'Listen,' I said. 'Cast your mind back. Remember one of our late friends whom we are to meet in court tomorrow telling us he was in the police force once? What more natural than that he should ask some of his old pals to keep an eye on us? Rumour has already stirred minions of the Ministry of Transport and the Customs out of their lairs, it's hardly likely to have passed our late friends by.'

Frank came down to earth. 'Maybe you're right,' he said, 'but I still think it unwise and unnecessary to go back.'

Feeling oddly alert and ambushed I crowded into the telephone booth and listened to Frank putting through the call on which so much depended. I heard the makers say, in tiny telephone tones, that there was no spare available, heard them offer to make a new part, ready in six weeks' time. 'No thanks,' said Frank, hanging up the receiver.

Back to the ship again. I made a rapid exploration – 'Don't think anyone has been aboard.'

'Of course not,' said Frank, 'people can't do those sort of things.'

'People can't do these sort of things either,' I said grimly, 'but we're going to. From now on it will be as well for one of us to be aboard till we get away.'

So I stayed whilst Frank took the broken part to the welders. A few minutes after he had gone I heard him talking on the quay and peeped through a hatchway to see who was holding him up. It was getting pretty late in the afternoon. What if he left it too late and the welders were shut down when he got there? He was holding earnest conversation with our bank manager. Fifty pounds on the wrong side, that is what it will be about, I thought, dammit, we're doing our best. Though I did not suppose Frank was explaining how. And I fumed lest he should miss the welders.

Eventually they parted. Frank strode off. Leaden-footed the minutes dragged by.

He returned after an unconscionably attenuated length of time, looking infinitely weary.

'More delay,' he said, 'the boss was out – the men can't say whether they can do the job or not. I am to go round first thing in the morning – they reckon he'll be in then.'

'And what did the bank manager have to say?'

'Oh, you saw us talking? Decent chap. Came round because he thought I should know what people are thinking. There are rumours we are getting ready to run away.'

'Who says so? Our late friends?'

'Yes. Very excited apparently. They say we've taken on enough oil to cross the Atlantic.'

'I wish we had. What did you say?'

'Told him we were getting the ship ready for sale – true enough in a sense. . . . It's a bloody business.'

'No time for false sentiment,' I said brusquely, 'we're doing our best. Were you convincing?'

'God knows.'

It was hard on Frank. His was a most forthright, downright nature. Subterfuge comes easier to women, it is a part of their make-up and I had learnt early on in life that ruthlessness is the only form of defence.

Night brought the expected change of weather with the grumblings of thunder. On the morning of May 17th Frank went round to the welders.

The boss was in. He looked at the broken part and dismissed any notion of the possibility of its being welded. Then offered to make a new part.

'When?' asked Frank.

'Ready between three and five this afternoon.'

High tide three-thirty.

'I'll be round after lunch,' said Frank.

During the morning he came raging to me in the saloon, waving a telegram.

'Look at this! Look at this!' he cried.

I looked. It was a belated offer from the curious Irish enquiry. The working alternative. Working? An offer of £1,500 for the 'world cruiser' – £50 more than we had paid for *Reliance* as a hull. That then was the value of the work we had put into her, the money we had spent on her, the price of our hopes and ideals. Not enough to meet our engagements. I dropped the telegram on the floor of the saloon, where it stayed to be trampled underfoot as became an insult. An insult which simply served to harden our resolve.

The weather matched our mood. A steadfast gloomy drizzle. We were in the saloon tuning in for a weather forecast when we were interrupted by the sound of footsteps on deck. I swept up the portable radio and ran down to the chartroom with it, whilst Frank prepared to receive boarders. In the chartroom with the door shut I strained to hear the report. Frank came bursting in: 'Only a social call. Chap brought photos of his son's ship. Say they're nice.'

'Nice,' I said, 'say I'm changing. . . .'

Atmospherics were bad. The radio had a tendency to scream. Keeping it tuned to a whisper I listened: '. . . area . . . Irish Sea. . . .' Frank came in again. With a telegram.

'What's the report?' he asked.

'Lousy, I expect,' said I, switching off irritably. 'What's that?'

'War drums,' said Frank, 'our representatives in Manchester say ring immediately. All over bar the shouting.'

I kept watch while Frank went ashore to the phone box.

'As I said,' he broke out on return, 'all over bar the shouting. They've won. Plaintiffs are telephoning the Sheriff at Blackpool. I am told we can expect trouble with a capital T any moment.'

We snatched a quick and anonymous lunch – it might have been sand and sawdust for all we would have noticed – then Frank sped off to the welders and I stayed on watch. On tenterhooks.

At three o'clock he returned. Triumphant. He looked at his watch, said, 'We can just make it.' And then as though time had no part in the play set about fitting the new part. 'Good,' he murmured. And taking it over to the workbench, 'Just a bit here . . . and here . . .' He set to work with a file, whistling tunelessly.

Once again I heaved oddments into lockers and got out charts and navigation instruments. Made a last check on stores. Looked over the packing of the eggs. Restlessly tapped the barometer, studied the barograph, examined the charts. And made nothing of any of them. Indecisively I carried the radio from one cabin to another trying to find somewhere safe and accessible to stow it. Abandoned it finally on a settee in the saloon, wedged roughly with cushions, and dashed on deck . . . 'Sister Ann, Sister Ann, can you see anyone coming?'

There was no one in sight. Not the shadow of a detective, Customs official or a sheriff – my knowledge of the last being based solely upon those depicted in Wild West films, I could not rid myself of visions of a stout horseman in a ten-gallon hat.

Clouds were right down. Ceiling zero. Glad I'm not flying today,

I thought. And remembered. No good for a compass check. Frank had managed to get one on Blackpool Tower from where we lay, and had hoped to get others as we went out.

The tide was in. It would soon be on the turn.

I dropped down through the hatch into the engine-room.

Frank was assembling the pump.

'That's a damn good fit,' he said with satisfaction. 'How's the time?'

'Half an hour past high water. . . .'

We went through the ritual of starting the engine: listening to the frightful cacophony; watching the pressure rise slowly in the gauge; watching the minutes tick slowly by. Waiting without emotion. Coldly waiting for the moment to arrive. The moment which, depending on whether the engine started or not, would decide the course of our lives.

Standing by the auxiliary, with one finger on the compressor release valve, automatically shutting it off as the Norman laboured, I drifted into a timeless coma, until Frank was suddenly beside me, shouting in my ear: 'No one in sight – hauled ladder up – they'll have a hell of a jump to get aboard now – nothing to do but slip the warps – if she'll start. . . .'

'The boats – what about the boats?'

There were a couple of small boats moored outside us. We didn't want to drag those to Cuba.

'I've moved them up to the quay astern of us.'

I went round to the compression taps and opened them for Frank to lever the flywheel round into starting position. He gave a few turns on the lubricator box handle, a few pumps on the fuel injection levers. Smoke poured down from the open taps. He looked across at me and nodded: 'Taps closed.'

Contact! He pressed the starting lever –

And the engine was going.

Simultaneously we bent over the oil-pressure gauge.

Chocks away – first stop Cuba!

We checked up on all the gauges, pressures, feeds and controls as though it was just routine. A daily occurrence. As though we were in the habit of blazing off into the blue with five thousand miles ahead of us.

'Let her run for a while,' said Frank, and led the way into the saloon, where we rolled a cigarette apiece.

He leant against the mast smoking his and I stood looking round the cabin as though seeing it for the last time, sharply aware of every detail. As though I was going away and would never see it again. It was inconceivable that I was going away and taking it with me.

Frank listened to the throb of the engine, a faint smile on his face. There was confidence about him now, a youth and eagerness replacing the doubts and uncertainties, the long-drawn anxieties of the long-drawn months past. He moved to flick the ash off his cigarette, and I watched him too, as though seeing him for the last time. His shirtsleeves rolled up – under, not over in the usual way. Everything about him, yellow hair, china-blue eyes, inexpressibly dear – indelibly printed on my mind.

He came over and put his hands on my shoulders, looking down and smiling:

'Well, my Ann, this is it. No regrets?'

'No.'

'Good-oh! Look after that engine then – we're awa'!'

And I stood looking at the empty saloon which had gone suddenly bright and blurred.

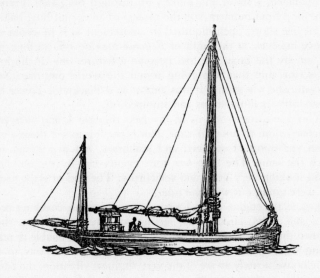

17

WE got under way with extraordinarily little fuss. In fact I did not even know we had gone until, in the engine-room 'looking after that engine', I happened to glance up through the open hatch and saw the quay wall sliding away. In a detached manner I had heard grating noises as the shafts and wheels and cogs of the controls from the wheelhouse went into action; had heard the hubble-bubble of the propeller churning the water – but, so hard is it to grasp realities sometimes, I thought Frank was simply having a last-minute check-over. But no, there was the quay wall rapidly receding. He had quietly slipped the warps and we were away.

Fascinated, I stood and looked up through the hatch. Framed there for a brief moment was the picture of an errand-boy, halting his bicycle short, open-mouthed in amazement as if he could not believe his eyes, at the sight of *Reliance* moving off. So long had she lain by the quay she had become a fixture, one of the local sights, the ship that was going round the world one day. Now suddenly she was going. It was almost as if Blackpool Tower had upped with its foundations and stumped off.

'You don't know half of it, my lad,' thought I, and went into the chart-room to note the time, half expecting to see there a sur-realist sprouting of seaweed and seahorses, but everything was much the same. The time was four twenty-five by the bulkhead clock, looking very brass and seaworthy. The end of slack water. We were going out with the tide.

Back in the engine-room I went over the engine, checking pressures and feeds, circulations, feeling for any undue heat; then, satisfied that Tuo-Lung was behaving properly and unable to resist seeing what Frank was up to, I went along the alleyway to the wheelhouse, acutely aware of the very slightest vibration; the barest perceptible movement underfoot – almost as if *Reliance* had come alive and was breathing gently.

'That's the best sight I've seen for many a long month,' said Frank, nodding his head in the direction of Fleetwood.

Reliance had come round the bend in the river and was turning into the Channel, leaving Fleetwood astern fading into the mist. It was a vastly different departure from the one we had always envisaged, but for the moment nothing mattered. We were outward bound. Whither bound, whence we had come, all the tortuous whys and wherefores dissolved before the fact we were taking *Reliance* to sea. Living at last after those deadly months of mouldering by the quay.

'Gosh,' I said, 'I forgot all about posting those letters.'

'Want me to turn back?' said Frank with a grin.

'Not on your life – they'll have to wait until we get somewhere – Tuo-Lung is going like a bomb. How is the ship behaving?'

'Like a cow,' he stated, pointing to the bomber tyre, the invaluable fender, which still hung over the side, dragging in the water, protesting every inch of the way. 'Get it off presently – when we are out of the Channel. . . . Hullo,' – as he glanced aft – 'I see we have company.'

I spun round apprehensively, expecting – what? Sheriffs in ten-gallon hats, maddened creditors, fast cruisers in pursuit? I don't know, but I was prepared to fight for our spell of freedom. However, it was the steam trawler fleet coming up astern, overhauling us. Frank laughed at my relief. 'They can lead us out now and save us trouble,' he said.

One by one the trawlers overtook us. The fishermen staring intently at the stranger in their midst, though not half as agog as they would have been had they known of our intentions. These could hardly be guessed. With the bomber tyre outboard, her decks cluttered with the hangover of the refit, sails heaped on the engine hatch, the twenty-foot ladder, stayed from shrouds and boom, pointing dramatically upwards like a warning forefinger, *Reliance* looked a tatty job on trials, not in the least like a vessel setting out on a transatlantic crossing.

At the end of the Channel we rounded the burnt-out remains of the Wye light and turned on course for the Lune lightship which was invisible in the mist.

Frank said: 'Here, you take her. Keep her as she's going. I'm going to have a look at the engine and clear up some of the mess,' and departed with a purposeful expression.

Grasping the wheel, with a sudden appalled realisation of the whole undertaking, I thought, This is an Atlantic crossing, and this is me doing it.

Reliance seemed enormous. Bigger by far than she had ever seemed lying quietly by the quay. To my confused and horrified gaze her decks appeared to stretch ahead illimitably – as far as the eye could see. She pulled and yawed like a hard-mouthed horse, demonstrating her power and my utter ineptitude. Never had I felt so humbled. Here am I, came the thought, half the crew, five thousand miles to go and I can't even keep her straight. As the water was as still as a mill-pool the voyage promised to be singularly exhausting.

Then Frank came on deck grinning at the ship's aimless wanderings as I tugged at the wheel, and started tackling the bomber tyre. As he struggled to bring it aboard, the holding ropes sheered under the strain and the great tyre vanished in a rush and flurry of water. Immediately *Reliance* stopped pulling and settled down. The verge ring compass on the port side of the wheelhouse shelf in front of the wheel was in my line of vision just where the compass had been in some of the aircraft I had flown. With this homely touch the ship seemed somehow to shrink to a manageable size. I felt at home. And unspeakably happy.

Frank, for whom straightening-out parties were a particular delight, cast the ladder overboard with a farewell salute as it floated away, and then began a positive orgy of jettisoning, reminiscent of Davies of the *Dulcibella*. And *Reliance* looked a lot more like a ship and less like a secondhand store in consequence.

We passed close to the Lune lightship, about which gulls perched in mournful array, and there turned south into the open sea.

Frank checked the course, streamed the log, and looking aft at the lonely lightship fast disappearing in the mist, said with a sigh of infinite satisfaction, 'Now, at last, we are on our way.'

One of the lesser incalculable joys of that rather wonderful first day out was to experience *Reliance's* transition from a houseboat to a thoroughgoing seagirt vessel. Down below, the saloon, galley, all the cabins and their offshoots looked much the same as they had done for the past eighteen months. A little sterner, perhaps, shorn of their ornamental oddments, but reassuringly familiar. No suspicion of a sea-change, nothing suggestive of Davey Jones or anything like that. But go on deck – and Hey Presto! Instead of the vista of mud and wall, cranes and smokehouses, chimney-stacks and railway lines, there was the sea. A grey and somewhat dingy sea at the onset to be perfectly honest, but genuine honest-to-goodness salt water reaching through the rain haze an Earth away.

As a matter of fact the bloom of wonder was severely rubbed for me about nine o'clock that evening when I went below to cook supper. The mirror-like surface of the water had given way to a smooth oily swell. *Reliance* glided along with a smooth oily roll. A pungent smell of warm diesel oil permeated through to the galley, to mingle subtly with the smells of methylated spirits, paraffin and cooking. The galley evinced an unpleasant disposition to spin. In an anti-clockwise direction. The glory of the sea was dimmed.

I finished supper preparations in mad haste and bolted back to the wheelhouse before half the crew had time to disgrace itself.

'Supper all ready – and it's all yours,' I said firmly, reaching out for the wheel.

Frank stood aside grinning unsympathetically.

'Seasick?'

'No,' said I with great dignity, 'and I don't intend to be.' It was, I knew from past experience, simply a matter of Fresh Air and Exercise. Keeping One's Mind Above It. Once physically adjusted to living violently sideways on, the sea could do what it liked without disturbing me. Meantime it was Fresh Air and Exercise and all that.

Just before dark Frank returned, replete, and unperturbed by smells or swells, which, though shaming this lesser half of the crew still more, was just as well. He checked on the Skerry lights, which blinked in the right place at the right time in a highly satisfactory manner. And Frank said responsibly, 'I'm taking the night watch. You turn in. I'll call you about two, just before light.'

The limitations imposed by lack of headroom precluded the construction of upper and lower berths in our sleeping cabin. But, oh dear, thought I, rolling uncontrollably from side to side across a nautical version of the Great Bed of Ware, a double bunk at sea is a mistake. I tried wedging myself with pillows and gripped the side of the bunk, but my muscles continued to work and flex with every movement of the ship, so that I could not relax. And being unable to relax could not sleep. I went over 'rules of the road' at sea. . . . 'When both lights you see ahead, starboard wheel and show your red.' And reflected on the dismal fact that it did not convey a very illuminating picture to me as to how to Avoid Risk of Collision at Sea. But then I have never found jingles helpful. There is one connected with magnetic variation that I don't remember as it is always super-imposed in my mind by another one: East, west, Home's best. Which has a sound ring of truth after all. Especially if one's home is cutting through the water bound for far-off distant shores. ...

I listened to ship noises: woodwork creaking; ropes fretting; the swoosh, slap and gurgle of waves against the side of the ship, most intimately near my ear.

I wondered how Frank was getting on in that strange other-world on deck. What sort of a night it was. Whether there were many ships – there had been few that afternoon. Then suddenly my secret dread rose to confront me like a spectre of the night. Man overboard. Frank overboard. Mentally rehearsing what action to take, I lathered at the thought. And took myself in hand. Such a thing was not impossible but it was highly improbable, especially on a night like this.

So? said my unsensible self, you know what Frank is for doing a thing and telling you about it afterwards. He might see something that needed doing on deck, and not call you because you are supposed to be asleep. He might slip. Anything might happen. He could be overboard and you know nothing about it until you went on watch and found him gone. ...

Good God, I thought, sitting up in a panic, this is absurd.

It was the first time in my life I had ever been inflicted with a runaway imagination, the type that sees a mortuary behind unpunctuality. What you need is a good night's sleep, my gal, said I to myself, and pulled the blankets over my head.

Frank called from the wheelhouse. Urgently.

Ah!

I bounded out of the bunk, thrust my feet into slippers, and, laces flying, sped down the alleyway, buffeted from side to side as *Reliance* inexplicably swerved. Madly.

The wheelhouse was cold and dark. Frank, dimly outlined against the windows, was watching something intently, pulling the ship first one way, then the other.

'What goes on?' I asked, clambering up through the hatch.

'See that ship?' he said sharply. 'Wherever I go she follows.'

A host of lights glittered ahead to port. They were swept aside as Frank pulled *Reliance* away to starboard. I caught hold of a window-sill to keep my balance.

'What do you make of it?' he said.

'Nothing. Just a ship.'

'Pursuit. . . .'

'Oh, come. . . .' I watched the ship and tried to follow her movements, but found it difficult to do so, as I had not yet got my night eyes and I was in any case unaccustomed to judging speed and distance in the dark. Frank did not make matters easier by taking violent evasive action.

'Following me about,' he fumed. 'What sort of a ship is she?'

'Goodness, I wouldn't know. She's just a bunch of lights to me . . . a biggish job I should say. . . .'

'Yes, yes, is she signalling?'

'No.'

'She was. . . .'

He still seemed anxious, so I went on deck to get a clearer view. After all, his fears might be justified. It was possible for our departure to have been notified as we sailed: we were only about eight hours out from Fleetwood. In these days of radio . . . I peered into the mist. The steamer lights were fading. She was drawing away. When I was certain of this I went back into the wheelhouse and said, 'She's on her way.' Then irresistibly pompous, added, 'It's all right – Green to green and red to red, perfect safety, go ahead.'

Frank let out a bellow of laughter. 'Perfect safety! . . .' then lapsing into broad North Country, said, 'Ee, tha'a rumm lass, Ann.'

'Did you bring me from bed for that?'

'No. No, she foxed me. Steamed right up and signalled, and when I turned off course to avoid her she followed me round. Wherever I went. Or so it seemed.'

He confessed he thought it might be a fishery cruiser on our track.

'Could be at that. Probably enraged because we are not showing proper fishing lights or something,' I yawned. 'The trouble with you, my lad, is that you are suffering from a guilt complex.'

For which I was ordered off the bridge. 'Call you at two!' he shouted after me. This time I went to sleep almost immediately and it seemed but a moment later when Frank called me to go on watch.

The morning was still dark and indeterminate. Dawn was late abed and reluctant to appear. Frank on the other hand was reluctant to disappear. He hovered in the wheelhouse delivering a profusion of instructions, and not until assured we had the sea absolutely to ourselves did he descend through the hatch. There he stood head and shoulders above the coaming. 'And call me at once if you are unhappy about anything. . . .'

'Go away,' I said, 'I'm extremely happy.' And I was. Best of all I like handling things. Things in action. Driving fast cars, riding wild horses, flying an aeroplane. Now I was at the helm of a seventy-ton ketch, steaming into the future, with the engine throbbing.

Occasionally a pinpoint of light appeared, to flicker uncertainly and vanish, but otherwise there was nothing to disrupt the serenity and solitude. I was soothed into a peaceful state of coma.

Suddenly out of the corner of my eye I glimpsed something huge and red. Anything as big as that would have to be near. I pulled the wheel hard over and ducked. Then I looked out again. At the moon grinning redly through the morning mist. Hm. Half the crew had better do better than this. Wide awake, I pulled myself together, thankful there was no witness of my humiliation.

A grey ragged dawn listlessly lifted heavy curtains of mist and cloud to reveal a grey and restless sea. Sea and sky met and inter-mingled. We moved in a centre of a circle . . . 'whose margin fades forever and forever as I move . . .' Time stole by, marked only by the steady beat of the engine. I stood at the wheel, shifting my weight from one foot to the other, absently surprised at their aching. The hypnotic effect of watching the compass, watching the endless greyness of sky and sea, listening to the soothing rhythmical beat of the engine, was inescapable. I drifted into another stupor.

A dim, dark shape materialised out of the haze, coming our way, overtaking us. I watched at first with interest. It rested the eyes, as it were, to have something definite to look at. Then I watched with growing suspicion. Contact with the civilised world was fraught – She came persistently nearer. I edged off course a little to draw away. And watched her continue to bear down on us. I made a definite alteration in course. Still she came. I turned right round and reined in the horses. Still she came. I whipped them up and drove smartly away. She followed.

Hackles up I called Frank.

Then together we solemnly watched the passage past of a wholly disinterested tanker. She must have thought we were mad.

'Ho,' said Frank, smiling, his right eyebrow lifted to the point of stall. 'Some people I know would suggest that was the outcome of a guilt complex.'

It was not the time, I thought, to mention my contretemps with the moon.

162

18

GREYNESS predominates the recollection of that Wednesday, our first real day out. Grey dawn, grey day. Grey sky, grey sea. But we were far from being grey in spirit. Frank was particularly pleased with life because *Reliance* was making six and a half knots, which was one and a half better than he had reckoned she would do under power. 'At cruising revs, moreover,' he exulted, 'wait till we get her under canvas – then she'll move.'

It was an uneventful day, spent mainly in getting into our stride, so to speak. Accustoming ourselves to a sea life whilst *Reliance* bowled south into a south-west wind. Frank and I did not see much of each other. Our carefully thought-out system for keeping watches went by the board, and I spent most of the day at the wheel, putting in ten hours at a stretch. It suited us both very well. Frank had a hundred and one things to see to, apart from attending to the engine, charging batteries, working out navigational problems, and cooking himself meals – a subject in which I had no practical interest just then. This mildly disturbed Frank, and when he discovered I had given up smoking as well, he was quite upset thinking I must be seriously ill, cigarettes being my equivalent to the staff of life. 'But think of the stores and tobacco we're saving,' I protested. And strangely enough as long as I was at the wheel occupied with keeping course and getting the feel of the ship I felt no distress whatever – except at the end of the day when my feet ached excruciatingly and I sympathised with those who have to stand for a living.

All day the sky was overcast, and as the day wore on it lowered, the sea rose and almost imperceptibly the wind hardened. We had lived long enough by the weather to read its signs and warnings automatically. The portents were not good and we prepared accordingly, consoling ourselves with the thought that in a few days' time we would be out of the depressions and into the sunshine.

Towards evening we picked up the dark rugged outline of the Irish coast and made a last check – on the Tuskar light.

Frank took over again at nightfall, and I turned in to find sleep strangely elusive for one who had been up and about since two in the morning. The motion was more pronounced and I rolled and tossed in the wide bunk, and started the idiotic fuss about Frank again, until shortly after midnight, fed up with myself, I joined him in the wheelhouse. He was surprised to see me so long before time, but nodded when I explained the fears that kept me awake.

'Yes,' he said, 'I know it's foolish. But I have a similar trouble. If I can't hear you, I worry, and if I can hear you I wonder what you are up to. It's just one of those things we have to get over – like your seasickness.'

'But I am not seasick.'

'Well, get yourself something to eat then.'

'No, thank you.'

In fact, it was one of those things we did not get over. Throughout the voyage we were hampered by an unshakable confidence in our own immunity from disaster, whilst extending towards each other the nervous concern of a hen intent upon keeping an improvident duckling away from the water.

And so through another night and we wandered into Thursday. Time was already getting out of hand. Already we had to think back to when we sailed to find out what day we were in. It is easy enough to keep track of the days when you go to bed on the night of one and wake up in the morning of the next. Sleep makes a definite break. But snatch sleep when you can, see every dawn, and live through that interminable no-man's-land of time between an early sunrise and eight o'clock and you find individual days soon lose their identity. They become nameless and memorable only for events.

Dawn of Thursday was sullen and threatening. There was a fairish sea running and *Reliance* was lively.

Sometimes during the early morning we crossed the steamers' lanes leading into and out of the English Channel. For the first time we saw plenty of shipping. Liners, freighters, ocean-going vessels that seemed huge to our eyes used to fishing craft, went their ways, east or westward bound, grandly indifferent and keeping as unswervingly to an invisible track as road traffic on land. Two grey MFV's intrigued me vastly. Hove-to alongside one another they sat fatly on the water with an absurd air of intently watching something at the bottom of the sea. I stifled an impulse to plough up to them and ask to have a look too. Normally it is a joy and delight to watch other ships at sea, but we wanted more than elbow-room and were glad when the steamer lanes and shipping were astern of us.

It was on the Nymph Bank south of Ireland that we got the first real intimations of the bad weather in store for us. So far we had only been warned. There we ran into an ugly little cross sea. Steep round-topped hummocks of water rushed hither and thither without any unity of purpose, which bothered *Reliance* no end. She charged them aggressively and flopped into the troughs, and rolled and pitched with exasperated fury. There seemed no way of tackling these angry white-headed mounds of waves that came from all directions. *Reliance* knew far better how to deal with them than I did, hanging on to the wheel, going through the motions of being a helmsman and receiving a vivid insight into what it must be like to be the tail of a kite. Frank came into the wheelhouse, watched the gyrations for a few minutes, said she was a bit of a bitch and would be steadier under canvas and that things were coming unstuck below, and suggested I might like to tidy them up. In other words he would take over for a while. I went below and found things were coming, had come, considerably unstuck, but did not notice any lessening in the violence of *Reliance's* antics under the touch of the master hand. Which, though gratifying, made tidying up a painful process – very bevelling to one's personal edges.

It is extraordinary what a shaking-up at sea can do in the way of disorganisation, no matter how well one may have stowed, packed, fidded and battened down. Everything with a lid, door or drawer in it will burst open and scatter the contents, a surging, seething jumble, on to the floor.

The chartroom was a mêlée of heaving papers, the saloon a sliding heap of books, the wardrobe locker door flew open as I passed and swinging overcoats sprang out to embrace me, the engine-room rang with the clatter of displaced tools on the check-plate flooring, and the galley – oh, the galley! Brass rails had jumped their holders and pickles and syrup, coffee and tea, bottles and cans and bags of flour churned in horrid confusion at my feet. I salvaged what I could and scraped the rest into the slush bucket, prepared lunch and left it to cook slowly on the small stove, a left-over and rather prized possession of the island days added to the galley equipment just before sailing, on account of its ability to sustain a low heat unattended which the larger, official stove, would not do so reliably.

Tidying up and lunch preparations had taken some time. I was not yet accustomed to living on a helter-skelter, and unable to anticipate the ship's next hectic move wasted a lot of time sprawling, lurching and clutching, picking myself up from amongst the conglomeration of oddments I was trying to put away. So conditions had changed somewhat by the time I returned to the wheelhouse. For the worse. The seas were bigger, more meaningful and threatening, pyramidal in shape, but still very much at cross-purposes. Cleaving your way through endless ranks of countermarching pyramids is rough work.

Frank, feeling the general outlook called for it, went out and fixed a life-line from mizzen to main shrouds, whilst I clucked quietly at the helm – these fishing boats have nothing much in the way of freeboard aft, *Reliance* had less than a foot, which brought the angry ocean pretty close to. He had just come back into the wheelhouse and was busy unrolling a chart, when I spotted a wisp of smoke floating out of the open main hatch. It was snatched away by the wind, and followed by another and another – smoke poured out of the hatch.

'My God,' I shouted. 'Fire!'

Frank looked up, rocketed out of the wheelhouse and up the deck. Leaving *Reliance* to look after herself I shot after him. The galley was ablaze. Through the main companion doors we could see the wicked flames leaping under the rising palls of smoke. Guessing what had happened – that the stove had broken loose, rolled over and spilt the paraffin out of its tank and set it alight – Frank dived into the galley with the intention of removing the stove. But it was a little inferno in there. He burnt his hands – grabbed the fire extinguisher at the foot of the companionway, found it would not work and leapt up on deck again, shouting for water.

Meantime I was feverishly disentangling fire buckets lashed to the port pin rail. Frank darted for the steel hatch and dropped into the engine-room, returning, breathless, with the engine-room fire extinguisher as I succeeded in releasing the buckets. I threw one overside on a line, heaved it slopping aboard, and together we fought the fire.

The flames ducked as we attacked, threw up a smoke-screen

and leapt up again under cover. The extinguisher spent, and the fire still raging. Frank changed his weapon, seized another bucket and continued to fight with water.

Reliance pitched and rolled with giddy abandon, but we slipped on the wet deck, slithering from side to hatch and back again, hardly aware of her wild antics, conscious only of the urgent, vital necessity of quelling the fire.

Then, suddenly, resistance crumpled. The fire was under control. It was out. And, as if at a given signal, the galley extinguisher, left rolling at the foot of the companionway, snorted into action on its own and added a quota of foam to the shambles below.

Breathless, speechless, thankful, we waited for it to stop, then went down into the galley.

We stamped out the final embers and tore up the smouldering remains of the floor covering and threw it over the side. We tore up floorboards and minutely examined bulkheads for signs of smouldering and spreading elsewhere (an inspection repeated at intervals throughout the day as a safety measure).

Everything was hot and the stench appalling.

The galley was blackened and blistered from floor to deckhead. Some of the woodwork was charred. The fire had cost our fruit and vegetables, whose cinders rolled on the floor, whilst the light ashes of tea-towels blew over everything.

The wiring of the electric grill and ventilator was burnt through. Frank, looking at the ventilator, said, 'If that had been on we *should* have been crisped.' And he disconnected the line to obviate any risk of a short circuit and the possibility of another fire.

The damage looked worse than it was. The contents of tins, bottles and cupboards were unharmed, though containers had lost much of their smart appearance, what with the knocking about they had received in the morning and the searing effects of the fire. But restoration of the galley was mainly a matter of soap and water and an eventual coat of paint. Except for the grill, ventilator and small stove, everything was in working order. The remains of the stove were jettisoned as soon as they were cool enough to handle.

Awed at our escape, a fire at sea in a wooden ship being a grimly inescapable disaster if it gets a hold, and anxious to avoid a repetition of the experience, we checked over the fastenings of the other stove very thoroughly indeed, until assured that nothing short of a seaquake would dislodge it.

Then *Reliance* caught us off our guard and pitched us summarily across the galley to remind us she was on her own.

'Go up and see to her,' said Frank, 'I'll clear up some of the mess.'

Later he joined me in the wheelhouse and asked for something for his hands. This was the first I knew of his having burnt them. His wrists and palms were painfully seared. I dressed them as best I could with acriflavine, but he flatly refused to have them bandaged, saying he could not work with them all bound up. Unprotected, they were always soaked in diesel oil and salt water, which seriously delayed healing and must have given considerable pain. But he rarely complained, though usually a fractious sufferer. A failing we shared and accepted in each other. It was so seldom either of us ailed in any way that if we did we roared about it under the vague and baseless impression that pain was less painful if accompanied by fuss.

In the days to come when time got really out of hand, and our departure from Fleetwood became small in the past seen through the wrong end of memory's telescope, that Thursday was remembered by us as the day of the galley fire.

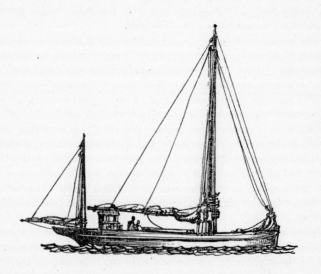

19

ANY tendency towards taking time off for brow-mopping after the fire was curbed at once by the pressing demands of the ship – ever the bane as well as the blessing of seagoing.

'Cripes' – or probably 'Eee', being a Lancashire lass – 'look at this,' gurgled *Reliance* delightedly. 'Real ocean stuff – watch me!' For the baffling cross-sea of the morning had given way to row upon impressive row of towering grey waves rolling up from the south-west, from half-way across the world, and grown stern and forbidding on their journey. But *Reliance* loved them, and challenging, roared to the top of their high white crests, poised, and plunged dizzily down into the troughs, then gathered herself for the next upward flight and dive. As if she had been waiting for this all her life.

The wind hardened towards nightfall, but there was plenty of sea-room, and no traffic about, so, for the first time I took a night watch. And what a night! It was splendid, with the splendour of a diamond's fire against black velvet. Dark as pitch, with a roaring wind and the gleam of white-topped waves high above the wheelhouse windows, and *Reliance* flying like a Pegasus through the night.

Her forward speed was probably negligible, but the sensation of speed was terrific – exhilarating beyond anything I had ever experienced before. In a queer way it was speed combined with lightness – all that flying should be and is not, except for that brief moment of becoming airborne. It was glory and power. An exquisite distillation of living. The span of a lifetime condensed into a few hours.

Frank came tramping up from below: 'God, what a night. Can't sleep in this.' And pecked about and said, testily, 'Slow her down a bit – do you want to run the guts out of her?' – which was pretty deflating.

That was our introduction to a three-day session of heavy weather in the Atlantic – what I would have called a storm but for the mocking shadows of real seamen who never admit to anything more than a breeze of wind, though they may allow it to be the worst for forty years. I had witnessed worse in the North Atlantic, from the deck of a ten-thousand tonner which seemed like a leaf in the wind, but never before at quite such close quarters. For a small ship in a big sea brings the weather right to your feet. When it is not sloshing over your head. Thank God for the wheelhouse, we thought as seas broke over the ship. Conditions were exhausting enough in all conscience and without the protection it afforded we should have been in even sorrier plight.

Together we watched through the last of that glorious black night – the opening bars to an oceanic opera – and together we saw the wild break of day. As high marbled seas rushed past racing the low grey sky overhead, we said, Well it can't last forever.

But in a welter of cloud and water time lost all meaning and became a jumble of events.

At first *Reliance* mounted the waves with the ease of a good horse flying a big fence. But all the time the fences were getting bigger. At the top of them we looked quickly round and pointed monsters out to each other – 'Gosh, look at that one!' Then the course got too stiff and *Reliance* faltered. She put in a short one and rose too late. She took off too soon.

Sometimes caught off her guard she went hurtling down a wave like a tin-tray down a flight of stairs, to land with a crash at the bottom which would have shaken Nelson off his column. And which would bring Frank ramping up, if he was below, to count heads and find out what was going on.

As the weather grew worse and *Reliance* more unmanageable, the fuel header tank needed more and more frequent attention. Diesel oil was fed to the engine by gravity from a twelve-gallon header tank, which was normally good for four hours, and was then refilled from the main tanks by a hand pump. But in a violent seaway the header tank could not be filled right to the top; if it was, extreme motion brought oil snorting in a deluge out of the breather pipes, to shower all over the engine-room. The wilder the sea the less fuel in the tank therefore, and the more frequently it needed pumping up, which kept Frank hopping from wheelhouse to engine-room like a jack-in-the-box.

As the gale hardened and the waves grew ever higher and

steeper, breaking and more vicious, there could no longer be any question of keeping to a course and driving *Reliance* into it. The engine was throttled right down, and the ship drifted, broadside on to the seas, rolling with savage abandon as if utterly out of patience with the whole proceedings. Waves crashed down on her and frothed aft, looking for scupperholes and a way out. The slow whispering thud of the exhaust changed to loud bang-bangs of protest as it was rolled under. And the ship's bell spontaneously rang up a good one, to be echoed by a hoarse croak from the hooter. A fire-bucket broke loose from the pinrail and racketed about the deck with an infuriating clatter. Every time it vanished under a deluge of water we hoped it had gone for the last time, but always it reappeared to continue its maddening cacophony. Why it should have been so particularly irritating I do not know, but it was. At last, beyond endurance, I slipped out in a lull (Frank was at the wheel) and secured it.

Frank was enraged: 'There is enough,' he said, 'to think about without you adding to it.'

Which was precisely how I felt about the bucket.

Watching the main mast whipping with incredible rapidity from side to side across the low leaden sky, my husband shook his head. 'This won't do,' he said, quietly, '– roll the sticks out of her. We'll try running.'

Going with the wind and sea gave a momentary illusion of peace. It seemed as if silence superseded sound, as a curious hush supersedes the roar of an engine in an aircraft on the point of stall. With her engine barely turning over *Reliance* tore off downwind and the wicked waves reached after with breaking crests curling over like overhanging cliffs.

'And this won't do either,' said Frank, 'for long.'

Then we put out the sea anchor and had respite until the warp fridged through with strain and the fight was on again.

The nights were the worst, when we had fatigue to contend with as well and sleep stood hypnotic at our elbows.

Standing at a wheel, pumping up a header tank, attending to the wants of an engine, perhaps heating up a pot of coffee, may not sound exacting duties. But to accomplish such things in a seaway with your ship plunging and bucking in a manner to give a broncho the staggers with envy, when even to keep your balance entails unceasing muscular control and the slightest relaxation of effort means you will be flung viciously against the nearest solid

– and inevitably pointed – object, makes heavy demands on one's physical and nervous energies. Heavier than can be met at times. We were soft physically, and tired mentally, from those long anxious months mouldering in port. We were bruised and stiff from head to foot from being pitched hither and thither. And it was a dubious sort of rest to take the helm. The sea does not let up for a moment, and the wheel being heavy at the best of times, grew heavier and heavier as the sands of our energies ran out, until but a few spokes of a turn took all the strength one could muster.

The night watches were short. Towards dawn they got shorter and shorter, as we could only stick about ten minutes at a time. To remain on hand in case of need, we did not turn in off watch, but rested at the end of the alleyway, under the wheelhouse, aft of the hatch, between the companion ladder and sail locker, where there was just space to lie cramped. A more uncomfortable roost it would be hard to devise, but we were beyond caring about such things.

At the wheel it was hard to keep awake – I dozed off several times on my feet – yet below it was impossible to sleep. Of over-riding importance was the necessity of not failing the other fellow, so one lay cramped and alert, listening.

It was on one of these spells I first became aware of the ship's voices. All wooden ships talk. *Reliance* spoke in a multitude of tiny voices that came from behind bulkheads, under floorboards, every-where all round, chattering, gossiping, gabbling incessantly and shrieking with gnomish laughter.

I spoke to Frank about them when I went up to relieve him and he seemed a bit startled, obviously thinking the strain was getting me down. But then he heard them himself and that was all right.

Daybreak was magical in effect. A potent restorative. As the darkness lightened so did the burden of our weariness, until we grew to recognise this fact and counted the heavy hours to dawn, knowing it would bring us mysterious strength to carry on.

As the gale reached its height an incident occurred which gave me the fright of my life.

The wheel suddenly locked solid. The rudder was operated by a chain from the wheel to rudder bar. The chain had slackened off, slipped off the pulley on the rudder bar and jammed beneath it. Frank went on to the counter with a crow-bar and I stayed in the wheelhouse to turn the wheel as he eased the chain back into place. I stood with my back to the wheel and tried to watch him through the window aft but it was too high. Out of control and uncontrollable, *Reliance* drifted helplessly before the savage onslaught of mountainous waves. Suddenly she was swept upwards, as if caught in the grip of a giant hand, and flung down . . . down. . . . There was a flashlight impression of the ship on her beam-ends, starboard bulwarks buried in a white smother – I clawed to the door, staggered out, as she came up, water boiling along her decks, swirling round the counter. Not a sign of Frank. I yelled for him, terrified. Looked wildly at the towering grey walls of water. Then to my indescribable relief he got up, dazedly shaking his head, dripping, from the very end of the counter, almost under the horn timbers. As I stumbled towards him he motioned me back.

'Who did that?' he grinned, in the shelter of the wheelhouse again, taking the wheel and giving it a turn, 'good-oh – she's OK now. Fixed it before that big fellow got us. What a party!'

But I kept saying, 'I thought you'd gone, I thought you'd gone,' and knew I was babbling and found it extremely difficult to stop. Fear for oneself is nothing. Fear for another reduces one to drivelling idiocy.

The dawn of the third day revealed minor havoc wrought about the ship. The masthead lamp wrenched from its steel platform by a force sufficient to cause the shearing of massive bolts (which ought to have held down a tram, said Frank) swung by its electric cable forty feet in the air. The riding light on the port trussle tree leaned at a drunken angle with its nine-inch holding bolts bent over like copper wire. Its electric cable, torn loose from fastenings to the shrouds, bellied furiously in the wind. The main halyard was down. The log line was gone. Ropes and halyards were white with chafing. Blocks swung to and fro, barging into the mast, the forecastle hatch, winding round the shrouds and off again.

Below, of course, it looked as if Pandora had been opening up that box of hers – in a very great hurry.

'As if we hadn't enough on our plate,' said Frank. 'Still, we can fix all this when the weather lets up a bit. We've got all the gear – it might be worse.'

He frowned thoughtfully. 'For all I know it might well be worse,' he added. 'All this is nothing in itself, but it is a warning. The sensible thing to do would be to put in somewhere when we get the chance. This isn't good enough, you know. Unknown ship, untried gear. Damn it all, I *don't* know the ship. She's taking a hell of a pasting. I have no idea how much she can stand. But it will certainly be more than we can.' He looked out of the wheel-house windows, peering up at the sky. 'No sign of it abating yet,' he said, and continuing the argument, 'If we nip into a quiet French port, we'll be able to straighten the ship in comparative ease, rest, which is most important, and be off again before anything catches up on us.'

'All the same I think we'll stir up a lot of trouble for ourselves going into port,' I said doubtfully, the idea of a night's sleep – only *one* night's sleep – being as alluring as the smell of cooking to a starving man. I was exhausted now, more dangerously than I knew. For the danger lay in not knowing. I thought I was just tired and being a bit cissy. But I had not eaten since we left Fleet-wood, four – nearly five days ago. Had not drunk either, not so much as a glass of water. The queer thing was that I felt, or thought I felt, perfectly normal, but there were no standards for comparison, for Frank was in not much better shape. He had managed a few scrap meals, but conditions had hardly been suitable for the pre-paration of anything substantial, and his was the burden of re-sponsibility, most wearing of all. And neither of us had had nearly enough sleep. We were both dead beat, and I had not the wit to realise it. Frank did, though; he said: 'We'll maybe stir up a whole lot more if we go on as we are.'

Between the devil and the deep sea, in fact. It was decided to turn back when opportunity offered, for there is always a chance of bluffing the devil, and none whatever of fooling the deep, dark sea.

As the morning broadened and grew into a day there were indications of the weather abating slightly. There was not the same force behind the wind. The seas were as high as ever, yet they tossed sullenly about the ship as if pursuing an argument from which the temper had gone.

We had no idea of our position. All we knew was that we had been going round and round in the depression, travelling with it in a north-easterly direction whence we came. The sky was as solidly overcast as ever, there was not a hope of getting a sight. The clocks, both the deck watch and chartroom clock, had stopped. Time and space had ceased to exist. Resorting to slap-happy naviga-tion of early aviation practice, we put *Reliance* on to a back bearing 'with a bit of east in it', gave her the merest breath of engine, and ploughed off on a search for a good pull-up for pirates.

After slogging on for about an hour Frank started nattering again. 'We're in a tricky position,' he said. 'If it blows up again, we might buy it.' Then added hurriedly, 'If we should see another vessel – do we signal for assistance? Abandon ship?'

Completely taken aback, I stared at him.

'Whatever for? What's the matter with *Reliance*? She seems as tough as old boots to me. Not made a drop of water in all this –'

'Not a drop,' said Frank.

'Well, then. And the weather looks more like easing up than getting worse now . . .?'

Avoiding my eye, he said: 'I dragged you into this. . . .'

'If that's all you are worrying about,' I interrupted, 'forget it. I'm here of my own free will and not at all inclined to pack up on account of a little rough-and-tumble.'

He grinned widely. 'Well, don't say I didn't give you the chance.' And departed for the engine-room.

As if to test our sincerity, shortly after, a large buff-coloured liner with a squat raked funnel appeared ahead over the crest of a wave. Close, and materialising with the sudden completeness the Cheshire Cat must have done before Alice. Captivated by the sudden sight of her I forgot all about *Reliance*. We were running with the sea on our quarter. She broached to. As everything went ring-a-ring-a-roses, all-fall-down, I gripped the wheel with the apathetic confidence of fatigue, waiting for everything to sort itself out. Frank, having just stumbled back through the hatch, was furious, and seized the wheel. 'What the hell are you playing at?' he shouted.

The giddy kaleidoscope stopped spinning. *Reliance* clawed back on to even keel. The liner hove to.

'What is she waiting for?' I asked.

'Us,' said Frank grimly. 'Change your mind?'

I shook my head and reached for the glasses hanging under the shelf, and then found it required two hands to focus, two hands to hold on. I needed to hold on. I needed to hold on to focus. Muttering 'Spiders,' in disgust, I gave up. So we never made out who she was. With our masts describing wild arcs against the sky we passed slowly astern of her. She picked up speed, mounted a last wave and was gone from sight as suddenly as she came.

A miniature sea lashed back and forth across the deck of the wheelhouse, freezing our feet. I thought of all the hot drinks and

warm beds that were steaming away to the West. Frank cursed the
lack of flags, wished we had been able to signal 'no thank you'
at least. He was very much ashamed of my lapse in helmsmanship.

Distinctly and detached as if someone else had spoken it aloud,
the thought came into my head, 'There goes your last chance.'

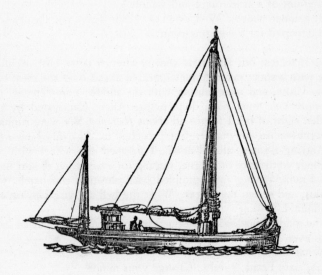

20

'TEA!' said Frank triumphantly, climbing carefully through the hatch with a steaming mug – quite a feat in a seaway – 'And you needn't look as if it was a libation offered by a Borgia.' I had not felt the slightest bit seasick for days, physical adjustment was complete and the Mind had been Kept most relentlessly Above it, but the habit of nourishment had disappeared. And I do not like tea. If it is strong it is nauseous, and if it is weak it is tasteless. But that mug of tea was the most delicious drink of my life, which only goes to show what a few days' fast can do. Apart from that it was an event to be able to make tea at all; conditions had eased considerably that afternoon.

Darkness approached with torrents of rain. A large steamer, looking indefinably French, surged across our track ahead and disappeared in the half-light to the west. A scattering of twinkling ship lights and an alteration in the character of the sea suggested we were in the region of the entrance to the English Channel. Altering course to follow more or less the direction taken by the eastbound traffic, we shrugged off the inevitable drowsiness which accompanied nightfall, and ploughed cautiously towards what we hoped would prove a quiet haven in due course. After making landfall would be the time to choose our port; meantime, sustained by the promise of rest to come, we kept wary watch, Frank at the wheel, and I standing by as an extra pair of eyes. If our surmise was correct, there were plenty of traps in the region of the Channel entrance we had no wish to fall into.

Night advanced and visibility deteriorated rapidly. Suddenly all signs of shipping vanished. Wiped clean off the slate. Except for one, a pinpoint of uncertain light ahead. The seas whipped up into baffling confusion. Broke in a brilliant spread of foam about us. The pinpoint light dipped and danced, flickered, gradually grew larger. As we drew nearer it became manifest as several lights. Three white lights in line with another above the first. Like huge eyes they were, round, unwinking and malevolent. A vessel of some sort, at anchor. But what? A lightship – no beam. Frank said: 'Look on the chart, it may be a mark of some sort.'

Before I could move, *Reliance* heeled under a shattering blow as a gigantic wave crashed down on deck, breaking high on the port shrouds, sending down a glittering spray of seafire to swirl aft in a silver stream. Crash followed crash as waves, coming invisibly from every direction, burst upon the ship in a blaze of phosphorescence. We plunged in a boiling of white water.

'Shoal, by God!' said Frank.

A resounding crash came from under the counter, a shock which travelled from stern to stem, and shook my hold from the window-sill so that I spun across the wheelhouse. Frank said: 'We're on.' *Reliance* wavered, lifted her stern with spinning prop and raced on. Pitching into a black bottomless pit. Hurtling down a cliff-face, crashing from one colossal boulder to another, shuddering, jarring, racing. Flashes of phosphorescence, bright as lightning – tumultuous stretches of iridescent foam illuminated our mad flight.

With one hand I groped on the shelf.

'What are you doing?' said Frank irritably.

'Looking for the torch. I was going to look at the chart.'

'Christ, never mind that now. Where's that ship?'

'Astern.'

'Are we going away from it?'

'Y . . . es.'

On and on we tore through the vicious sea, unable to stop, not knowing which way to turn for safety, not knowing what lay ahead, expecting every moment to strike, impatient with the little headway we made getting away from the ship which seemed to be the centre of the hell's broth.

'Get the charts,' said Frank changing his mind, 'we've got to get out of this.'

I pored over the charts by torchlight in the alleyway below so as not to dazzle him, and returned to the wheelhouse no wiser than before.

We were heading straight for the ship.

'Where the hell are you going?' I shouted.

'Can't help it,' he snarled – 'bloody wheel's jammed again.'

He groped on deck for the crow-bar. 'Bring her round as soon as the wheel gives.' The door slammed behind him.

Spindrift struck the wheelhouse with the rip of gunfire. Tossed like a log in rapids *Reliance* plunged towards the lights. Bigger and

178

bigger they grew. Wilder and wilder the sea. The wheel gave in my hands. I started pulling her round. Frank was beside me again, and the relief was so great I had hardly strength to turn the wheel. Slowly the lights slid past. We turned and headed away from them.

Frank took over again and I went back to the charts. As I searched relief gave way to reaction and I could barely keep my eyes open. Struggling to keep awake I searched the charts from the Lune light to the Bay of Biscay and could find nothing to give us a clue of our position.

A shout from the wheelhouse – 'Look! What's that?'

Wide awake, I scrambled up. 'What?'

'Port bow – a light. . . . '

A tiny pinpoint.

'Yes – there's another – starboard ahead.'

'Buoys,' said Frank.

Now what?

'You're getting back to that ship.'

'I know, I know. What's that ahead?'

'Another buoy. . . and there's another over there.'

'They're bloody well all round us.'

All round us. Whichever way we turned. Ringed in. Trapped. Unable to face up to any more problems my mind shut down. I was overwhelmed by the desire for sleep. Ached from head to foot with longing for it. The Pole was right – 'like drunk'.

'If we got in, we can get out'. I heard him speak as if far away. 'Surely you can find this on the chart,' he said.

'Can't find . . . a . . . thing . . . that fits this . . . layout.' And I heard my own voice far off. It was an effort even to speak.

How long we rocketed round and round that bewitched circuit, circling those fantastic lights like a giddy moth, I have no idea. I was fighting a losing battle against sleep. Then suddenly we were out free. The mystery ship astern of us, and gone. The buoys vanished. Almost as if it had been a nightmare and this was the awakening.

'There,' said Frank, making out that he knew how it was done, 'I said if we got in we could get out. But, where do we go from here?'

The sea was not so brilliant now, nor so viciously wild. Hooded by night mist, with only the glint of dark waters visible either side of the ship, we crept ahead, feeling our way. Frank held a course for twenty minutes, then handed over to me and departed for the engine-room. I plodded up and down that course, twenty minutes one way, twenty minutes back again, not taking any chances. He came back and said: 'Can you stick it for another ten minutes? I'm all in. . . . Ten minutes – that's all I want.'

Thus we spent yet another night of brief rests and watches, as we ploughed up and down, waiting for dawn. There was quite a sea running in the wheelhouse which slopped over the hatch coaming. We had to give up roosting beneath and used the bathroom instead, lying on the raised floorboards there, legs stretched across the alleyway, folded oilskins for a pillow. As usual I drowsed at the wheel and dwelt upon sleep, longed for my ten minutes to come to an end and then ached with anxious insomnia below.

The dawn was chill and dreary, but the morning stretched with daylight, clouds lifted, sea settled, the horizon widened. Restored once again by break of day we lengthened our watches to half an hour at a time. I began to feel so good I let mine tick on into two hours and watched a match-stick on the horizon, coming towards us, grow into the mast of a fishing boat. It seemed an opportunity to find out where we were. I opened the throttle, but long before coming within hailing distance the fishing boat turned off and sped away too fast for *Reliance* to overtake her. I swore, and Frank, coming up full of apologies for having, as he thought, overslept, looked after her and said, 'Never mind, we'll make landfall before morning's out.' There was a long low bolster of cloud on the horizon over to the north-east. The sort of cloud that hangs over a coast. We made towards it.

There were no signs of the 'lightship' or encircling buoys. Last night might never have been.

Below for a two-hour spell, I dropped on the bathroom floor and went out like a lamp.

A beam of light shone full on my face and woke me up. Sunlight. I stared at the golden beam and thought how wonderful it was to see sunshine again. *Reliance* moved steadily, with a sibilant hiss instead of the turbulent rush and roar of the past few days. I sat up yawning, and stretched. All this talk about going into port – no doubt we could get in somewhere easily enough (I wonder where we are) but could we get out again? Why put our heads in a noose? Someone might pull it tight. The sun was shining. The sea was calm. Why not rest and refit at sea? Must have a word with Frank.

What a difference the sun made. Everything so peaceful. I could hear Frank clattering in the galley. – *I could hear Frank clattering in the galley!* No engine? *No engine?* What goes on?

I went to find out.

He was shuffling pots on the stove and looked round gaily as I entered the galley.

'Hullo,' he said. 'Coffee just coming up. Had a good sleep? You *were* out – I walked over you several times and you never stirred. Ship like a doss-house, bodies all over the place.'

'Only one body . . . look, Frank, the – '

He lifted a pan lid and inhaled noisily.

'Mmmm. And my girl, you are eating today, whether you like it or not. Captain's orders. This is soup – that is whale-steak, and here' – performing swift legerdemain with the coffee pot – 'is a cup of coffee.'

'Thank you,' said I taking it mechanically. 'Frank, listen. The engine. It's stopped.'

'It has and all. Take your coffee on deck. I'll hand the other things up to you. We'll feed in the sunshine.'

'Why?'

'Because it's a nice day.'

'No . . . why has the engine stopped.'

'Ah, there you have me. I'll tell you about it later. Don't worry, I've put up the staysail and *Reliance* is sailing herself. Lot steadier, isn't she? Here, take my coffee as well. I'll have that while the whale is getting hot. Be with you in a minute.'

I sat on deck just for'ard of the main hatch, balancing a cup of coffee in either hand and relaxed into the peace of a blue and golden day. *Reliance* lopped along with an easy swing. Blue waves with gay white ruffles danced by, occasionally throwing a bubbling crest aboard, where it ran down the salt-washed deck in a darkening stream. It was grand to be sitting on deck, I was beginning to think I was a wheelhouse fixture.

The warming sun, the sparkling sea, the whisper of wind in the rigging – the contrast of mood was enchanting, yesterday's wrath, today's rapture. I held to the moment, marking it that I might remember. . . .

Just behind me was a rope mat, put out that morning by my energetic husband to dry. I was debating whether to risk standing the cups on it, for Frank was taking an unconscionable time, when something, gentle as a mothwing, brushed the back of my neck, caressed my shoulder-blades, stroked my spine and landed on the mat, where it stayed, solid and immovable. Cautiously I leant against it. Pressed against it. It was as hard as a rock. Still balancing the cups I looked over my shoulder.

The monumental masthead light had come down. A forty-foot drop. 'Whoops, Frank, you nearly lost your wife!'

He popped his head through the hatch. 'What?'

I jerked my head back, and he stared at the lamp, then looked up at the mast.

'Good God, did it touch you?'

I nodded. 'But so lightly I hardly felt it, not even a drop of coffee spilt. . . .'

He came on deck. 'Here, give me mine before anything else comes down.' Then bent to examine the copper lamp. Soberly he said, 'You'll never be closer than that.'

At the end of a thoroughly enjoyable and inelegant meal – for me the breaking of a five day fast – eaten by spoons from basins, sitting on deck with the ship heaving gently beneath us, we lit cigarettes and grinned blissfully at one another. Frank said, 'I've been thinking . . . why go into port when we can rest and refit out here. . . . What are you laughing at?'

'You. Preaching to the converted. I woke with all that in mind this morning, but the silence of Tuo-Lung put it out of my head. By the way, what is the matter with the engine?'

'That I must find out' – and explained it had stopped quite suddenly when he was in the engine-room attending to the fuel. At first he thought he might have inadvertently knocked the fuel switch off whilst refilling the lubricator box which was just by the switch, but on trying to lever the flywheel round to starting position he found it was immovably solid. He thought the trouble was probably in the gearbox. Then he put up the staysail, lashed the wheel and started cooking. 'I thought it was about time we looked after ourselves,' he said.

'Why didn't you call me to give you a hand?'

'No need. And you were dead beat. But you can give me a hand now to get up the mizzen.'

We put it up without mast rings and it hung like a bag. I said *Reliance* looked more shippy with it up, but Frank said it looked bloody and was undecided whether to tackle the mast rings or the engine first, and finally decided on the engine.

It was a good day. A very good day. The sort of day we had looked forward to in imagination when first planning a world cruise. We discovered we had acquired our sea balance at last and could move about the ship without being flung about. We did not achieve half the things we meant to, being more tired than we knew and slow in consequence, but we had a taste of contentment that afternoon which we had not known for months and would never know again. We attended to smaller details first, tidying Pandora's upset below, putting bedding on deck to air, sorting through stores and gratified to find the eggs still intact, which seemed nothing short of miraculous. Then whilst Frank concentrated on the engine I washed up, marvelling at the number of mugs in the sink, and baked, and cooked quantities of porridge, and made gallons of coffee, so that there should be something in hand in case the weather went back on us again.

It was an accomplishment of simple things that afternoon which was so intensely satisfying, as the ship rolled on under a clear blue sky. The commonplace in the unusual, which is the essence of romance.

We did not know where we were and could not care less so long as we had sunshine, solitude and serenity. Time enough to take up the grimmer threads again when the engine was going; meantime we pottered and enjoyed the rest.

By nightfall the cause of Tuo-Lung's paralysis had not been traced, except insofar as the gearbox was found to be guiltless. It did not worry us unduly, there was another day coming. But instead of the restful night we had looked forward to we were kept on the hop, watching and figuring out the host of lights which appeared in the offing all along our lee. I fussed quietly because, with inoperative engine and inadequate sail, our position was not a very happy one. But Frank took a broader view. 'Lights are signposts at sea. We can find out where we are.'

Lights may well point the way when you see what you expect to see, but we did not know what to expect. We pored over the charts until dawn, timing flashes, taking bearings, drawing gradually nearer, perplexed at the unaccountable difficulty in locating our position. Or the lights on the charts. It was difficult to time the flashes accurately. They were just apparent over the horizon and were frequently obscured at a crucial moment by a wave or the rolling of the ship. Eventually we concluded, with reservations, we might be off our old friend the Skerries. 'And how the devil did we get back here,' said Frank. 'What a drift! I suppose it could be possible in that wind.'

'Snakes and ladders,' I said gloomily. 'We got on that beggar at 98, and here we are back at the beginning again.'

At dawn the lights went out, but there was no land to be seen. We started right in on the engine and found the for'ard piston seized.

Gummed up with a glue-like carbon, a deposit due to slow running in the gale. The cylinder head was removed, no light task in a seaway, and a drastic-looking attack with a brass drift and a sledge hammer had no effect whatever. Nor the application of petrol or paraffin. Methylated spirits proved a dissolvent, and it took an inordinate amount, which was disquieting, for meths was necessary for priming the cooker; ungumming cylinders had not been allowed for when computing quantity. It took hours to free the piston. We poured meths round the edges of the piston top, where it seeped down between the piston and the cylinder wall and got to work on the gum. Then with our combined weight on the lever we strained the flywheel round, moving the piston down about half an inch. The area of cylinder wall uncovered was rubbed clean with meths, lubricated, and the flywheel sweated back and forth until the piston moved freely over that small area. The process was repeated right down the length of the cylinder.

By nightfall the piston was free. And we were exhausted. The temptation to leave the reassembling to the next day was almost irresistible. But it was blowing up again. Somewhere to leeward was land, so we resisted the temptation, and not until the engine was together and ready for starting did we feel free to take our reward. Then we supped in virtuous content in the companionable warmth of the galley.

Later we went on deck. The sky was dark and starless. The broad seas rolled in dark solitude from horizon to horizon. Not the twinkle of a ship nor a flash of a light. Tomorrow we would renew the voyage in earnest. Tonight we would sleep.

'In dry blankets with hot-water bags,' said I, 'and to hell with the rough sailor stuff.'

If it is necessary to suffer in order to be beautiful, then by God, it is necessary to endure in order to enjoy, I thought, drawing the warm blankets up round my ears and relaxing in the exquisite luxury of bed. I had drawn first spell below. The sheer blissful comfort of a pillow beneath my head – 'Art thou poor, yet hast thou golden slumbers?'

Poor perhaps. . . the veils of sleep dropped before my eyes. *Sweet* content.

'Ann!' Frank barked sharply from the wheelhouse.

I hopped out of bed, thrust my feet into slippers, grabbed the rest of my clothes and hurried along the alleyway, dressing as I went.

Golden slumbers be damned.

21

'SORRY to disturb,' said Frank, as I climbed into the cold dark wheelhouse. 'See those lights? – We'll have to go about.'

There they were, flashing like a firework display, a fresh lot to aggravate us. A group of two flashing white on our beam, a red winking on the port bow, and another white flash appearing just over the horizon behind the red. *Reliance* had picked on the red as a goal and was making for it with utmost despatch.

Frank tended sheets and I brought her round. She jibbed at going through the wind, got behind the bit and played up. She had to be turned full circle downwind to get her on to the other tack, and she wasted as much sea-room as possible in the operation. I was loathing her volubly when Frank came aft.

'You're absurd,' he said; 'you're not happy unless you've got several hundred miles between you and anything else.'

'That's a beautiful thought,' I said, disgustedly grieving for my warm bunk – getting colder every moment. 'I could get some sleep –'

'Right now you'd better get the charts and we'll try and sort this lot out.'

Once more we went through the motions: timing flashes, even more difficult tonight, for the wind was fresher, *Reliance* livelier and the waves more obscuring; taking bearings, scanning the charts and trying to make the results add up.

If our previous guess was correct and it was the Skerries we were off last night, then there were lights on the Welsh coast which corresponded with some of these lights – *if* our timing was correct – but not all.

It was bewildering.

It also meant we were sailing into a bag.

Meantime wherever we were we were getting too close for comfort. *Reliance*, with crabbish purposefulness, was making a lot of leeway and sidling towards the area dominated by the red light.

We gathered up the charts and made our way to the engine-room. Frank said: 'It only goes to show you can't leave anything to chance. If we had left the engine reassembly to tomorrow we would have been looking rather sick.'

The heat and noise of starting preparations pulped our weary senses, so that the whole operation seemed twice lifesize and correspondingly slow.

The engine started first press of the trigger. The flywheel flew over and stopped with a resounding bang. Frank bounded to the fuel panel and switched off.

'Christ!' he shouted, pointing at the flywheel, 'one of those bloody fool things you do when you're tired.'

The long steel lever had been forgotten, left in the flywheel, had swung round with it and jammed; embedded in the asbestos wrapping of the exhaust pipe, and the back of the refrigerator.

Immediately I shot on deck to see how much time we had. The red light was closer. Wind mocked in the rigging. Wherever we were going we were getting there fast.

Back in the engine-room Frank was trying to manhandle the lever free. Together we tried, with all our might. It would not shift. 'Hacksaw,' he said and looked at me sharply. 'Getting any nearer in?'

'Yes.'

'Number one didn't fire,' he said, starting to dismantle the atomiser of the for'ard cylinder. I lifted down the hacksaw, he nodded, and climbing aboard the flywheel I set to. There was only one way to get at the two-inch solid bar and that brought the weight of the cut portion down on to the blade, nipping it. Sweating, I sawed away automatically whilst waves of heavy sleep billowed over me.

Half-way through. A touch on my shoulder. I turned to stare stupidly at Frank. 'I'll finish that,' he was saying, 'you clean the jets.' He had dismantled both atomisers, and I cleaned the tiny jets, a job he always jibbed at, because he was getting a bit short-sighted, though he hated to admit it, and there were already too many monocles in the bilges.

Before starting on the jets I went on deck again to see how far we had travelled meantime. The red light was no longer a red dot with a wicked wink. It was a large round orb suspended in the night, which closed its eye slowly, deliberately, prescient of all sorts of nameless horrors. But it had lost its power to terrorise me. I was emotionally expended. If we were going to pile up then we were going to pile up. Meanwhile there were the jets to be cleaned. A dense curtain dropped between the necessity for cleaning the jets and all else, and it was an immense relief. Like getting a second wind running.

The atomisers were ready and reassembled by the time Frank had finished cutting through the bar. Then a new bar had to be found as the old one was too short to give sufficient leverage. There was nothing aboard, but a jury lever was rigged out of a couple of lengths of steel piping. The mouth of one being opened to allow the end of another to be fitted.

Frank took a look out and said dispassionately, 'We can make it – if the engine starts.'

We went through the roaring rigmarole of head-heating and bottle-charging, giving the heads their full fifteen minutes – and started the engine.

We watched the flywheel spinning, listened to the tom-tom beat – Frank turned off the blowers, smiled. 'Away with you to the wheelhouse and get her to hell and gone from here.'

Still wearing mental blinkers I traipsed up to the wheelhouse and was astonished to find daylight had arrived. The lights had vanished and there was no suggestion of land in the offing, but the horizon had drawn in again, and there was a grey lumpy sea snarling round the ship. The dawn sky was overcast, mutinous, and streaked with yellow, giving promise of yet more wind to come.

I set a course to take us away from the invisible land. Frank came up and altered it, back to the invisible land . . . 'Pick out a landmark and find out where we are. . . .'

Reliance yawed heavily because I was weak. My arms ached abominably and felt dislocated at the shoulders. I handed her over to Frank. Within a few moments she was back to me. His sore hands were bothering him. After a few more minutes weaving I was powerless. Back she went to Frank. And for once daylight seeming to have lost its recuperative magic for us; worn out, weary, irritable and exasperated, we took turn and turn about steering.

Then all hell broke loose. There was a thundering of canvas and the mizzen sail came down. We dashed on to the counter, to find the head of the sail in the sea, and inched it back aboard, clawing at the iron canvas. Frank stayed to hold a post mortem and I went back to the wheel.

'Look at this!' he cried a moment later, trumpeting with wrath and waving a chunk of metal, 'goose-neck sheared through. Look at that crystallisation . . . glass hard. Modern bloody workmanship!' He pitched it into a corner.

Fortunately there was no damage to the sail itself. The bolt rope was torn asunder, but that was an easily reparable matter. The sail could be hoist on the topping lift, but it was decided not to put it up again until mast rings were fitted, so it was temporarily lashed down on the counter.

We picked up land later on in the morning. Clouds had rolled back by then and hung puffily over the coast, which appeared first as a thin blue line and deepened as we approached. It was turning out to be a bluish, boisterous sort of day, rather pleasant. We brought porridge and coffee up to the wheelhouse, and breakfasted there with the door hooked back, and listened to *Reliance* chattering.

She was excessively vocal that morning. Something for'ard – in the rigging or somewhere – kept asking 'You ready, George?' And something in the rudder trunking produced a nervous cough so realistically it made us jump every time. We thought this frightfully funny and felt a lot better. Frank suggested we should find a quiet bay, drop anchor and lie up for the night. It seemed an excellent idea.

The coast proved to be fairly high and looked placidly neat and picturesque from a distance. We closed a long, rocky point with a bright white lighthouse on it. With only the most cursory glance at the landscape on the chart, Frank pronounced it to be Holyhead.

'Are you sure?'

'Of course. Seen it dozens of times.'

He then went below to refuel. His reaction should have been a warning. For normally he was a most meticulous man. Exact to the smallest detail. Normally he would have taken bearings, checked and double-checked, and I would have been surprised had he not done so. But the supposition that we were off the Welsh coast had become, subconsciously, an *idée fixe*. Therefore a rocky point with an imposing lighthouse on it was Holyhead. From appearances alone I could not quarrel with his statement because I had never seen Holyhead in my life. But it never occurred to me to do so. The bearings did not seem to tally, but I was too tired to argue.

The pole was not quite right – extreme fatigue does not produce a condition 'like drunk' so much as one 'like drugged'. We were both drugged with the same deadly dope and prone to make the most fantastic mistakes.

Reliance surfed joyously that afternoon with a snorting breeze abaft the beam, her red staysail tugging like a horse. We peeked indecisively at bays and inlets after the manner of a motorist who hesitates to pull up because there is bound to be a less crowded stretch of road further along. We threaded through what seemed to us to be an extraordinary amount of shipping, all shapes and sizes. Normal traffic, I suppose, for the area, but it looked a lot to us, after days of empty waters, and more than we cared to see. Suddenly a black motor vessel, fishing-boat type, with derrick mast unshipped and leaning against the wheelhouse, detached itself from the coastal background and made swiftly towards us. A forbidding-looking bunch of Burberry's and felt hats stood in the bows and watched us keenly. There was no doubt it was the *Reliance* they were after. What for, whether it was a pilot boat, fishery vessel – *Reliance* still had her fishing numbers up – or something, from our point of view, infinitely worse, we did not stay to enquire. We opened the throttle wide and sped. The black boat followed, drew almost level – I was just getting ready to repel boarders – then inexplicably she turned back, pitching exaggeratedly and throwing up clouds of spray that drove the Burberry's to shelter.

The incident was unsettling. We gave up the notion of finding a quiet bay; the likelihood of finding one quiet enough seemed less probable. On the other hand uninterrupted rest was an urgent necessity. And we were not likely to get that either in these waters. The wind, obstinately south-west, was hardening, backing very slightly. The clouds were unrolling rapidly, spreading across the sky, and lowering. The promise of the ugly dawn was to be fulfilled. A dirty night was certain. Frank set a course from what we took to be St David's head to Ireland – 'We will try our luck over there' – a course that should bring us south of the Tusker light, whence we would creep, possibly to Waterford (though I disliked getting so far up a river, it savoured too much of a trap), but we left the final decision of what we would do when we made landfall on the Irish side.

It was growing dusk by the time we made our departure from 'St David's Head'. Frank went below to the engine-room. I looked at the course marked out on the chart; looked at the compasses; looked at the angle at which the coast lay from us. It did not agree with the angle made by the coast and the drawn course on the chart.

As it looked to me, the way we were going would bring us out somewhere by Arklow, and not south of the Tusker light. As soon as Frank returned to the wheelhouse I pointed this out to him. He would have none of it. We argued heatedly, angered by one another's obtuseness.

'We're almost going back on our tracks,' I said.

'Nonsense. *Look* at the chart. Check up for yourself. *Look* at the compasses . . . if they're wrong, they agree in their error.'

Which was unanswerable. But I held my point.

'The angles are wrong,' I insisted, maintaining it was something I should know something about; I had not been flying all those years in vain. 'You'll see, Ireland will appear over there' – pointing to port, ahead.

'You're not in an aeroplane, now,' said Frank testily; 'things look different at sea. Ireland will appear there' – stabbing a finger over to starboard – 'and we won't have to wait very long for it, either.'

By this time clouds were down on the dimming cliffs. The coastline was vague and indeterminate. Then a line squall swept down and blotted everything from view. We churned in a horrible sea, with screaming wind, and horizontal hail rattled about the ship like shot. When the squall passed over darkness was nearly complete. We caught a glimpse of a darkling bluff; a corner of coast which ran roughly westerly, parallel to us, and away to the north with a glint of dark waters. It was impossible to make out any decisive features. Frank looked at his watch – 'What did I say?' I was utterly and completely bewildered. 'You win. But it still does not make sense.'

It made even less sense as I stood by with the chart and tried to locate the lights as they appeared one by one. It was a fierce illtempered night. Huge waves threatened to thrust *Reliance* towards the shore. She struggled in the grip of an angry tide and made little headway. A light, now astern, and which should have been the Tusker, was not. A lightship should have turned up, and did not. A light, out to sea, should have been easily identifiable, and was not. Baffled, we crawled along, buffeted by a tempestuous beam sea, with the knowledge that nothing prevented us from being swept on to a lee shore but the steady thump of the engine. An anonymous red light gleamed on the coast ahead. We plunged on. The red light was abeam, turned white. Then it was astern and red again. Frank said it made him giddy, swore we were going round and round it. My reply was succinct and Anglo-Saxon.

He cried, 'God! What's that?'

The loom of a bluff like a blockhouse dead ahead. Thrown in relief by the flash reflection behind it. Slowly, agonisingly slowly, *Reliance* came round. Clawed out to sea. Plunging and falling for interminable hours in the red sector. We inched out and inched past the bluff and met full in the face the blinding flash of the revolving light. It was so shocking, so terrible in its brilliance, our instant reaction was flight. Flight? In that sea? She barely held her own facing it. We were forced to continue westwards along the coast, and made very little headway.

Suddenly, inexplicably, we were heading straight for the light . . . tearing headlong towards it . . . Frank swearing . . . heaving at the wheel. . . . 'Governor!' he gasped, 'jammed – can't hold – see what you can do.' I tore down to the engine-room and in ten seconds saw that I could do nothing. Back to the wheelhouse. Frank's unnecessary injunction to 'bring her round' as he dropped through the hatch. Spoke by spoke. Arms like jelly. Mouth like dust. Must be scared – and can't feel a thing. Except withering exasperation with this camel that won't come round – A change in the engine beats. That's better. Hard over. Ah. . . . Slowly, reluctantly she turned her head. The engine stopped. She swung back and flew towards the light on the wings of the wind.

Frank sprang into the wheelhouse. Flung open the door, looked out. 'Bloody hell . . . quick . . . anchor, decklights – '

There were about a dozen switches on the switchpanel in the wheelhouse. I turned the lot on. The wheelhouse, lit from within, looked eerily cosy, like a dancing cottage as we raced up the deck. We tore the lashings off the bower – it was already shackled – we picked it up from where it was stowed on the port side, carried it across, stepping over the bowsprit, and threw it over the port bulwarks. It hung, caught by a fluke on the cover board. We hitched it up one hand apiece, cast it free, and leapt back as the chain ripped out.

'And that was a shot of adrenalin,' said I.

Seventy fathom of chain roared out. There was a flip, something glinted, a splash and silence.

I laughed. What was the use? 'Bitch knows all the answers.'

Frank stood in an aggressive attitude, looking towards the land as if he would fend it off with a boat hook.

High and dark loomed the cliffs above us. High and white broke the spray against them. We lifted on the towering waves and the dreadful beam revolved overhead.

Rockets, flares, lifejackets – I leapt down the main companion. Dashed about below gathering oddments. A round ribbed box of waterproof matches. A torch. The last four one-pound notes, which I stuffed in my trouser pocket. A snapshot for luck, and smiled at myself as I did so. Picking up the rocket tin from behind the wheelhouse companion I was petrified by a peal of demoniacal laughter – God, what a time to ventriloquise! Cursing *Reliance* I shot into the wheelhouse unhooked two lifejackets and was on deck again.

Frank was heaving at the staysail halyard.

'One chance,' he shouted – 'might sail her out – – '

Might hell. I dropped the tin and jackets, marked where they rolled and threw my weight on the halyard. I felt as strong as a horse. Together we heaved. Nothing happened. 'Is it the ship or the sail we're trying to hoist?'

Frank ran forward. The foot of the sail was in a cluttered heap in the bows. He bent over it and let out a bellow: 'The chain! It's the chain holding it!'

So it hadn't gone. Dazedly I looked round, all my sudden strength draining away now it was no longer needed. I shivered and patted my clothes. 'Soaked,' I said in surprise.

Reliance had come round and was lying as she chose to lie, broadside on to the seas, rolling ferociously.

A small light winked anxiously from the top of the cliffs. Frank came and put his arm through mine. Together we looked at it owlishly.

'Too late,' said he, 'we fixed it.'

I gathered up the rocket tin and jackets and took them back to the wheelhouse. Twenty yards astern was a rock about two cottages high.

'How did we miss that?' I said, 'and what of what we can't see?'

'God knows,' said Frank, 'and there's nothing we can do about it.'

22

'I THINK this might be termed an emergency,' said Frank, digging into the wine-bin for the half-bottle of rum.

Water crashed upon the decks overhead and swam across the decklights like the windows of an aquarium. We sat on the floor of the saloon amidst the surging chaos of our books, drinking rum and discussing the incident with hilarious exaggeration. As though it was closed. For all the world as if we had just come through a sticky flight and were swapping horrors in the bar ('and there I was weaving in and out of the chimney-pots . . .') instead of pitching at precarious anchor within shouting distance of a formidable lee shore with a rock astern of us bigger than the ship. . . .

'Gosh . . . that anchor! It might have been a piece of cheese – what does it weigh, Frank?'

'All of two hundred pounds. More. Two and a half hundred-weight.'

I thought of our struggles getting it aboard at Fleetwood.

'By the way, what stopped the engine?'

'I don't know,' said Frank candidly, 'I didn't stay to find out – I was working the throttle by hand, you know, and it is very sensitive that way.'

We debated what could have gone overboard coincident with the chain running out. (Later we discovered it to be the cap of the mushroom ventilator over the forecastle; apparently the chain caught it, but it was odd it should do so at the very end.)

'Thought we'd had it then.' I showed him the contents of my pockets. 'Shipwreck gear.' He grinned at the matches. 'Where are the cigarettes?'

'Those are waterproof. For flares.'

We then had a look in the chain-locker and inspected the grunting chain shackled to a colossal ring bolt in the samsonpost. Satisfied that all was well that end Frank went on deck to see what was happening up there. I went into the galley to get supper.

I decided on fried eggs and chip potatoes. Of all things – it can only have been a gesture of defiance to the Fates. A heavy sea of fat washed over the sides of the pan, which I was obliged to hold on the stove with one hand whilst I held down the coffee pot with the other. I leant against the sink, and jammed myself there with a foot against the opposite bulkhead. But chips were achieved and placed in the cupboard below the burners to keep hot whilst the eggs were fried. When these were ready I tried to open the hot cuboard door. The knob turned, but the latch was immoveable, and the chips for all practical purposes might have been locked in. At once I was filled with a terrible rage, tearing at the knob, shaking the stove, and swearing at the top of my voice.

'Easy. Easy,' said Frank coming into the galley. 'Whatever is the matter?'

'Door jammed, God's teeth! Chips!' I shrieked.

'All right, all right. No need to get excited.'

He applied himself to the knob and in twenty seconds was frantic. Eventually we had to dismantle a burner and get the chips out through the top of the hotplate.

We ate supper sitting on the galley floor. Frank told me he had found the governor fault. A bent split pin. 'For the want of a nail the shoe was lost. . . .'

With his last chip poised halfway to his mouth he went sound asleep.

Gently I woke him. We took a last look round on deck, and turned in fully dressed, dead to the world, and slept, conscious, but heedless of the continual thunder of the waves above.

It was daylight when I awoke, somewhat surprised not to find water lapping round my ears. I lay pondering this and listening to footsteps on deck.

Footsteps!

Pummelling the bundle of blankets that was Frank I babbled urgently 'Someone aboard! Someone aboard! Wake up. Someone aboard!'

'Crackers!' he shouted through the bedclothes.

Tramp – tramp came from overhead. The sound of voices. A warp thrown down heavily. The mutter of a boat alongside. The hustle and clatter of people boarding.

Frank sprang up, listened, and was gone. He went on deck through the engine hatch. 'HulLO!' he said. I followed him to the engine-room, heard a surprised voice say, 'hullow, mate, didn't know anyone was aboard – and drifted back to the stateroom to wait. That was not fighting talk. I was quite prepared to do battle if necessary, but not for a social occasion.

Eventually the footsteps shuffled off – 'Sure you don't want help?' Frank shouted, 'No, thanks!' An engine started, roared, thumped away.

Frank was back in the stateroom.

'Well,' he said, 'that was the lifeboat crowd. They had been told by the coastguards here that there was a ship in distress. The coastguards apparently thought we had abandoned as there was no sign of a dinghy aboard.'

He threw the cigarette machine on the bunk. 'Ciggy. You make them better than I do.' As I rolled a couple of cigarettes he went on: 'They offered to help ... to give us a tow back with them ... to Newlyn, I think they said. ...'

'Where's that? Newlyn ... I seemed to know the name. It's not Irish anyhow.'

We plumbed the depths of memory's well, but the buckets came up empty.

'But I told them I was a poor man and could not afford salvage. ... I said we had just had a little engine trouble' – Frank was a master of understatement at times – ' ... and would soon get it fixed. I tried to get tidal information from them, but it wasn't any use. They kept on saying it was dangerous here, said we would get no second chance. If the engine failed again it would be curtains. I told them the engine would not fail again.

'They were very concerned to know if I had anyone with me. I said I had a mate aboard, and they were appalled that there were only two of us to handle this ship.'

We grinned fondly at one another, feeling very proud, brave and foolish.

Then he laughed. 'You should have seen their faces when I told them we turned in after dropping the hook. 'What,' they said, 'no one on watch?' 'Watch!' said I, 'watch that stuff! Blow me, I'd seen all I wanted in ten minutes. ...'

We smoked in silence, contemplating 'that stuff,' then I said, 'Darling, that beard, it's bloody.' At the same time Frank said, 'Our whereabouts will be all over the place now' – and his comment won.

'Why?' I asked.

'Whenever a lifeboat goes out, it is reported to Lloyd's, whether they pick anything up or not.'

'Glory be,' said I with a sigh, 'then we had better get cracking.'

~ ~ ~ ~ ~

After coffee and porridge, Frank fixed the governor, we started the engine, and leaving it to warm up, wandered on deck to size up the situation. The coast seemed only slightly less forbidding by light of day. The cliffs were high and precipitous, rock-bestrewn at the base. There was a wreath of radio masts and rows of houses atop, and although the houses looked inhabited there were no signs of the inhabitants. 'But I bet every window bristles with binoculars,' said Frank,' and they'll be all saying if I'd a been I wouldn't a went.'

Reliance had moved, riding at the full scope of her chain, and further away from the big rock. The red light turned out to be a slender white lighthouse at the end of a perfectly frightful rocky point. The coast ran in a north-west, south-easterly direction. Frank had not asked the lifeboatmen where it was because he confessed, somewhat diffidently, it seemed so silly not to know.

The sea had moderated, but there was still a strong wind from the west. As we should have to beat out on the starboard tack it looked as if we might have some fun clearing the rock and the lighthouse point.

Whilst Frank had been fixing the governor and checking over the engine generally, I had been doing a little research with the charts. We realised by then, of course, that at no time had we ever known where we were. Not that that was much help. We had plenty of charts. Apart from those concerned with the West Indies I hardly knew where to begin. It is inconceivable how difficult it is to find a place when you have no idea where to look for it. Newlyn niggled at the back of my mind like a face one knows well enough and cannot put a name to – or rather a name one cannot put a face to. I did not find Newlyn.

It was not until we started winding in the chain that we dicovered just how tired we were . . . how much we were paying for the phenomenal energies expended last night. The chain kept riding up on the gipsy and had to be hammered free. At first this was necessary with every other link and was killing. We wound, stopped and hammered, working at the end of a see-saw that rolled as well as pitched. We got in ten feet and stopped, panting, spent.

Frank said, 'Ten fathoms, then a stop for coffee.'

We took hold of the winch handles and ground on. The blood

pounded in my ears. I thought if I did not die I was doomed to spend the rest of my life slaving at that winch. It got harder and harder, needing a spurt of effort to move the ratchet into the next cog. We roared in our breathing like broken-winded horses. Frank, working the starboard handle, said, 'Is the chain straight up and down?' This had no special significance for me: I looked over the side. 'As a matter of fact, it is.' He nodded.

Then we waited until the ship plunged, and wound like fury, taking in the slack of the chain until she rose again and brought us to a sudden stop. The ten-fathom mark was just coming up when, try as we might, we could get no more. Our efforts produced the alarming result of lifting the winch six inches off the deck.

'Chain fast on the bottom,' said Frank. 'You'll have to steam up on to it' – and arranged a system of signals so that I could follow his directions from the wheelhouse.

A DH Rapide circled overhead. Press photographers. 'Vultures,' I muttered, not without a certain amount of sympathy, opening the throttle and slipping into gear.

Slowly steaming on to the chain, alert for signals, I saw Frank swing round, wildly wave his arms and shout in a manner which was not in the programme laid down. I opened the throttle wide and steered as close to the wind as I dared. Frank raced back to the wheelhouse.

'Chain's gone!'

The Rapide dived and flew round us, very low.

Frank looked up at the aircraft: 'What a break for the cameraman!'

As we battered our way out from that inhospitable coast, clearing the lighthouse which gave us the willies to look at, I grieved over the loss of the bower anchor and sixty fathom of studlink chain. Frank was more inclined to take a generous view. Maintained it was cheap at the price. We still had the old fisherman anchor, the kedge, ten fathom of chain and a wire cable.

'We've saved the ship,' he said, 'and what is more, my Ann, we did it ourselves. . . .'

He added: 'It may be hell . . . but, what a story!'

I could wish it savoured slightly less of a penny-dreadful serial. One can have too much of hanging by one's teeth waiting for the next instalment.

'Don't tell me farming is hard work,' I said, 'you do at least get some sleep o' nights. After this it is pigs and chickens for me.'

Illogically, we immediately began to discuss our next boat. I stuck out for a wheelhouse. We should have been in a pretty fix without this one. Frank said he wondered why we had bothered with so much accommodation – 'As far as I can see, we want nothing more than a galley and wheelhouse for ourselves.' He thought a fifty-fifty motor-sailer a mistake – 'We will concentrate on either sails or motor next time, with one or the other definitely auxiliary, and then make sure that the main motive power is one hundred per cent operable.'

With *Reliance* as she was, the engine was not quite powerful enough. She would probably do considerably better with the help of the mainsail, but conditions had not favoured our fixing the main halyard, and it was a task we both funked in our weakened physical state.

Frank said it was proved we needed a crew on future voyages. But I disagreed. 'You cannot judge anything from this voyage. Our circumstances are peculiar. If it wasn't for this damned business of being hunted, we could do the job on our ear.' He was pleased at that.

There was one interesting, though highly inconvenient, outcome of our last night's adventure, and that was the extraordinary amount of water which had found its way, via the tight flush-fitting brass screw filler-cap on deck, into the paraffin tank. In all the previous heavy weather this had not happened. But I wished I had discovered it before filling the stove tank. It was only through the evil behaviour of the stove that I discovered it at all. We drained paraffin from the storage tank tap into a can and the presence of water was noticeable. Afterwards we used bottles and poured off the water, usually two-thirds of a bottle-full. It added disproportionately to the burden of chores.

We ploughed steadily back along the coast the way we had come the night before and discovered the point of land, so dangerously misconstrued as Ireland, to be the westerly point at the entrance to a huge bay. Chagrined, Frank said, 'You were right' – which was no comfort, as we were no wiser as to our whereabouts. It was singularly discomforting to think that probably everyone in England knew that but ourselves. We wanted to get away from the place and did not know where to go as we did not know where we were going from. We would like to have found shelter and to have anchored, to rest and put the ship in order; in fact we timidly peeped into the bay with that in mind, but dared not do so. The feeling of being hunted was strong upon us, and we had no intention of giving in. Upon that we were irrevocably resolved. But such was our apprehensive state of mind, upon lesser matters we were incapable of making a decision.

By nightfall we reached the eastern point of the bay. There Frank dug his toes in. 'I am not going round that,' he declared, 'until I can see what lies on the other side.'

We spent an intolerably weary night steaming back and forth across the mouth of the bay, waiting for dawn. A course beset by steamer traffic and bounded at either end by a light, which remained maddeningly anonymous. I hated lights anyway; not surprisingly they had become an obsession, and there was a wicked set towards them. *Reliance* pulled hard-mouthed. If one relaxed for a moment at the wheel she made off for the nearest light, at a hard gallop, hell-bent for destruction. Or so it seemed. We were frightfully tired, but so tightly wound up it was impossible to sleep, and our watches were spent below in the galley drinking coffee and making a fresh brew for the next one.

Dawn came at last, cold, grey and very angry.

We made for the point.

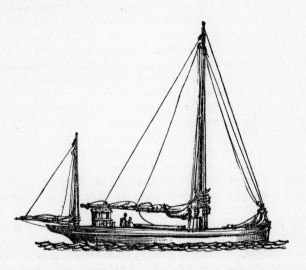

23

'DID you ever see anything like it?' marvelled Frank. He was at the helm, and I was standing behind him, perched on the hatch coamings, holding on to a window-sill with one hand and the door-knob with the other; a stance one automatically took up in the wheelhouse, other than at the wheel, to keep one's balance. I was waiting with inordinate anxiety to see what lay round the point. As if it hid something of supreme importance.

With engine throttled down, borne there by wind and tide we were nearing the point: high brownish cliffs, fearsome outlying rocks; the lighthouse; and outspread, sprawling coast-guard buildings. But it was the sea that brought forth Frank's comment. It boiled and frothed, a hideous devil's-cauldron of a sea. The wind was dead aft, and again I was aware of that unearthly silence, an evil silence that transcended sound. White serpentine waves snaked swiftly past the ship. I felt myself pressing against the starboard side of the wheelhouse as if by doing so I could push the ship out to sea. Away from the coast and its monstrous waters.

A light winked down from the cliff-top. Very slowly it delivered its message. As one speaks to a foreigner. I stared stupidly at the winking light, heavy-lidded with relentless fatigue. I could not read what the coastguards had to say, but I could guess.

'Aren't we getting too close?' I ventured.

Frank said, as if he had been thinking the matter out for some time and come to a sudden decision, 'Hold tight. I'm going out to sea.'

With the quiet confidence always manifest when he was at the helm, he turned and edged out across the precipitously vicious waves, handling *Reliance* superbly; transformed into a nautical centaur, he and the ship were one. Fascinated with admiration, I thought of my own ham-fistedness, how *Reliance* would react in such conditions with me, and was filled with envy.

Another bay opened out; a thickly-wooded coast; and a vista of coastline, bays and headlines stretched, illimitably it seemed, towards the east.

'God,' said Frank with a sideways glance, 'what a hell of a sea . . . some race or other. . . .'

Race? That was the key I wanted. I sped down to the chart-room, the door in my brain unlocked at last. One corner of England neither of us knew, had never seen, visited or flown over. . . . I hastily turned over the charts, found the one I wanted, English Channel West, and went straight to the spot now I knew what I was looking for. Yes. There it all was. Newlyn, the lights, the bay. . . . Obvious. Of course. Just too tired to think straight. I returned to the wheel-house with my tidings.

'That was Land's End where we nearly piled up the night before last.'

'Not in the least surprised,' said Frank. 'End of the world if you ask me.'

'I am not fooling. I've found us at last. That point there is the Lizard.' I looked at the compasses and the lie of the coast at home now. 'If we go on as we are we'll sail slap into the Eddystone.'

'Oh. And how far off is this Eddystone?'

I took the wheel, *Reliance* restively impatient with the change of helmsman, and Frank studied the chart, one eye on the sea.

'But Frank, why are we going *up* the Channel?'

He chivvied me out of the way and took the wheel again. 'Because,' he said, somewhat drily, 'we have no alternative.'

I could not think what he was driving at. Now our position was clear there seemed no reason why we should not turn about and head for the Atlantic, renew the voyage in earnest, surround ourselves with sea-room. Thousands of miles of blessed landless ocean. Frank snorted, pointed out it was blowing a gale. A sou'wester that blocked any passage west for us as surely as if there was a solid barrier at our back. It took a minute or two for this to sink in, which was not due to bravado or stupidity on my part; it was just that I had got so used to bad conditions I could not recognise when they worsened.

Even so, I petulantly argued the advisability of turning and fighting our way out, for gales weighed nothing with me beside the calamity of being trapped in the Channel. Frank said patiently that that would simply be an exhausting waste of time and, most important of all at this stage, fuel. 'We have got to conserve it now,' he

said. 'I reckon there won't be more than two and a half days' left.'
A point I had overlooked entirely. Problems piled up and seemed insuperable. So insuperable my brain shut down and refused to consider them. I was engulfed in an awful tide of weariness. Frank, with some sense left, realising how beat we were and that the necessity for rest was urgent if we were to carry on, said we would make for France.... 'Stress of weather, we'll bluff it out somehow. Go down, look out a port and work out a course I can steer in this.' It seemed a stupendous responsibility in my half-witted state, and I was reluctant to take it. But he would not leave the wheel. 'You won't be able to hold her,' he said. 'You'll have to look after the engine today.... And bring back the tidal atlas for the Channel when you come. It's a large flat blue book ... somewhere in the chartroom.'

'All right,' I said, ' "the farther off from England the nearer is to France" ' ... and kept on saying it all the way to the chartroom. The chartroom was knee-deep in books and papers, surging back and forth, with the swivel chair adrift and rolling on its side. ('Will you, won't you, will you, won't you, will you join the dance?')

'Look at you!' I shouted at the mess. 'All over the place again' – and peevishly hunted among the heaving papers for the charts and things I wanted. The refrain in my head changed – 'No one, he said, could call me a fussy man ... fussy man ... fussy man....'

'What is this?' I said aloud, infuriated, 'a chartroom or a kindergarten?'

I found the buried chart, the dividers, parallel rule, pencil, paper, put them on the desk, righted the chair, sat at the desk. And stared at the chart.

('The farther off from England ...')

What a coast! Rocks and rocks, and lights and islands. It would be dark by the time we got to the other side....

The ship lurched violently and the chair went over backwards. I grabbed at the fidding on the desk to save myself. The chart, rulers, everything, slid past me on to the floor.

('Fussy man ... fussy man ...')

'Shut up!' I shouted.

Was it possible. Could anyone be as tired as this?

I scrabbled through the chaos, found the things, and started again.

'We're here' – I made a pencil mark on the chart, and fell forward on the desk asleep. Raised my heavy head. Blinked. 'Why am I

here? Oh, my God, yes.' The chart was on the floor again. I was holding on to the edge of the desk.

This would never do. Must make an effort.

I forced my eyes to stay open – it was a physical effort – and they would not focus. Forced my wandering brain to attend. It registered that there was a lump of France sticking out into the Channel making a fearful bag with the Channel Islands therein: a bag to be avoided in the dark. In this state of fatigue. The whole coast looked lousy anyway, and with that my wretched brain tried to shut down again. I drove it back to the problem. If we followed a course to miss that lump . . . we could stooge around till daylight (What's another night of this among so many?) then find somewhere. See what we were doing. I struggled with the parallel rule. Everything slid. The rule slid. The chart slid. The chair slid. I slid. In a flash of temper I threw the rule away. And found it again in a panic. Then dug out my old Douglas protractor, relic of flying, and felt more comforted. With brow raised, taut, to keep my eyes open, I puzzled over variation, which meant nothing. Somewhere at the back of my mind there were warnings about the tides round Le Havre. And that meant nothing too. Nothing had any meaning at all, except that I was hoving on the edge of a deep dark pit of unconsciousness. A pit into which I must not fall, though I was longing, *longing* to.

Then my brain brought out a new dodge to get the rest it was determined to have. I was in the act of picking up the dividers, blacked-out, and came to, still picking up the dividers. There was no warning, the blackout was as sudden and complete as the snapping of a shutter.

It was terrifying, absolutely uncontrollable, and happened again and again. The whole of that day was a fantasia of flickering film.

Eventually I took a sheet of notepaper up to Frank on which I had written a course, a distance and ETA. Though how long it had taken to do, and what sort of nonsense it was in fact, I have no means of telling. And in any case it had all been a waste of time. The problem of going anywhere in particular was submerged by the greater one of survival.

It was a mighty weighty wind that blew that day. Great grey perpendicular walls of water reared up and rushed the ship. Each one presenting a special problem. And they came relentlessly, steep and swift. Breaking, with spray blowing off their crests in hard horizontal streams. So there was not much visibility and no horizon to speak of, only the top of the next wave, and the next and the next.

Between blackouts, of which I made no mention to Frank, I was comparatively alert. I read, aloud, the Channel tide book, all its warnings and portents, from cover to cover, and was immeasurably depressed.

By about midday conditions were appalling. We were caught up in a frightful sea raised by opposing wind and tide. And whilst plunging and rolling in this mix-up we saw a large brown buoy, which we thought rather disturbing, because it did not seem to serve any definite purpose according to the rules, but we could not think that it had come there of its own accord. Concluding, from the white fury that raged round us, that we had been swept on to the fringes of the Portland Race, and remembering all the tide book had had to say about it, we were more depressed than ever. But there was nothing we could do about it.

The steering chain jammed again. Seeing what the trouble was from the aft window, I seized the crowbar, kept on hand for just this emergency, went out into the bluster and roar, and fixed it. Frank was livid when I got back. It was the only time I saw him really upset, otherwise he seemed such a tower of stength. I knew perfectly well how he was feeling, which was why I went out myself. I just could not face that worry.

We each ate a packet of dates, horribly cloying, but cooking was out. The stove tank was still half-full of water and refused to keep alight, and it was no time to fiddle about with a recalcitrant stove.

Much of my time was spent in the engine-room. The header tank needed frequent attention, of course, and filling the lubricator box was a lengthy process. Lubricating oil was stored in a forty-gallon oil drum lashed to the bilge pipe that went up to the hand pump on deck. This had to be unlashed, upended and oil poured into a wide-lipped gallon can. A job that wanted about six hands in a seaway. The drum was about half full. For some reason the blackouts were more persistent below, and I frequently came to, one arm round the bilge pipe, in the very act of pouring oil from the drum to can. Temporary unconsciousness added considerably to the difficulty of the manœuvre, but strangely enough I did not lose much oil. The procedure was further complicated by the dismal discovery of water in the oil drum, and then it had to be filtered as well. How the water had got in I had no idea. But what really got me worried was the amount of water in the ship. And still coming in. *Reliance* was taking one hell of a pasting; she had sprung a leak somewhere under the counter, and water was spurting in around the mizzen step. It streamed down the alleyway. Rose in the engine bilges until the flywheel threw up a jet as it spun. Floorboards were afloat in the cabins. Throughout the stormy voyage *Reliance* had been wholly admirable, all that the old men said she was and more. The hammering she had withstood would have pulverised a lesser vessel long before. And although she had been a damned uncomfortable ship, she had been an exceptionally buoyant one, like a lifeboat. But there is a limit to everything. Now she was losing some of her buoyancy, there was a sluggishness in her movements. The bilge pump coupled to the main engine chose this moment to choke. I took it down and tried to clear it, but failed. I was running the auxiliary engine at the time to charge the batteries and thought I would turn it over to the auxiliary bilge pump, but it was such a complicated set-up I could not sort it out and went along to Frank to find out how it worked.

It was late afternoon by then and worse than ever. He said when I entered the wheelhouse, 'There is something I want to tell you. One of these chaps may get us.' But I was too concerned with problems of my own to take that in, and asked him to explain the layout of the auxiliary pump. He was silent for a while and then said he was too tired to explain. I made to go on deck to the hand pump, my mind running along a single track, whereat Frank roused himself in a fury and roared that under no circumstances was I to go on deck. I offered to take the wheel so that he could go down and sort out the bilge pump. But he would not have that either. 'You couldn't possibly hold her,' he said.

'But the bloody ship's half full of water,' I said, 'she must be pumped out.'

'Can't be helped,' he spoke thickly, 'have to put up with it, hope for the best.'

My God, I thought, he's shot. The only useful thing I could think of to help him was a hot drink. I searched feverishly in the turmoil in the spare cabin wherein were stored oddments that would not stow in lockers. I found an old Primus and gimbals, and set them up in the galley. It should have been done before, but somehow there had never been an opportunity. With some difficulty I filled the Primus with paraffin and essayed to clean the jet, blacked-out holding the jet to the light, came to holding the jet to the light, pricker poised. But the pricker was broken. I went into the engine-room, now pretty well awash, where I knew there was a tube of

207

spares on the work bench. All the time there were resounding crashes on deck. The motion of the ship was indescribable. Yet although I was exhausted beyond reason almost I moved about with a sureness as if *Reliance* was a chromium-plated motor cruiser ploughing up the London River. I seemed to have acquired a sense of balance that operated without conscious direction.

None the less, I went for six in the engine-room looking for the spare prickers. *Reliance* gave a monstrous lurch. It *felt* as if she had fallen off the top of a cliff on her beam-ends forty feet below. Everything movable in the engine-room detached itself and flew through the air. I went over backwards on to the flywheel; fortunately the safety gate was shut. Christ, he's weakening, I thought, hastening to get the Primus going. The prickers were found, the jet cleaned, the stove lit. Inevitably, despite careful filtering, some water from the paraffin storage tank had found its way into the Primus. . . . It was dark by the time I took a mug of coffee, stiffly laced with rum, to the wheelhouse.

Frank downed it in one. 'That's *good*,' his voice was a croak. I offered to give him a break at the wheel, but he refused almost savagely. I had to go back to the engine-room then, it was time to refuel again, and told him I would try and cook up a can of soup. He said, 'Good. Don't be long coming back. I'm so goddamned tired. Can hardly keep my eyes open . . . helps to concentrate to have . . . someone to . . . talk to.'

But it was two hours before I could get back. Two hours of juggling with the watered oil in the drum, with the watered paraffin, with the temperamental stove. And half the time it seemed as if I was unconscious, blackouts followed so swiftly one upon another. Grown super-sensitive to the movements of the ship I noted a change in her antics, they were wilder, more erratic. And labouring withal.

I had been working with the lights on below. By contrast the wheelhouse was pitch dark.

'Soup,' I said, holding the mug out and touching the back of his hand with it.

'Soup?' said Frank.

'Hullo,' I said, 'there's a light . . . over there . . . port bow. . . .'

A pale bluish light shone faintly through the salt-sprayed windows.

'Light?' said Frank.

Then we were both flung across the wheelhouse and the soup was spilt. Back to the galley I went and refilled the mug.

'Here, drink this before you lose it.'

He drank it, holding the mug in both hands, leaving the ship to herself; then placing the mug carefully on the shelf from where it promptly slid on to the floor, he stepped back and took my hand.

'Tell me,' he said gently, 'there's something wrong. What is it?'

'Something wrong?' I could hear my voice climbing. 'I should say so. It's blowing one hell of a gale. . . .'

He shook his head.

'Please tell me . . . what is it?'

He moved forward to the wheel, leant on it, then abruptly: 'See those yachts?'

Wave crests breaking white as they sped past the wheelhouse window.

He caught my arm. 'Tell me. *What is it?* What's wrong? I . . . can't remember . . . only darkness . . . and . . . the rain in my face.'

Shocked beyond belief or comprehension, torn by an overwhelming pity, sick with fear, I did not know what to do. I listened to my mind, accusing, 'You left him too long, you left him too long'; reminding, 'The header tank needs filling, the header tank needs filling.'

'The header tank,' I said aloud, 'needs filling. I must go and fill the header tank. Do you understand? The header tank . . . I won't be long. I won't . . .'

Under the shadow of horror I pumped up the header tank – there was enough oil in the glass gauge to last a while, so I left that and hurried back to the wheelhouse. He was crouching in a corner, and I gave him a cigarette, wanting an excuse to see his face by the light of a match. I had to know. . . .

Reliance battled on alone, sluggishly. The pale light danced ahead.

The match flared. I held it to the end of his cigarette, and raised my eyes to his face. And dropped the match. Frank had driven himself beyond the breaking-point. There was piteous blank unreason in his eyes.

24

I STOOD at the wheel, oblivious of the sea thunder, automaticall
easing the ship into the tumult, watching the lights go on below
one by one, throwing yellow pools on the dark deck as they shon
up through the round decklights. It had been extraordinarily diffi
cult to persuade Frank below. How long a breakdown of this natur
might last I had no idea, but I knew there would be no cure withou
rest and sleep. I dare not beg or plead or entreat; the suggestion tha
he should turn in had to be made as though it was the most natura
thing in the world. Only his world was not natural, and he did no
seem to understand. He stood looking down through the hatch s
long that the horror of it was like a creeping paralysis and made m
say sharply, 'What's the matter? Don't you know the way to th
stateroom?' Whereat he snapped, 'Of course,' and went, climbin
very slowly down, and leaving the lights burning as he went for'ard
The galley light went on and I wondered anxiously what he wa
doing there. Then the lights went off one by one and he was back i
the wheelhouse, saying, 'All in the dark?' as he switched on the ligh

The lost look had gone from his eyes but his expression was ver
strange.

Keeping a tight hold on myself so that I should appear calm,
said the light was dazzling, asked him to turn it off. I said, as w
swung and lurched to the tossing ship, that the gale was moderatin
and he might as well take the opportunity of turning in. Ignorin
all that, he said, 'Had a bit of a party, haven't you?', then shoute
menacingly, 'Ship's a bloody shambles.'

Mildly, I pointed out she was bound to be; it was blowing a gal
He snarled, 'Don't think you can get away with that. You can'
fool me.'

The wheelhouse reeked of soup. It was all over the place, on th
shelf, on the wheel, on the bulkheads, on the deckhead even.
wondered at one mugful spilling so far.

Suddenly he sprang at me, gripped my arms, raved – shouting at the top of his voice, wild-eyed.

Reliance staggered wearily, unresilient, dazed by ceaseless onslaught of the sea.

Jesus, I thought, what am I to do? I can't handle this alone. Not Frank and the ship. Must get help.

The blue light still gleamed, wraith-like, ranging from astern to ahead on the port hand as the ship lunged aimlessly. The light was blue only because of the water-laden atmosphere. I was sure it was an outlying shore light. A lighthouse light. And to this vague agency I intended to appeal. Breaking from his grasp, I sprang down the companion, seized the rocket tin from behind the ladder and was back in the wheelhouse, not daring to leave him alone.

He watched narrowly as I opened the tin. They were flares, and I wondered why I had always been under the impression they were rockets. Then before I could stop him he had seized the lot and was making for the door. Terrified lest he should get on deck, I grabbed him by the coat and we fought, horribly. He got the door open, threw the flares out, over the side, whisked away by the screaming wind. With a supreme effort I thrust him aside and slammed the door. He threw himself upon the wheel, opened the throttle wide, and in a paroxysm of frenzy pulled the wheel first one way and then the other.

Something had to be done. And quickly. With the vain hope that a counter-shock might restore his senses, I screamed at the top of my voice, simulating hysterics. And thought at first it had succeeded, for he quietened and slowly throttled down: said, 'Ann, Ann, this isn't like you.'

At this point the engine stopped.

'My God, you've stopped it!' The words were out, in a whisper, my hysterical act forgotten. He had turned the throttle wheel too far.

He said in a perfectly normal voice, 'I'll tell you something' – I turned to him hopefully – 'we are not at sea at all. We're in harbour. Tied up along a quay.'

Anguished, I could only stare helplessly.

Then the whole ghastly nightmare started up again. Shoutings, ravings, preposterous accusations against which I had no defence for there is no reasoning with hallucination. Frenzies that I could not pacify, having become an enemy. Pitiable struggles – for he was bent on 'going ashore' – pitiable in that he was so pathetically weak, and it was I, not he, that had the strength of ten. Betimes, he held his head in his hands and said, 'What a horrible dream.'

It went on for hours. A life-time.

I dare not leave him and so could not get stuff to make flares. Nor signal with the navigation lights, for their switch was in the engine-room. I thought of signalling with the stern light, the wheel-house and the decklights, but he was leaning against the switch panel, and any move I made, anything I said, was suspect, and enough to drive him into terrible furies.

And all the time the ship rose and fell, rose and fell, growing heavier and heavier. But I dared not go down to see where the water had risen to. Nor yet on deck to pump her out.

Suddenly he caught me off my guard as I was wracking my brain for some solution to the dreadful problem, and was out of the wheel-house door, shouting he was going ashore and I could not stop him. I was after him, terror-stricken, and had him by a bulldog grip on the arm. But he would not come back, and it was no place to fight out there. I thought if he saw what it was like, felt the force of it, perhaps the truth might penetrate to his tired, blind brain. We made our way, step by step, up the heaving, pitching deck, with spray stinging our faces, wind tearing our hair, clutching our clothes, water swirling about our feet. Nothing of which he seemed to realise. Right to the stemhead we went. It had moderated, of course, or we should never have got there. And we stood, I fast hold of his arm, he shouting to imaginary boatmen to take him ashore.

I wondered what they might reply . . . but they would not, could not, hear. And I suggested he should go below and wait for day-light when it would surely be easier to get a lift ashore. And hoped that in his other world it was also night.

Unexpectedly he acquiesced. Allowed himself to be led to the main companion. I halted there and stood back to let him go down first, fearing otherwise he might make some unpredictable and unpreventable action and go over the side. But I, oh God, had become a foe of incalculable designs. He hesitated, laughed and with indescribably heartbreaking bravado led the way down into the saloon.

Getting help was uppermost in my mind. I did not follow, but went into the galley, snatched up the towels and tea-towels there, the bottle of meths, and returned to deck. In my pocket was the box of waterproof matches. They were not proof against anything but lighting. I threw them overboard. Dived into the galley for a box of ordinary matches. Returned to find the towels washed away. Of course, they would be. What was I thinking of? Down again for more material. This time through the wheelhouse, along the alleyway, into the stateroom, hastily gathering the first materials to hand. Woollen sweaters, pyjamas, anything. Then back on deck, pouring meths over the articles wholesale. A boarding sea swept them out of my hand, carried them away and me into the scuppers. I picked myself up and clung to the mizzen shrouds to get my breath back, and wondered if I would ever do anything right.

Think, I ordered myself, think. Use your wits.

I knew one should use paraffin for flares, but there was no time to fiddle about filtering it; Frank might appear on deck any moment and the paraffin was too intermingled with water to be much use without filtering. Petrol! That was it – But the petrol can was below: oddly enough in the bathroom. It would be wise, first, to find out what Frank was doing. Cautiously I opened the main hatch doors. He was leaning against the steps. Absolutely out. In his state of exhaustion he was likely to remain so for some time. Quietly closing the doors, I went below via the wheelhouse for the petrol can, and more material.

With a petrol-soaked flare bundle tied to the lee mizzen shrouds, I was crouching to light a match, then the next thing I knew was being flung into the bulwarks by a welter of water, and the bundle was gone. Defeated, I crawled into the wheelhouse and there bethought me of signalling with the lights.

Snapping the switches off and on, flashing an sos, I appealed to an empty world. The light shone palely back to me, seen and unseeing. Slowly realisation came: there would be no help. There *is* no help, save what comes from within, and searching there I found none.

All I knew was that somewhere on our lee was land, and there was danger of drifting on to it.

At least I could prepare for that eventuality. I unlashed the Carley float from the side of the wheelhouse, moved it over to the side and leant it there, propped against the bulwarks with the painter fast to the mizzen shrouds. Put the paddles into the wheelhouse together with the lifejackets, and left the problem of how to get us both into the float if and when the need arose.

By this time it was dawn. The wind had abated considerably, but *Reliance* was drifting stern on to the seas. They rose high, broke, and crashed on her counter with the repetitive force of a steam hammer. I did not see that she could stand much of that, and brought her round, surprising me by answering the helm, so that she was broadside on – she would go no closer – where she rolled and wallowed horribly, but did not take such a pounding. I lashed the wheel and went on deck to the hand pump.

Frank appeared through the main hatch. Uncertainly I went to meet him, not knowing what there would be to contend with. He looked inexpressibly haggard. We smiled at one another and I said, 'Hullo, are you you – or two other people?'

He seemed somewhat surprised and said, 'Why, me, of course.'

He stood holding on to the shrouds, gazing round as if he had just come aboard and was looking things over for the first time.

Blue hills of land were visible now, a few miles to leeward. How far it would be difficult for me to say, but in our thoroughly helpless state the coast looked a lot too near. There was a lighthouse to seaward of us. The Eddystone, and we were off Plymouth, but I did not register that at the time, being wholly concerned with Frank.

Watching him closely I could see the dazed expression fading from his face as he came to himself, but stemmed the rising flood of my relief by asking how I had managed to anchor on my own.

At once every nerve was strung out to breaking-point – 'Anchor?' I cried. 'Look about you, man!'

It was just enough to bring him right back to normal.

'What has been going on I don't know,' he said, 'you can tell me later . . . but I can see what will happen if something isn't done about it.'

There was no uncertainty about him now. The situation was his and he was in control of it and himself as though last night had never been.

What happened after that I do not know for I blacked-out completely. Shock of relief, I suppose, at Frank's amazing recovery. Reaction. It was no longer necessary for me to keep my wits about me, therefore I could not, and the exhaustion which had been simply shelved during the night overwhelmed me. Frank said afterwards that I went below under my own power, but I have no recollection of doing so. I remember standing on deck, looking at Frank, saying, 'He's back, he's back,' and then next thing I knew was waking, alert and panic-stricken, lying on the bunk.

I had no idea of how long I had been there, and terrified at what might have happened meantime, I leapt off the bunk, and was swinging up the engine-room companion, when I heard a strange voice hailing the ship, and Frank's footsteps on deck. Peeping through a port in the coaming I saw a small fishing boat making towards us. The sea (heavens, how long had I been out?) had moderated considerably; was calm compared with what we had become used to. Frank was standing by the bulwarks, hands on hips, a stance of incredible ease and confidence.

A fisherman shouted: 'Want any help?'

And Frank shouted back with a cheer in his voice that warmed me through to hear: 'No thanks. Just drying out after a bit of a pasting last night.'

25

FRANK had restored order in a remarkable manner whilst I was unconscious. He had pumped the ship out, by hand, working the long stiff arm of the deck pump, an exacting job at the best of times, until *Reliance* was dry and riding buoyantly again. He had put up the stay-sail, a headsail of number-one canvas and no pocket handkerchief to handle. He had – how like him – cleaned down the inside of the wheelhouse ('Distempered with soup. What has been going on?'), had made coffee and porridge for breakfast. Found out where we were, which must have been a bit tricky for him under the circumstances, and set the ship to sail herself with lashed wheel out to sea. Apparently *Reliance* had drifted, early on, very nearly to the entrance to Plymouth, where he had tried to anchor, using the kedge, with main halyard for a cable, and somehow lost them both. He was exceedingly put out by this, which he said was rank carelessness on his part. The fact of there still being the spare bower available and a spare halyard did nothing to appease him. It was after this he hoisted sail. He had even made a simple and ingenious little gadget to drive the water out of the wheelhouse and keep it drained, which worked most successfully.

It was altogether an astounding achievement for one who had but a short while before reached the ultimate in exhaustion, but Frank had more guts than anyone I ever knew. It made me bitterly ashamed of my recent lapse and I was never so humbled in my life.

Over breakfast whilst *Reliance* lopped slowly out to mid-Channel, we did some mental overhauling. Throughout the meal we kept up a pretence of cheer, but there was this thing between us, and when he said abruptly, 'What did happen last night?', I was glad of the chance to bring the horror into the open. We had shared all else, and could share this too. Better by far to bring it out and have done with it than to leave it rotting in the recesses of our minds. Or so it seemed to me, and I told him all that had happened. He listened silently, holding his head in his hands, and looked up, when I finished. 'How awful,' he said, 'how bloody awful. My poor Ann. To think that I . . .

'But you know,' he went on thoughtfully, 'it is extraordinarily interesting. I must tell you my side of the story.'

Which was totally unexpected because somehow I had imagined he would have no recollection of what had occurred.

He remembered the gale as I did up to the time I brought him the coffee. By then he was mentally and physically beaten. Dizzy with looking out of the window, back to the compass, out of the window again. Worn out by the bellowing assaults of the sea. . . . One of the most subtle tortures and unrecognised contributory factors to fatigue on a small ship in heavy weather (if it goes on long enough) is the utter inability to relax. For all the time muscles are in play, flexing, working, contracting, whether you are awake or asleep, upright, moving or sitting down. On they go, automatically, relentlessly, never letting up for an instant – until you could scream. . . . He was worn out by sheer physical exertion at the wheel – *Reliance* was just about as heavy on the steering as it was possible to be, the only bad thing about her. After I had left him he had passed right out, and came round lying on the wheelhouse floor with water swilling over him. It was pitch dark and bitterly cold. He had not the faintest notion of where he was or what was going on. He thrust his head out of the window and was stung by flung spray, and was utterly and completely lost.

After that it was a phantasmagoria of the macabre.

He unfolded a nightmare tale to me there in the galley, standing as it were on the borderline of sanity and looking both ways.

He knew who I was when I came into the wheelhouse with the soup, but otherwise his mind was a blank. All he knew was that something was wrong. His mind was shut against reality, so that nothing I said about the gale had meaning and he thought I was keeping something dreadful from him. Then when he went below he passed out again in the saloon, and came round with the conviction he had been attacked and laid low by a blow from behind. The chaos in the saloon being evidence of a fight having taken place there. He knew, as one knows in a dream without question or reason, there was a plot afoot, in which I was involved together with other unknown invisible persons (presumably responsible for the attack) to deprive him of the ship. Make away with him, in fact, and take *Reliance* off on some unspecified, nefarious purpose.

When we went up the deck together he was convinced we were

in harbour, tied alongside a quay-wall, dear God! But after he passed out for the third time, he awoke to normality but hazily.

It was the most terrible experience I ever heard of. And it showed clear in his ravaged face.

'Dingbats,' he said, when he finished his account, '. . . and to think it happened to me.'

'But of course,' I said, desperately anxious to settle this and drive the fear of it from his mind, 'it would happen to you. Look what you have been through since we sailed. Before we sailed for that matter. Look at the mental and physical energy you expended yesterday. And on what? When did you last sleep? I don't suppose you averaged more than an hour a day since we sailed. And when did you last eat? There is a limit to endurance. You reached it and went beyond. A less conscientious person would have packed up long before – like I did this morning – but you forced yourself on until your conscious brain could stand no more and the subconscious took over.

'And the subconscious can have a particularly nasty way of explaining things.' I grinned tentatively.

The psychology may have been shaky, but it had the desired effect. Frank brightened. 'Do you think that?'

'I know it,' I stated positively. 'I was in no better state, but it took me a different way.' And I told him about the blackouts. He looked very grave. 'It can't go on,' he said. 'This ship . . . she's had everything we possess. She's not going to have our sanity too.'

'She won't. Sleep and rest, and food. That's all we want. And we'll pull out, never fear.'

It was all very well to put on a show of heartiness and talk like a character out of a paper-backed adventure story. I never felt less hearty in my life. I was scared, not of dying or death or losing the ship or failing in our ultimate purpose, but of the thing that had happened to Frank. Until that, the voyage, for all its hardships, had been a kind of splendid fun, at once terrifying and magnificent (and there is a real retrospective joy in hardships overcome), but now it was as if there was an evil force at work, a malignant cancer in our adventure, against which we were helpless. And the horror of it brooded over us, for all we bolstered each other up with a brave display of heroics.

Plymouth was on our doorstep so to speak, but we never mentioned it.

Last night I would have thrown in my hand to save Frank, and today I withheld for the same reason. And the choice was mine, for he was at the stage of leaning on me for decisions and drawing on me for strength. To have put in to Plymouth would not have given us the rest we craved. It would have brought on legal miseries which might well, I feared, put Frank out of his mind for ever. I would see those lawyers, and ourselves too, for that matter, in hell first.

We were going to be fit before attemping to scale that mountain.

So *Reliance* plugged out to clear the Eddystone, whence we intended to beat out of the Channel. But the wind died and died away, just when we could have done with a bit, and I spent the day at the wheel juggling with every puff, steering between the lighthouse and Start Point. And fretted fearfully over Frank, who had agreed to turn in, and then spent the entire day filtering paraffin, sorting things out and testing the fuel tanks to find out how much there was left.

I dared not fuss and chivvy him off to bed, because it was essential for his recovery to show absolute confidence in him, so I held my peace in the wheelhouse and worried myself sick. He brought a cup of cocoa at dusk and we had a gusty meaningless row because we were so strung-up. We were clear of the lighthouse then, bobbing up and down in the Channel, like a rocking-horse not getting anywhere. So we left the ship to look after herself and went below for a meal, switching on the navigation lights as we went.

Afterwards we went on deck in the dark, to find *Reliance* had drifted into a steamer lane and ships were thick about us like trees in a forest. Bearing down was a colossal steamer winking wrath from an Aldis lamp. There was hardly a breath of a breeze to stir the staysail and we were powerless to alter our course in any way. The steamer steered round us, flashing fury with the lamp turned aft, and continued to do so as she stormed on her way down Channel. I leant over the bulwarks and bellowed, 'And you!', which was entirely wasted, but an eminently satisfying thing to do.

Frank turned in then, saying, 'Don't worry about these guys – we're under sail, they have to get out of our way.' And I spent a hectic night drifting, not quite out of control, but very nearly, across the bows of outraged steamers. There must have been some pretty fruity commentaries taking place on various bridges that night. *Reliance* was a pigmy among giants and the giants were not looking for navigation lights at her level. After a few heart-twisting turns I switched on the riding light, stern light and decklights as well, which may have been unorthodox, and illegal for all I know, but at least rendered the ship visible.

By dawn we were across the steamer lanes and rid of the ships.

I was exceedingly tired. The wind started to fuss and moan after its quiet night, then grumbled and blustered, whipping up a steep little sea, in an early morning temper. *Reliance* became rather a handful. The staysail lunged and jerked and thundered whatever I did. Frank had had about eight hours' sleep, so I thought it fair enough to go and ask his advice.

He was sound asleep and bounded up in a great fright when I touched him. 'What's this?' he rasped. 'You've got the cable running out freely, haven't you? It's buoyed, isn't it? Well, then, what's the trouble?'

With sinking heart I tried to explain what I had come about, and wished to God I had not disturbed him.

'I don't see what your worry is.' He was very brisk. 'There's nothing jamming the cable, is there?'

'No,' I said wearily, 'never mind. Go back to sleep.'

'Nonsense. You come to me with your troubles, then you won't tell me what they are.'

'I'll tell you in the morning.'

I went back to the wheelhouse wondering if it would be wise to put back to Plymouth after all. But the thought of the lawyers intervened. Best to wait and see how he was later. He wasn't properly awake then; he would be all right after plenty of rest and sleep. I decided to wait and see. . . .

The wind grew no stronger but steadied and *Reliance* settled down. I lashed the wheel and went on deck to tidy up. Ropes and halyards and things were loose and swinging. There is a technical jargon for doing things to ropes just as there are technical names for the ropes themselves, but I never got round to learning the language. I knew roughly what the various ropes did – and what they shouldn't do, so I tightened them up and made proper little hanks of their running ends and hung them on their cleats and belaying pins and felt very responsible. Then Charles gave a bit of bother and broke away. He was a tremendous block with a hook to hoist the jib. I christened him Charles after a friend, whose wife in a moment of stress had once referred to him as being 'so big and angry', and I never knew anything so big and angry as that block when it was at large. I caught him eventually after an exciting dodge and chase (one cosh from Charles, bigger than a man's head, and you'd had it), and hooked him into an eyebolt in deck and knitted a cat's-cradle round him to keep him there, which it did, and wondered very anxiously about Frank.

He turned up about six in the morning, looking remarkably cheerful.

'What were you nattering about this morning?' he asked. 'I wasn't awake properly. Damn funny. Thought you were foreman of a cable-laying gang.'

'Frank,' I begged, 'for Pete's sake, don't do it again.'

'No,' he said sombrely, 'I won't.' And he didn't.

It blew steadily all day (from a westerly direction of course, it never blew anything else for us, unless it was south-west) what would have been a good sailing wind if we had had any sails, but the mizzen wanted mending and the main halyard was gone and the spare needed rigging, a task we boggled at, neither of us having the strength to play the daring young man on the flying trapeze or hoist the other in the bosun's chair; so we slogged on the long beat down Channel as best we could under the old red staysail.

A test heave on the flywheel lever confirmed the suspicion that the for'ard cylinder was seized again, gummed up through slow running; the reason for the engine stopping when the throttle was closed. Fuel was so low now that it was to be conserved against the time we chose to make port – or an emergency. But we shirked the job of an overhaul until we regained the strength to handle the heavy engine parts, and spent the day catching up on our food intake, preparing and gobbling prodigious meals. At the end of each one Frank fell sound asleep.

By nightfall we were doodling off the French coast, marked by a long row of shore lights. Just where it was exactly escapes me now; we seemed to know at the time, but were more directly concerned with the rapidity with which *Reliance* was approaching. So we came about, and the staysail rent asunder. Whereupon *Reliance* with an air of saying that will be all for tonight, drifted smugly out to sea. Up Channel. I could have taken an axe to her.

We stooged about till dawn and got up the jib, Charles being rather more than we cared to handle in the dark just then. As it was he was exceedingly obstreperous, swinging us off our feet and slinging us into the mast or anything solid at hand. It was a relief to get him up out of the way.

There were one or two fishing boats at work in the vicinity. A large blue one came up to us, attracted no doubt by the tatty appearance of our ship. An immense crew hung avariciously over the side and offered to help. Frank refused and offered to buy some fish. I had hopped below at their approach and hopefully counted the four pound notes. But they said they had no fish and went away. They returned later offering to tow us into some place or another, and were quite disgruntled that it was not their day for easy money and they had to go fishing after all.

We concentrated on the mizzen sail; Frank fixed the mast rings, and I stitched the bolt rope on the sail. *Reliance* rolled nowhere in particular in a merry-hearted fashion, scooping up small bucketfuls of water which sloshed playfully down the deck. We hoisted the mizzen on the topping lift, using the handy billy to help with the last few feet, and had it set just as the blue fisherman was making towards us for a third try. Evidently the fishing wasn't too good that day. But when he saw the mizzen go up he realised we were no good either and departed.

We lashed the float in place again against the wheelhouse, and generally the ship looked less of a shambles. But Frank seemed very depressed, and to set him up I said with ample food and water aboard we had every chance of completing the voyage; talked glibly about putting into Lisbon or the Canary Islands if we found it was getting beyond us. I have no idea whether I believed in this myself, being quite beyond faith in anything, but it was a show of confidence, and cheered Frank no end, and that was all that mattered.

A row of red lights turned up at night, still on the French coast, to give us light fever, and we stood watch and watch about. Frank slept all right on his watch below, but I could not, and spent the time in the galley listening to the radio.

Actually after that last deplorable blackout I did not close my eyes in sleep aboard again.

Our time was drawing to an end. There were but three more days of our voyage left, though we were not to know that of course.

We strove desperately to get out of the Channel, beating from side to side against a relentless westerly wind and with available sail not getting much forrarder. Had we been at the top of our form we should have done better. We were inundated with offers of assistance from passing vessels of all sorts, from small fishing boats to large steamers. It was most embarrassing. Frank used to deal with them, whilst I (having become a very desperate character) watched from a vantage-point below, ready to launch a surprise attack in the event of any funny business. This amused Frank vastly. He said there was no likelihood of any trouble from that kind at sea. But I have no faith in humanity. He always tried to buy fish off the

fishermen, but either the fishers are mean or the fishing in the Channel is bad for we never got any. The last fisherman to accost us asked if we intended making port; Frank said no and he grinned, saying, 'I wouldn't if I were you.'

We got trapped by wind and tide in Lyme Bay and flogged up and down between Start Point and Portland Bill, unable to clear either point, and seeming likely to spend a Flying Dutchman existence in the Bay for the rest of our lives. We then put up the balloon jib which was really too light a sail for the weight of wind blowing, but it pulled like a horse, and *Reliance* sailed closer to windward. It seemed at last we might clear Start Point. Towards nightfall (this I think would be June 3rd) the wind increased, and the question arose as to whether we should take the big jib in. It was obvious that the blow would continue, which suited us fine if it got no worse, but it was just as much as the sail could stand. If we replaced it with the smaller headsail then we could not clear Start Point, and faced the prospect of at least another day ploughing up and down in Lyme Bay. On the other hand if we were to take it in, now was the time to do so.

Frank said furiously, 'Whatever I do will be wrong,' decided to play for a straight win and left it.

So it blew up into a snorting gale; the silk sail burst with a clap of thunder and flogged itself to ribbons.

We spent another night in the familiar bellowing maelstrom of a maddened sea. Hawklike, I watched Frank with anxious intensity, but there was no need. He was undistressed. By dawn we were tossing in an ominously green sea in the south-western corner of Lyme Bay, with the Devonshire coast far too near, and getting nearer every minute.

Charles had taken the opportunity to create an inextricable tangle above the hounds and refused to come down. We wrapped the remnants of the sail round the winch and wound him down. So that the twist would not be transferred to the sail Frank made a rope grommet, and strenuously we hauled up the little jib, by hand and by winch.

By this time we were so close in I was yawning my head off in exasperation at the difficulty of it all. *Reliance* refused to turn through the wind and had to be gybed round, losing valuable sea-room. The water looked positively translucent. Then we were slogging up towards the Bill once more.

'What a game,' said Frank.

225

26

INEVITABLY the wind eased off: we bucketed slowly away from the shore, out of green into grey water, up towards Portland Bill. If only we could clear one of the horns of this damned Bay and get into mid-Channel again. If only this infernal wind would blow from another direction. . . .

It was in melancholy mood I waited in the saloon for a weather report from the radio. The sky had been still full of wind at dawn, and I hoped to hear that the sky was a liar. The radio bleated a song popular in my early flying days, 'There's a Small Hotel', evoking a host of memories – was life really so gay, so carefree? – and sounding both appropriate and incongruous. It had changed to 'Put Your Shoes On, Lucy', when Frank came in and we giggled at it foolishly.

We listened to a gale warning and Frank said, 'We'd better fix the engine in that case.' He seemed quite brisk and cheerful. I picked a book at random from the top of the pile at my feet. *Ulysses*. Flicked the pages – '. . . made weak by time and fate, but strong in will to strive, to seek, to find, and not to yield.'

Not to yield. I followed Frank into the engine-room.

It was an easier task to free the piston this time, knowing exactly what the trouble was and how to tackle it. We felt when we left it ready for starting that it was a good job done and that we were catching up on the work bit by bit. But we hadn't got round to the mainsail yet. It was still pretty wild though not yet the gale of the warning and we were too jellyboned to cope with a halyard up the pendulum-swinging mast. Tomorrow, we promised ourselves, if it is fit.

By night we were coming up to the Bill, having pinched and scraped all the sea-room possible. The sou'westerly wind had hardened considerably. *Reliance* under jib and mizzen was tugging away to clear the Bill, upon which the light flashed brightly. Frank took a last look round; satisfied that all was well, he turned in. It was tacitly understood that rest for him was all-important.

For a while I stayed in the wheelhouse watching the Portland light and our steady progress. We were going to have ample margin. The movement of the ship underfoot had become second nature and I did not notice it. Nor hear the shrilling of the wind. But I felt the cold and lashed the wheel and nipped below for a cup of coffee.

As one is oblivious of the noise of a well-known engine and is instantly aware of a change in the beat, so I recognised when *Reliance* changed direction. Immediately I was on deck to see what she was up to.

For no known reason she had swung off course and was belting downwind for the Bill.

Knowing her reluctance to go through the wind and the amount of sea-room she required gybing, and desperately anxious not to lose all we had gained, I called Frank.

As she was coming slowly round, Charles, way up at the top of the mast, played his ace – the rope grommet parted and the jib blew over the side.

Reliance drifted stern first.

'Engine,' cried Frank. On the way down I slipped into the galley and turned off the stove. It was bound to be an all-night session. It always was. And I knew the situation was going to be tough by the waves of drowsiness that swept over me. A sure sign.

As the torches roared I looked out of the hatch. Bright were the lights behind Chesil Bank. Bright were the lights on the Portland radio masts. Brilliantly swept the beam of the lighthouse.

The tide was making six knots, or more. Taking us with it. . . .

'We haven't much time,' I said to Frank, who nodded as if I had said it was raining.

The engine started on one cylinder. I went to the wheelhouse and Frank wedged the fuel injector on the for'ard cylinder. There was no time to play around. We had covered an amazing distance whilst the heads were heating and were very near to the high cliffs of Portland Bill. But half-power was not enough. With the throttle wide *Reliance* was going astern. Stern first she passed under the light, its white beam slicing the night sky overhead.

Frank took over and put her into reverse in the hope she would steer better.

I looked out of the door aft. Black waves were breaking high and white on outlying pinnacles of rock. Right in our path.

'Don't think we'll make it.'

I felt faintly surprised and automatically unhooked the lifejackets. Each time she lifted we listened – waiting. . . .

Ahead or reverse it made no difference. *Reliance*, fast in the grip of wind and tide, passed under the end of the Bill, missing the rocks by a matter of inches. The swift immutable current swept round the point and up the eastern side of the Bill. *Reliance* went with it, stern first round the point, then broadside, bow on to the cliffs, closing nearer and nearer in every long-drawn minute.

We dropped the mizzen, and Frank went to try and clear the atomiser on number one.

'Bring her round,' he said, 'if you can.'

With unusual docility she turned, was coming round, was nearly round, then a sharp bark, and the engine stopped. She swung back to face the cliffs. And plunged towards them, inexorably.

I thought: I know this. I've been through it all before.

As Frank bounded up through the hatch, cursing, I switched on the deck-lights and together we ran up the deck. The anchor was already shackled to wire and chain, but as we tore at the lashings, he looked up at the towering cliffs above us and straightened.

'No use. No time,' he said. 'We'll have to look to ourselves. . . .'

Quickly he got the paraffin and as I handed him a bundle of garments for a flare, he hesitated – 'Won't you want these again?' – and laughed shortly and soaked them in paraffin.

The flare cast an orange glow over the deck and by its weird light we unlashed the float and moved it over to the lee side, ready for launching.

We were putting on lifejackets, Frank grumbling he couldn't work in one, when she struck. Lightly at first then harder and harder. We were in front of the wheelhouse. He shouted, 'Hold tight!' and we grabbed the mainsheet. Jolting and bumping on the bottom, louder and louder she crashed. Each crash the knell for our hopes and beliefs. Sounding the end of all for which we had laboured and endured.

And I could believe none of it.

I heard Frank saying, 'What a shame, what a shame,' as the ship rent beneath our feet.

Then the tall cliff face was upon us with a tremendous splintering crash. The bowsprit snapped like kindling. The flare was out. The night was dark. We clung to the mainsheets in a pool of light thrown by the lamps in front of the wheelhouse. She began to roll. From side to side, rails under, with incredible speed, as if she would roll right over. A colossal jolt; the shock travelling from stem to stern. The mainmast sagged, came over, seemed to hang suspended. The boom dropped and we leapt from under. Before our horrified eyes the bows of the vessel buried into the very face of the cliff.

And above the roaring sea came the terrible noise of a dying ship.

Frank yelled: 'Float!' and we heaved it over the side. It swung in the water, level with the deck, in the depths below, streaming away under the counter.

'Jacket OK?' he shouted. 'Over you go!'

I swung over the side, facing it, and, as the ship rolled, felt out with my feet for the float, missed it, and was left hanging by my arms. He leant over and gripped my wrists. But the ship, rolling prodigiously, flung me off. I shouted: 'Let go!' and dropped into the sea.

In the float I got a leg fast in the ropeworks. Each time the ship came over, the mizzen boom on the counter rail drove within a hair's-breadth of my chest. I was trapped, helpless and infuriated. Frank, not seeing this, shouted, 'Right?' and without waiting for a reply climbed on to the bulwarks and leapt overboard.

I happened to look up, got an imprint of him silhouetted on the rail high above – the ship having rolled the other way – then he jumped clear into the sea, swam to the float, clambered aboard and handed me a paddle as, panting and angry, I wrenched free. Muttering about the dangerousness of the rope-works in the float (incomprehensible to Frank) I dug in a paddle and sculled away to the end of the line out of reach of the boom. Frank said, 'Got your knife?' and cut the painter.

It struck me as an unnecessarily dramatic gesture, just as making a flare from a bundle of real clothes had appeared to him. It was impossible to believe in our predicament.

As far as we could judge – it was too dark to see more than the faint outline of the cliff-tops and the white smudge of waves dashing against the face – *Reliance* was aground at the foot of a bluff round which the coast fell back a bit. There was no landing for us there, the cliffs were sheer, and the high-flung spray of the bellowing breakers warned us to keep off. We struck out along the coast in the direction of Weymouth, taking care to keep clear of the boiling turmoil at the foot of the cliffs.

Our queer little craft was a lozenge-shaped ring of cork, or some other unsubmergeable substance, canvas-bound and painted red and yellow. The ring was woven about with an intricate system of lifelines, and in the centre of the ring, suspended by a rope network was a wooden box. It was in this network I had got entangled. The box was double-sided, with two compartments either side with sliding lids, for the containing of provisions (a point we had not taken advantage of, unfortunately). It was immaterial which way up it floated, for both sides were the right side.

We sat on the ring and paddled, with our feet on the box and water up to our knees. Sometimes the water swept across our laps. The float swooped gamely to the top of a wave and dived down into the trough. Frank said she was a good little craft – but wet. We were very cold.

We were both wearing woollen sweaters and jackets but our clothes were soaked through, of course. Frank had cast off his shoes and his feet gleamed very white in the black water. I was still wearing the light rubber-soled sneakers that had hardly left my feet since we sailed from Fleetwood. In my pockets was the 'shipwreck' equipment carried since the night off Land's End, torch, four one-pound notes, watch, knife and lucky photograph. The watch was still going in spite of its immersion. We left the ship shortly after two a.m. and it did not stop until twenty-three minutes past eight. Then it stopped irrevocably.

As we paddled along the coast, careering up and over and down the swift waves, we saw terrific activity burst out on the cliff-tops. A rocket shot up with a bang, leaving a white trail against the night sky. Torch, bicycle and car lights appeared and ran about in a purposeful manner. An organisation was going into operation. We visualised telephonings, shouts, orders; a lifeboat launched, coastguards in action . . . because of a ship in distress. . . . *Our* ship, we realised, unable to rid ourselves of astonishment and incredulity. Simultaneously we looked back. A yellow pinpoint of light still burned at the foot of the bluff.

'What a shame,' burst out Frank, thinking of his beloved ship, 'what an utter, bloody shame.'

Right back to the beginning again . . . with four pounds and a pocket-knife. . . . No *Reliance*, no future, no hope. I made some boy-scout remark about everything going to be all right. But apart from the overriding surprise I was beyond feeling anything but a thankfulness that Frank and I were together and a yearning to lie down and sleep for about a week.

He said, 'Aren't we getting too far out?'

It was hard to say.

'No. Yes. We are a bit.'

There was a point a mile or so ahead along the coast, and we thought if we could get round that we might find a lee and a landing, and paddled towards it for all we were worth. Yet we seemed to draw no nearer.

A steamer making for Weymouth passed on our starboard hand, not too far away. We shouted, competing ineffectively with the roaring sea, and shone the torch, but the battery was almost spent, and it gave only a feeble glow. At the same time we spotted the lights of a lifeboat coming round the point we were trying to make for.

By now we realised that the fierce current that had wrecked *Reliance* was turning and carrying us out to sea. Inexorably, we were going back, some distance out, and parallel to the way we had come. But the ship's lights were consoling and the knowledge there was a lifeboat looking for us, comforting. We had complete faith in being picked up.

We could see the masthead light of the lifeboat rising and falling. From the tops of waves we could see the navigation lights. Then it moved close inshore, and passed us.

We yelled at the top of our voices and waved the torch. The torch went out irrevocably, and our shouts were drowned in the tumult of wind and water.

Our puny efforts with the paddles were no match for the sea. Drawn relentlessly away we watched the lifeboat work up the coast to *Reliance*, then down and back again, shining a searchlight on the cliffs.

Frank said peevishly, 'What the hell do they think we are? Goats?' And I said, 'It will be dawn soon, and then they'll see us.'

We passed *Reliance* . . . the end of Portland Bill.

When daylight came they did not see us. Nor by then could we see them. Only from wave-crests could we see land at all. The seas were tremendous, and very steep. From the top we looked down into impenetrable depths, from the troughs we gazed, awestruck, at huge walls of water. The cold was intense.

Wilder and wilder came the seas. Wilder and whiter. Instead of the float riding over the crests, the crests rode over the float. We paddled one-handed, holding on to the lifelines.

'I do not see' – I found it extraordinarily difficult to move my frozen lips – 'how anyone could pick us up in this . . . even if we were seen. . . .'

Frank did not reply, but looked round and round at the awful sea as if he did not believe what he saw.

⌀　　　⌀　　　⌀　　　⌀　　　⌀

The current took us into the very centre of Portland Race. The sea was white with insensate rage. Towering pinnacles of water rushed hither and yon, dashing into one another to burst with a shrapnel of foam – or to merge and grow enormous.

From the level of the sea itself it was as the wrath of God, terrifying to behold.

Seated on the bottomless coracle, filled with wonder and awe, we worked away with the paddles to meet the seas. Bravely the little craft tugged up the precipitous slopes and plunged into the depths. I was thinking I would rather be in her than in a dinghy, when suddenly I was in the sea, underneath the float, looking up through the centre where the water was bright green.

There was time to wonder – is this drowning? – and – How green the water is from this side – then I surfaced, found I was gripping a lifeline.

The float was swinging uneasily at the bottom of a trough. There was no sign of Frank. Terror-stricken, I shrieked for him at the very top of my voice.

He came up about ten yards away. Swam strongly to the float, still holding his paddle, whereon I realised I had lost mine.

We heaved aboard, and lay athwart the ring, gasping, clinging to the lifelines.

'What did that?' I panted.

'Don't know. This is *not* funny.'

Then we saw my paddle, swung upright and set off in pursuit, chasing it up hill and down stormy dale, but it remained forever out of reach.

Suddenly we were in the water again. Under the float. Green water above.

This time we were slower getting aboard. Took longer to recover. We looked at one another in great fear.

'What do we *do*? How do we fight this?'

The upset was so sudden, happened so quickly, we had no notion as to the cause of it. And that was the frightening part.

Dizzily the float tore up and down, swinging and swaying. Tensely we watched the advance of each white-headed mountain. Frank had lost his paddle in the last upset and we could not even make a pretence of fighting.

232

Then we were flung into the sea again. And this time saw how it happened. Saw with slow-motion clarity how the float was sucked up under a great overhanging crest, and thrown over backwards in the boiling tumult as the wave broke.

This time it was very hard to get back on to the float.

Frank threw an arm about my shoulders: 'All right?'

'Yes.'

'Good-oh.'

We got right inside the float, crouching on the wooden box with water up to our armpits.

There must be some way of stopping it turning over, I thought.

He shouted: 'LOOK OUT!'

Instinctively I leant forward, head down on the ring to meet what was coming. And we did not turn over. But took the full force of the wave as it exploded upon us.

I found myself shouting: 'That's it. That's it. Lean forward. Head down. That foxes 'em.'

Shivering violently with cold I remembered something once read about the mechanics of shivering and put up a great show of exaggerated shudders, partly to offset the numbing cold, and partly as a manifestation of triumph. Frank smiled wanly.

But the conquest was short-lived. The seas grew worse. Boiled in a white lather all about us. Breaking in endless succession. . . . We hardly recovered from the onslaught of one before gasping under the next. The weight of water and shock of cold were stunning. Each time a wave broke over us it was with the effect of an icy plunge, although we were actually crouching in water all the time.

Hours dragged out in immeasurable misery as the sea struck with a sledge-hammer to kill a pair of gnats.

No longer buoyed by the slightest hope of rescue we sank into an apathy of endurance, huddled together, heads on the ring, hands grasping lifelines with the prehensile, immovable grip of the new-born. Or the dying. Passively fighting for the lives which were a little less living after every blow.

In a comparative lull, from a wave-top, I glimpsed land, Portland Bill, thin and attenuated in the distance. Pointed to it. Frank slowly stood up and called in a whisper for help.

It was such a pitiful travesty of his usual stentorian bellow I was inexpressibly shocked, and with a surge of protective energy reached up to pull him down, dreading a recurrence of the horror of the other night. Then I saw it was not that . . . and looked wildly round for help. But there was none.

He did not speak. He put out a hand, pressed mine, reassuringly, smiled at me.

And gradually, the smile fixed and meaningless and terrible, faded into unconsciousness, into a slow delirium when, blank-eyed, he tried to climb out of the float. I held on to him and feebly tried to rub his hands, my own unfeeling.

A monster wave rose above the rest. Fury piled on fury. Curling foaming crest. Sweeping down on us. Inescapable. I threw an arm round Frank, leant forward.

The little float drove into the wall of water and was lost within it.

When it broke free Frank was dead.

I stared at the edge of the ring. At the ropes intertwined about it. At the froth and bubbles on the water.

Nothing mattered now. No point in trying any more. The fight was over. I laid my head on my arms and closed my eyes, engulfed in a blessed darkness.

EPILOGUE

BUT Fate, or whatever governs the chances that influence our actions, is entirely without mercy.

A wave thundered down on the float which should have been the end of me, but instead, woke me from oblivion to anger. A bitter impotent rage, so that I struck out, beating the air with my fists, fighting a tangible battle with an intangible foe.

It was the last wave to break over the float then, and I was left alive and miserable and waiting to die. Bethought me of the knife in my pocket and how the end could be hastened, but the knife was gone. I was too stupefied to think of the obvious.

(*That* only occurred three days later, when it was too late.)

So I waited.

A puffin landed near-by and sculled round the float evincing great interest in it. I had an unreasoning impulse to touch it, but it was just out of reach. It seemed entirely without fear and its presence was infinitely comforting. It made no effort to fly away, but drifted alongside, preening its feathers.

As I watched the bird thoughts came into my head, peopling an empty stage, and I listened to what they had to say and looked at their actions as though they were no part of myself. As indeed they were not, for they came without conscious evocation.

I saw the headlines ripping out – and vultures picking over the bones of our beliefs. Heard the speculations of armchair sages, wise to another's trouble, not to truth. Heard the baying of the wolves. . . .

And listened to rumours, whispers and suspicions. . . .

They say . . . You ran away. You purposely wrecked the ship. You dare not face your responsibilities. You could not face what was coming. You killed yourselves. Shirked . . . Ran . . . Suicide. . .

They say . . .

By God . . . No! Furiously I turned on the thoughts and scattered them for those of my own choosing.

There was one of us left. One to carry on what both had begun.

The application may have been unorthodox, but the principles were sound, of that I was convinced. To have faith in one's beliefs, to follow an aim to the end is a fundamental necessity. Otherwise the whole pattern of life is pure chance, a miasma and a mockery, and nothing is worth the doing or trying. As lief be a blade of grass and live out one's unknown purpose unreasoned.

To leave that which we had begun uncompleted, to give in without a fight to the very end, would be to nullify all that had gone before, admit defeat, and to a worthlessness of all we had tried to do, and be.

'All right,' I cried to the fleeting clouds, 'you shall have your blood money.' And to the empty sea I shouted: 'I'm going back. Going back. Do you hear?' And got up to stand on the float and shout it again, wracked with rage and madness and utmost despair.

As if some purpose had been accomplished the puffin flew away.

∽   ∽   ∽   ∽   ∽

As the long, long morning wore on and the sun climbed high, the sea moderated somewhat, the clouds swept away, and it turned to a day such as we had loved, blowing and blue, but the life-giving warmth of the sun had come too late.

I sat on the ring to dry out and the float hurried on to an unknown destination, taking me within twenty yards of a large brown buoy. Afterwards I discovered it to be twelve miles from land, marking a sunken aircraft. But I had seen it before, in a gale, and knew our surmise then had been correct. I wanted to tell Frank. Then the buoy moved away, disappeared over the leaping waves, and it was some time before I had the wit to realise that the float had changed direction. Turning to see whither it was bound I found land ahead and on the port hand.

Gradually features became discernible, recognisable as the west side of Portland Bill and the long strand of Chesil Bank.

The float was making straight for a beach below Portland town at the mainland end of the island. It looked to be a good landing, but there was a tremendous surf. Waves swept past the float, hurrying landwards without a moment to lose, growing bigger and bigger and roaring mightily.

About two miles off the float changed direction again as the current took it diagonally towards the Bill and out to sea. I broke off a wooden handhold attached to the lifeline, for use as a paddle and tried to work inshore. It was pretty inadequate but enabled me to steer to a certain extent. The stream ran in fairly close but at the same time carried the float seawards, sweeping down the coast, passing good landing places until there was nothing but sheer cliff, rock bestrewn at foot, where the sea dashed with huge columns of spray and smoking spume. It did not seem possible to land there, or even having landed to scale the cliffs.

Nearing the end of the Bill the float was very near in.

The place was a mass of rocks and giant boulders. The noise of the sea was thunder. But it was either that or making the whole miserable circuit over again.

Feeling, for God's sake let's get it over, I dug away with the handhold for all I was worth. Then was caught up in a blind white rush, hurled towards the rocks. The float turned over and I was flung into the sea. Surfaced for a moment, still gripping a lifeline. High overhead hung a wave, breaking. Instinctively I let go and was lost in a green confusion, rocks beneath, sea above.

The water receded. I was lying on my back on a rock with the float on top of me.

The float was empty.

I tried to push it off. Failed. Tried again and succeeded. Another wave towered. Tumult. Then air and peace and the float atop again. Again I pushed it off. Crawled to another rock, clung to it as the next wave broke.

Between waves I had glimpsed a cavern whose floor was above the level of the breaking seas, and between waves I worked towards it, pursued by the float, and thinking with idiotic simplicity, So this is how you land on rocks, cling like a limpet and keep your head down.

Then I was standing in the cave. Alone. No sign of the float. Nothing. I stood and looked at the sea and my thoughts were my own.

The cave was tall and vaulted, running parallel to the cliff with an out-wall protecting it from the sea, and it was open both ends.

I looked up at the cliffs, sixty or seventy feet, maybe not so much, I was in no state to judge, except that they were sheer and overhanging, quite beyond my capabilities to scale. I had come in to a small rock-ridden cove bounded by the cave and a precipitous wall of cliff. I knew it was almost at the end of the Bill but could not see what lay round the corner. There was no way of finding out except by going into the sea. I looked out at the other end of the cave. The entrance there was almost blocked by great rocks, and beyond was more sheer cliff, seeming to tumble down into the sea. There appeared to be no way out either way.

I shouted until my voice gave out and all I heard in reply was the scream of seagulls and the thunder of surf.

My pockets were inside out and there was nothing left but the lucky photograph and the useless watch with which to fight the fight I had come back for. So much for all that high-flown thinking. I laughed helplessly and blacked out and fell about until I had the sense to lie down and rest. It was cold and the cavern floor was wet. I thought of going below to get a coat, and stirred and found where I was.

A small brown bird was hopping inquisitively round my feet.

I was pretty far gone by then and knew if I stayed where I was there was no point in having come ashore, so I crawled over the boulder-blocked entrance to find a way along the coast and look for that place where the cliffs had seemed possible of climbing. I don't suppose the going was really as tough as it seemed. There were rocks and boulders to be surmounted all the way, some as big as cottages and presenting interesting problems for there was no way round with the sea on one hand and aloof heights on the other.

I came to the place I was looking for and started to climb. The surface was not rock but loose dry earth with here and there a patch of turf. It was very steep. Where there was nothing to give a grip, I dug out hand and footholds with my hands. Ten yards from the top I lost my grip and slid back for several yards, arms outspread, pressing hard against the side, until my feet were brought up against a small outcrop. It was a straight drop fifty feet into the sea, when I looked over my shoulder, and this was somehow profoundly irritating. I dug very careful handholds then and climbed to the top.

What I expected to find there I don't know. The reason for all this effort was lost in the effort itself. I was dimly aware of being geared-up for a fight. Though with whom or why was not clear. Maybe I expected to see the battleground laid out ready and waiting. I beheld a gentle slope of turf leading up to a radio mast. Nothing more.

Beyond?

Slowly I walked towards the top of the slope.